JOHN SMITH

JOHN SMITH
Old Labour's Last Hurrah?

EDITED BY
Kevin Hickson

Biteback Publishing

First published in Great Britain in 2024 by
Biteback Publishing Ltd, London
Selection and editorial apparatus copyright © Kevin Hickson 2024
Copyright in the individual essays resides with the named authors

ISBN 978-1-78590-823-1

10 9 8 7 6 5 4 3 2 1

A CIP catalogue record for this book is available from the British Library.

Set in Bulmer and Goudy

Printed and bound in Great Britain by
CPI Group (UK) Ltd, Croydon CR0 4YY

FSC
www.fsc.org
MIX
Paper | Supporting
responsible forestry
FSC® C171272

CONTENTS

FOREWORD

Dame Margaret Beckett MP

T HE CONVENTIONAL WISDOM SURROUNDING John
Smith at the time was that John, as leader of the Labour Party,
came across to the public like the ideal bank manager – someone
who might be friendly, not unsympathetic and would provide sound
advice on which you could rely.

While John was all the above, it does not fully capture who he was
or what he was like as leader. He had great energy and determination.
Simon Hoggart once quoted a colleague who described him 'steam-
ing down the Committee corridor like a small rhinoceros'!

I once saw a photograph of John as a boy that I would describe
as a *Just William* kind of picture. He had a wicked grin from ear to
ear, his tie around his ear. Colleagues who spent time in his company
had no difficulty in detecting that small boy in the statesman and the
leader.

John had eloquence and wit, as well as passion for the less fortunate. He was prepared from very early in his parliamentary career to

do what he believed to be right, whether or not it would be popular with the party hierarchy.

It was while shadowing the industry portfolio that he seems first to have identified a theme he pursued vigorously for the rest of his life and which has pervaded Labour's approach to economic policy ever since – though he is rarely given the credit he deserves. It is easy now to forget the conventional wisdom of the day, which was that you either had social justice or economic competence, not both. John, by contrast, argued that they were the two sides of the same coin – you have both or you probably don't have either.

John had another quality, so unusual in my experience as to be almost unique. He had calm, serene, almost untroubled self-confidence. He wasn't arrogant or cocky or conceited. He just knew what he could do.

Unlike many other politicians, he was never looking over his shoulder at the competition. He wasn't worried. Without jealousy, he enjoyed and celebrated the achievements of others without worrying that they might eclipse him. John had no difficulty getting on with everyone across the party, whatever the shade of their opinions.

I first worked closely with John after the 1987 election, when he chaired the economic and social policy group. Not only egalitarian, John was also non-hierarchical in his attitudes, willing – even eager – to hear everyone's point of view and open-minded about taking on board what he heard.

The impact of his egalitarianism and open-mindedness speedily became evident. Emma MacLennan, then a policy officer at Labour Party HQ, told me of an encounter with him. He said he had had an

idea about pensions he wanted to run by her, and Emma responded enthusiastically that it was a great idea. He stopped in his tracks,
swung round and said, 'NEVER do that again. I want to hear what
the problems are. I want you to think about the downsides. I don't
want to hear the downside in the Chamber.'

In the policy group, he was the same. He wanted to know what
everyone thought – even the most junior in the room. One idea was
abandoned when cogent objections were raised by a student on an
internship.

At about this time the party decided to enlarge the shadow Cabinet, and I was elected to join it in 1989. Neil Kinnock asked John, as
shadow Chancellor, who he wanted to take over from Gordon Brown
as shadow Chief Secretary to the Treasury – the enforcer of financial
discipline.

John said, 'I want Margaret Beckett.'

It may seem odd now, but the idea of having someone from the
left of the party in such a role and working with an acknowledged
'right-winger' was thought extraordinary. John was, characteristically,
not worried. As shadow Chancellor, he was both a formidable opponent in the House of Commons and an advocate for the less fortunate.

Immediately after the 1992 election Neil Kinnock resigned, and it
was clear that John would run for the leadership. My husband, Leo,
and I agreed that it had to be the best possible person. It was clear to
us that was John.

Within a day or so, I heard a BBC report that John and I were
running as a team. I was appalled. I rang the BBC and told them it
was completely untrue.

Then my phone rang and rang and rang.

By Monday morning, I had accepted what seemed to be the inevitable. John appeared. 'I came,' he said, 'to tell you that you'd got to run, but I hear you've already decided to.'

Once John and I were elected as leader and deputy leader respectively, John told me he wanted me to handle all aspects of our campaigning and to be 'a real deputy'. I wasn't quite sure what that meant, but I soon found out.

John had a very clear view and vision. The job of the leader was to set a clear direction and vision for the party – to concentrate on pursuing that and not allow himself to be diverted by day-to-day trivia.

It was during this period that the unifying benefits of John's approach to colleagues really came to the fore. He genuinely wanted, for example, to hear the views of the whole shadow Cabinet on policy. Genuine dialogue and debate without a preconceived conclusion were fostered – not interminably but thoroughly. Clear and firm conclusions were reached, and decisions, once made, were adhered to. Reconsideration of a decision thrashed out and concluded was not impossible, but you proposed it at your peril and you had to be very sure of the necessity and of your ground.

Over the subsequent months he embarked on a substantial programme of change. Within the party he proposed new structures, moving to a 'one member, one vote' system. He set up a Commission for Social Justice to independently reassess the full scale and picture of the nation's social problems and how they might be tackled. He committed himself to constitutional reforms, such as a Human Rights Act, greater freedom of information and greater devolution of power away from Whitehall.

Sometimes since his death it has been tacitly suggested that John was a status-quo man, content to wait for it to be Labour's 'turn' to govern again. But nothing could be further from the truth. In his view, the job of the leader was to set a clear direction and vision, and he did just that.

INTRODUCTION

Kevin Hickson

T HE DEATH OF JOHN Smith on 12 May 1994 was one of those events that sticks in the memory. He was cut down at the moment it looked as if he was set to become the next Prime Minister, after a long political career and after successive electoral defeats for his party.

Thirty years on, it is timely to look back on his period as Leader of the Opposition. The book is not a biography, not least because this has been done elsewhere very ably by both Andy McSmith and Mark Stuart.[1] Instead, it follows the approach of similar books I have produced on party leaders including Harold Wilson, James Callaghan, John Major and Neil Kinnock.[2] It seeks to bring together both academic writers and those involved in the political process as either politicians, advisors or journalists in the belief that the divide between academics and non-academics should be reduced. It also provides pieces from authors with different perspectives, in the belief that diversity of opinion is to be encouraged. It offers no overall argument and no concluding chapter, instead leaving the reader to make up their own mind – hopefully more informed by the time they have finished the book than when they started it.

The premature end of Smith's tenure as Leader of Her Majesty's Official Opposition has inevitably led to a series of speculative questions. Most obvious of all is whether Smith would have won the next general election, with most people concluding that he would have but disputing what the majority would have been. Whether he would have won subsequent elections has also been speculated on. Other questions are: what would Smith have been like as Prime Minister – would he have been presidential like Tony Blair or more consensual; what would he have done in response to particular events; and what policies would he have pursued? Though they are interesting questions to ask, none are particularly useful since there is, of course, no way of knowing for sure.

Instead, this book asks better questions – better in the sense that they can be answered more definitively. The book is concerned with how Smith became leader, how he managed relationships with key stakeholders such as his shadow Cabinet, the Parliamentary Labour Party and the trade unions. How he fared in opinion polls and in the electoral contests he faced and what his policy positions were. In other words, it discusses his time as leader rather than speculating on what might have been and in so doing offers a fresh account of his time in office.

The question that forms the subtitle to this book provides an overarching theme: whether or not Smith should be seen, as New Labour modernisers tended to do, as the last stand of Old Labour or whether he could have avoided the new tensions within the party which the modernisers created. Thirty years on from his death, debate on these points remains.

STRUCTURE OF THE BOOK

In addition to the foreword by John Smith's deputy leader Margaret Beckett MP, the book is divided into three parts.

The first part explores the context within which Smith served as leader. Keith Laybourn provides an account of Smith's aims and record as leader, looking at how he fits into the historical traditions of the Labour Party. Kevin Hickson then examines the framework of ideas within which his leadership occurred. In the next chapter, Philip Norton evaluates Smith's record as a parliamentarian. In the final chapter in this section, Mark Garnett and David Denver examine public opinion and electoral performance under Smith.

The second part goes on to examine policy development under Smith. Wyn Grant explores economic policy, while Ben Williams discusses social policy. Joseph Tiplady examines the evolution of Labour's education policy in the Smith period. This is followed by a chapter on constitutional reform by Jasper Miles, an issue which became more prominent at this time and on which Smith had a radical approach. An issue long associated with Smith is devolution and this is explored by Neil Pye. Finally in this section, Richard Johnson examines the nature of Smith's pro-Europeanism.

In the final part, a range of commentaries are provided by political practitioners including some of those who worked very closely with Smith. Ann Taylor provides an account of what it was like to be a member of the shadow Cabinet at this time. Bryan Gould, who was defeated by Smith for the leadership in 1992, provides a personal perspective. David Ward, who was head of policy in the leader's office, examines the nature of his leadership, finding the criticism of the 'modernisers' wanting. That critical perspective is then given a more sympathetic hearing by John Rentoul in the following essay. In the final piece, Andy Burnham sets out what Smith's contemporary relevance is.

PART I
CONTEXTS

1

TRIBUNE OF THE PEOPLE: THE POPULARITY, APPEAL AND LEGACY OF JOHN SMITH

Keith Laybourn

JOHN SMITH ENJOYED ONLY the briefest of moments in office as leader of the Labour Party. Yet during that period he transformed the political fortunes of the Labour Party, establishing a commanding lead in the opinion polls over the Conservative government and a substantial personal lead over John Major.[1] His untimely death provoked outpourings of grief across the nation and across political divides. Indeed, his early death has given rise to the suggestion that he was Labour's lost Prime Minister, the legacy of his achievements being seen in the subsequent success of Labour under Tony Blair. Yet his obvious popularity within his own party, the electorate and trade unions belies the fact that the policies he developed were often controversial and potentially divisive. This raises the question: why did Smith's Labour leadership become an almost overnight success? How was it that he was able to improve the fortunes of the Labour Party and turn a seemingly unelectable party into one of government? Was it simply due to the declining popularity of a Conservative government riven by sleaze and driven on by the neo-liberal policy of promoting inequality and a low-wage economy? Was it because of Smith's obvious integrity as a politician? Was it his commitment to widening participatory citizenship in a period of centralisation of government, his advocating for devolution, a Bill of Rights and modernising the Labour Party that proved politically attractive? Alternatively, was it simply that his inclusive leadership and intuitive understanding of people united his party and the nation?

Tangentially, it has been suggested that it is possible to see Smith's successful Labour leadership as a break from Old Labour and the basis of the emergence of New Labour. But was this so? Rather, was his period in office – a unique one of Labour leadership based upon himself – distinct from either traditional Old Labour or the emerging New Labour? Indeed, was it one in which he simply sought to reform Old Labour, trundling along established, recognisable and popular paths of support, but made it more an effective and democratically associated New Deal Labour, aimed at creating genuine citizenship?

Any assessment of Smith's popularity – a fleeting and transient concept in its own right – can at best be only tentative, but it is not unreasonable to suggest that it emerged from his personal qualities as a consistent opponent of Conservative sleaze and incompetence. As a man of integrity, his traditional Labour demands for a widening of citizenship resonated at many levels in society, and his leadership style of inclusivity was vital in his move to reform Old Labour while not actually encouraging the more specific social policies of New Labour.

Despite the controversial nature of the policies he promoted, particularly in the development of the European Community and the Commission on Social Justice, and his gradual, reasoned approach to change – which frustrated some like Tony Blair, Gordon Brown, and Peter Mandelson – he united and energised the Labour Party. Given that style of leadership was, and is still, so vital in British politics, it was possibly Smith's personal qualities and inclusivity that made powerful connections with the electorate. Indeed, it seems likely that his style of leadership and beliefs brought about a unique period in the Labour Party, which saw him attempt to reform the Old Labour Party and take it back to its democratic roots, rather than to define the contours of New Labour. It is often said that it is for governments to lose elections rather than for the opposition to win them, and John Major's government was a shrunken, pale imitation of a government, but in Smith's case his leadership would probably have won a general election had he lived on, even without Tory failures.

MYTHS, HOPES, ASPIRATIONS AND BEGINNINGS

Smith was a political enigma. Widely admired, he was a political leader of substance who demanded a change in the political system. Yet this was often against the particular interests of those who supported him, as with his support for one member, one vote (OMOV) at the 1993 Labour Party conference, which he made an issue of confidence in his leadership. To achieve these changes in the face of almost intractable odds required his own personal brand of Labour politics.

It is perhaps also a marvellous myth, perpetuated and embroidered over time, that his gradual reformism was a transient stage towards New Labour. The fact is that his gradual reformism was abandoned and superseded after his death. Nevertheless, Smith's calming, uniting and firm influence on British politics was able to inspire change by moving to reform the Labour Party and pressing for a more democratic political system and devolution, based upon increasing the right of citizens over the state and its institutions. That may explain his popular appeal as a radical, if moderate and conservative, reformer who sought to combine the traditional social democratic values of citizenship with a measure of cautious modernisation, ensuring the rights of the individual and community in the increasingly centralised state, which stripped local authorities of their powers and replaced them with state control and quangos, substantially unelected Tory-dominated committees with wide financial powers to determine expenditure in the community.

Indeed, his aim was to remove a system whereby, as he stated in his famous Charter 88 speech, 'We do have an elective dictatorship.'[2] In that speech he added, 'I believe we must replace the out-of-date idea of an all-powerful nation state with a new dynamic framework of government.'[3] This obvious desire to decentralise in an age of Tory centralisation certainly galvanised his appeal with the electorate, a vital factor in appeasing those within the Labour Party who might be adversely affected by his reforms. His appeal for the widening of citizenship and the democracy of the community certainly held sway in the early 1990s, embedded as it was in his desire to assert the rights of ordinary citizens in law and create a new constitution for Britain. Indeed, as one historian has suggested, Smith offered the message of 'democratic optimism'.[4]

Nevertheless, Smith began his Labour leadership role in the doldrums of defeat, following the Conservative victory in the general election of April 1992 when the Conservatives won 336 seats to Labour's 271. Labour's defeat, apparently grasped from the jaws of victory, was widely blamed upon the 'shadow Budget' which Smith, as shadow Chancellor, had put before the electorate. Driven by the desire of Neil Kinnock not to increase the tax of anyone earning more than £22,000, Labour's tax burden would have fallen on middle-income earners because of the intended rise of the top rate of tax from 40 per cent to 50 per cent. Those middle-income earners then voted against Labour, and the 3-point Labour lead in the opinion polls at the outset of the 1992 general election evaporated.

In the wake of this defeat, Kinnock resigned, and the mood message of Labour became 'bury the shadow Budget'. Despite this setback, Smith won the Labour leadership contest in July 1992, heavily defeating Bryan Gould, the British and New Zealand Labour politician, by a majority of more than nine to one: 91.016 per cent to 8.984 per cent.[5] This was achieved through his almost total dominance of the electoral system, which gave trade unions 40 per cent of the vote to the 30 per cent each enjoyed by the Constituency Labour Parties and MPs.[6] This success may have benefitted from the early 1980s exodus of those Labour figures from the centre-right of the Labour Party to form the Social Democratic Party – namely David Owen, Shirley Williams, Roy Jenkins and Bill Rodgers. Yet, given the runaway nature of the actions of the 'Gang of Four' it is an imponderable factor, and one doubts any one of them would have been able to unite and transform the Labour Party as Smith did. Indeed, Smith's metier was as a unifying figure in the mould of Harold Wilson who could unite the left, centre and the right of Labour, although he invariably expected loyalty from them all for the wider Labour cause. This might explain why critics such as Kinnock and Blair felt that Smith's leadership was slow to modernise, based upon the need to compromise and driven by a policy of 'one more heave', to use a phrase popularised by Peter Mandelson, which was soon widely used within the Labour Party.

When Smith became Labour leader he was determined to erase the stigma of his failed shadow Budget.[7] He succeeded in this. Smith's personal opinion poll rating was 6 per cent behind that of John Major in the summer of 1992, but by September 1993 he held an almost 30-point personal lead over Major, one which still remained high, at 21 points, at the time of his death.[8] The opinion poll ratings for the Labour Party moved similarly.[9] What had happened to achieve this remarkable turnaround in public opinion?

Vital to understanding Smith's success is his background and upbringing. Raised in Scotland in a Church of Scotland family and educated at Glasgow University, during which time he won the famous Observer Mace (which after his death became the John Smith Memorial Mace) competition for his debating skills, he became a solicitor and libel lawyer. He joined the Labour Party in 1955, contested various parliamentary seats and eventually entered Parliament as MP for North Lanarkshire in 1970 but represented Monklands East after 1983 due to boundary changes. He quickly gained ministerial office, rising to become Secretary of State for Trade in 1978–9 in the last throes of James Callaghan's government. Between 1979 and 1992 he held a succession of posts, although he is mostly remembered for his role as shadow Chancellor of the Exchequer between 1987 and 1992. During these years, Smith began to develop the views that were to shape his unique period of office.

The son of a Scottish headmaster and described as a son of the manse, Smith was a lifelong Christian socialist. That emerges strongly in his essay 'Reclaiming the Ground: Freedom and the Value of Society', in which he stressed his Christian faith and allied it with the moral activity of the community – exemplified in the work and ideas of R. H. Tawney, who had based his life on the moral principles of his Christian commitment, which made him an uncompromising ethical socialist.[10] Indeed, according to Smith, 'He [Tawney] saw British socialism as ethical, individualistic, parliamentary and pragmatic.'[11]

That influence led Smith to reject both rigid communism and unrestrained capitalism and to espouse democratic socialism, which sought to enhance individual freedom in a framework of collective common purpose and opportunity, in which fellowship was the bond of a community of equality.[12] Indeed, Tawney's socialism, and Smith's, was about citizenship and the active involvement of each citizen in the democratic process. This was a familiar strand in socialist thinking in the late nineteenth and early twentieth centuries and one advocated by Labour's early leaders such as Ramsay MacDonald and, most obviously, Philip Snowden in his lecture and pamphlet *The Individual Under Socialism*.[13] Here, Snowden supported both municipal and state control of industries and fair wages, which would guarantee the freedom of individuals and release them from excessive burdens of work for poor pay and consequent poverty. Such thoughts had also been evident in the writings of T. H. Marshall, whose three-stage evolution of citizenship in Britain – from male contracts to political rights and then social and industrial rights – ended with the idea that all people should have the right to join a trade union and be guaranteed a minimum wage and reasonable hours of work.[14] Similar thoughts were clearly evident in the thinking of Tawney and the mind of Smith when he further argued the need for an infrastructure of freedom provided by a collective provision by an enabling state to be 'the moral basis of democratic socialism'. He went on to state, 'It is sharply distinguishable from the anti-democratic and totalitarian forms of socialism against which Tawney was such a steadfast opponent.'[15]

Tawney saw that liberty-creating socialism was only possible in an environment of political democracy and freedom of speech and thought, which was something Smith also strongly believed in. Smith's commitment to the thinking of Tawney was reflected further in his R. H. Tawney Memorial Lecture on 20 March 1993.[16] Here, he attacked the Conservative Party notion that individuals conduct their lives 'on the basis of self-interested decisions taken in radical isolation of others', because that 'ignores the intrinsic social nature of human beings' that transcends the narrow idea of personal advantage. The whole purpose of his lecture was to explain 'why I believe that real freedom depends on the interdependence of the individual and society, and why this idea – which has long remained at the centre of democratic socialist thinking – retains its intellectual force and its capacity for popular appeal'.[17] Meaningful freedom to Tawney, Smith believed, 'was positive liberty – the freedom to achieve that is gained through education, health care, housing, and employment', based upon an enabling state and the 'richer conception of freedom for the individual in society that is the moral basis of democratic socialism'.[18]

Smith's ideas were long established within the political Labour movement and they represented a fusion of the noble and radical vision – the 'social contract' tradition in political theory and the socialist tradition. The first makes the fundamental assumption that no individual will be able to choose institutions that favour themselves in what is, in effect, a commitment to social justice. The second seeks to create citizens oriented towards community and altruism. Though paradoxically visions of opposite foundations, that they could work together for fairness to individuals is not incompatible with community service and altruism in creating citizenship.

Smith had already expounded his view that the individual rights of citizens were guaranteed through collectivism in a lecture on May Day 1987, in which he presented his view in the context of the destructive economic policies of Thatcherism in the 1980s, which were monetarist and anathema to inequality. He asserted that the New Right had argued that the inequalities of laissez-faire 'are truly more egalitarian because they will lead to more growth and greater prosperity', noting that Tawney stated, 'The argument is that the wealth of the few is the indispensable safeguard for the modest comfort of the many, who, if they understood their own interests, would not harass the rich with surtaxes and death duties, but would cherish and protect them.'[19]

A similar speech was given to the Labour Rally in Nottingham on 2 May 1987, in which he opened by stating that 'it breaks my heart to see what is happening in this country today'.[20] He added that 'this Tory government is shameless', asserting that it was claiming economic success that it had no right to do in the light of high unemployment, and declared that instead of running down the British economy, he, now the shadow Chancellor of the Exchequer, would establish the British Industrial Investment Bank to provide new sources of finance for British industry. He ended by emphasising that Labour believed in the people and that only Labour believed that people 'are our most important asset' for making 'our way in the world'.[21] He returned to the issue in July 1992 on becoming Labour leader, emphasising, 'Our values of freedom and fairness, and of citizenship and community, are far more relevant to the needs and aspirations of the British people that are the dogmas of laissez-faire and privatisation that continue to dominate the Conservative Party.'[22]

His strong commitment to Christian moral values, individualism and citizenship and his vision of a fairer distribution of wealth in society were developed further by his attitude towards devolution of central authority to national, regional and local bodies. In April 1976, as Minister of State at the Privy Council Office, he helped pilot through the House of Commons the highly controversial devolution proposals for Scotland and Wales. Having initially opposed the idea of devolution, he changed his mind, as he felt that the best way to ensure the continuation of the Union was to offer devolution, which, in the case of Scotland, would mean devolving powers to a Scottish Parliament in Edinburgh. In the event, Scottish and Welsh devolution did not occur, although the Kilbrandon Commission (1969–73) had found in favour of a Scottish Parliament and devolution. Separate bills for Scottish and Welsh devolution were passed in the House of Commons, but a Labour backbench motion required that 40 per cent of the total electorate had to vote yes or the Acts would have to be annulled. This filigree arrangement meant that when the referendums were held on 1 March 1979, though a majority voted yes, this requirement was not met. Despite this turn of events, Smith had steered legislation through the House of Commons and had changed his mind from opposing devolution to supporting it for the continuation of the Union, in the face of the SNP and indeed Plaid Cymru.

In the 1980s, while in opposition, Smith also emphasised his belief in strengthening Britain by it becoming a major member of the European Community, which Britain had joined under the Conservative premiership of Edward Heath in the early 1970s. Indeed, he was one of only five Labour MPs who voted against the Labour Party and for joining the European Community on 28 October 1971.[23] His strong pro-European attitude became even more evident in the debates in the House of Commons on 21 November 1991 when he revealed that he felt that British governments had underestimated the importance of the European Community in the 1950s and that the current Conservative government was doing the same when there was a pressing need to discuss the European Community's industrial and financial policies and the Social Chapter – these were to become a sticking point during the 1993 negotiations when the Maastricht Treaty on increased European unity was under discussion.[24]

Smith clearly saw that the idea of the nation state was outmoded and that a new form of government – the European Community – was a necessary, if not perfect development, in which national, regional and local democracy could thrive. In particular, the social aspects of the European Community had to be brought into British law, since he felt that the Social Chapter was vital in creating social citizenship.

THE FAILURES OF THE
CONSERVATIVE GOVERNMENT

Even before Smith projected himself forward to the British public as Labour leader, there is no doubt that he and the Labour Party benefitted from the incompetence and the sleaze of the Conservative government. Indeed, Labour fortunes were given a quick fillip by the disastrous actions of the Conservative government. Having set the exchange rate of the pound too high, the UK government was forced to withdraw sterling from the Exchange Rate Mechanism (ERM) after interest rates were raised twice and half the British reserves were spent defending the existing exchange rate.

There was instant newspaper criticism anticipating the end of the Conservative government, with *The Independent* going so far as to suggest that 'it is hard to see Norman Lamont continuing in his present post, John Major is gravely damaged'.[25] Most polls, which were volatile in the summer months, had the Conservatives and Labour running neck and neck. However, after 'Black Wednesday' there was a dramatic shift in polling intent, with the Harris/Observer poll of 16–17 September 1992 recording 44 points for Labour, a lead of 8 points over the Conservatives and a substantial increase from the 1-point lead in the ICM/Guardian poll of 4–5 September 1993.[26] At that point, Smith pointedly described John Major as 'the devalued Prime Minister of a devalued Government' and felt that the Tories were doomed after their debacle.[27] Thereafter, both Labour and Smith held persistently large leads over the Conservative government and Major without any real challenge from the Liberal Democrats, who had nothing to offer Labour in an alliance, despite the recurrent tendencies of Paddy Ashdown, in what David Steel once said would be a 'one way bargain' in favour of the Liberal Democrats.[28]

Increasingly, exposure of the lack of Tory integrity became a central theme of Smith's campaigning throughout 1993. He challenged the integrity of Norman Lamont, the Chancellor of the Exchequer, focusing on the disquiet and cynicism growing throughout the country about what he called the 'declining standards of government'.[29] He had not received an adequate answer from the Prime Minister after it emerged that taxpayers had paid towards the legal fees of the Chancellor of the Exchequer in evicting a tenant from his London house.[30] He felt that the Prime Minister was clearly out of touch with the anger of the public mood on this matter, stating, 'This is a government from which nobody resigns unless absolutely forced to do so by overwhelming pressure from the public, the media and their own backbenchers. They mislead parliament, they break the law, they jettison policies which once formed the cornerstone of their entire programme.' He added to this the charge of the arrogance of power and the movement of Tory politicians from 'senior positions in the Cabinet to influential posts in privatised industries'.[31]

On 12 January 1994, it was reported in the minutes of the Parliamentary Labour Party (PLP) Committee that 'the Leader referred to the Opinion Polls published that morning which showed the Party on 50 per cent', adding that 'he thought that the political situation was on the whole quite favourable'.[32] On the same day, Smith was determined to respond to the attack levelled by Lord Howe on the inquiry led by Lord Justice Scott into the long-drawn out Matrix Churchill affair, which revealed that businessmen put on trial for illegally exporting potential items of war to Iraq had been advised about how to avoid the restrictions by government ministers. Smith drew up a press release stating that he was appalled at the attack on Lord Justice Scott and his inquiry just four days before John Major was to give evidence: 'Lord Howe is attempting to discredit the inquiry which is likely to be critical of the Tory Government and Tory ministers and to protect the Prime Minister from further huge embarrassment that this will cause to him and his beleaguered government.' He demanded that the Prime Minister reaffirm his confidence in Lord Justice Scott, adding, 'If he does not, then I can only assume that Lord Howe's crude attack was made with the blessing of the Prime Minister.'[33]

In the event, the heavily redacted Scott Report, published in 1996, exposed the lack of accountability of government ministers to Parliament, the misuse of public interest immunity certificates and the extent of government obfuscation.[34] Two weeks after Smith's press statement, it was reported in the minutes of the Parliamentary Committee that 'the Leader said that some satisfaction could be drawn from the fact that the long drawn out campaign to get across the dishonesty of the Tory Party on the question of trust had begun to bear fruit'.[35] Blair added that 'the campaign against the Tories had been brilliantly successful'.[36]

SMITH'S EFFECTIVENESS AS LABOUR LEADER

Tory sleaze was certainly important in improving the fortunes of Labour, but the improved opinion poll ratings were also driven by

Smith's Labour leadership, which saw him establish control of his own party and the unions, whose recent record had been seen as a challenge to Labour control. Indeed, the first thing Smith did when he came to power was to start the process of reorganising and reshaping the Labour Party. It had been undermined by the defection of the Labour right to the Social Democratic Party in the early 1980s and under Neil Kinnock had faced the twin challenges of entryism by the Militant Tendency and an essentially right-wing trade union movement that exerted considerable control over the Party. Kinnock had sought to eject the first and reduce the power of the second, dominating Labour through its National Executive Committee (NEC) and his impassioned performances at party conferences. This did not work, and Smith therefore inherited from Kinnock a party whose hopes had been shattered and whose image was still one of being controlled by the unions, who were themselves adversely associated with the unpopular and demonised industrial conflict of the 'Winter of Discontent' of 1978–9. However, Smith was an entirely different character to Kinnock – much more the collegiate type of leader – and was famed for his wit in the House of Commons.

The first thing that Smith had to do was to demonstrate that he was in control of the Labour Party and that it spoke with a united voice. At his first meeting as leader, he spoke at the PLP Committee to announce that he 'wanted to build a collegiate attitude within the Shadow Cabinet, based on confidence and trust'.[37] For this he appointed his close friend Murray Elder, general secretary of the Scottish Labour Party, as his chief of staff; Hilary Coffman, previously press officer for Neil Kinnock, as his spokesperson; David Ward as his advisor and head of policy; and David Hill as Labour's director of communications, to ensure that party headquarters and the leader's office '[were] in tune with each other'.[38]

This last appointment revealed the style that Smith was to adopt. Unlike Kinnock, who sought to destroy his opponents, Smith listened to what his opponents had to say and tried to incorporate them into the party. He listened to the Labour left, such as Dennis Skinner and Clare Short, and even indulged Tony Benn, who had just been ejected from Labour's NEC after many years' service. Smith had never been elected to the NEC until he became leader but worked with it, through Elder, to encourage it to vote on issues but also to be in line with leadership policies. He launched new Joint Party Committees (JPCs) and a National Policy Forum (NPF) in November 1992. The latter could only offer policies to the JPCs, which Smith appointed. Despite allowing for different views to be expressed, it was Smith who controlled the NEC, and Peter Shore declared in 1993 that 'no previous leader had enjoyed such personal and institutional control over party policy'.[39]

Smith's real means of control was, however, the PLP, the corporate body of Labour MPs, which, until 1983, had elected the leader and deputy leader of the Labour Party. The PLP minutes are often terse, but they reveal Smith's strategy in controlling his MPs, as this was the forum for all Labour MPs and all the parliamentary divisions in Labour. Smith used the PLP as a means by which he informed Labour MPs of his policies and as a sounding board to keep abreast of the issues within the rank-and-file of the party.[40]

Party policy was opposed to the ideas of a Central European Bank, but Smith was committed to the Maastricht Treaty – which the Central Bank was a part of – as the best possible policy for the future.[41]

Many Labour MPs, including Peter Shore, felt that the Central Bank was undemocratic and not in Britain's interests and that Smith's amendment to support it was, in Bryan Gould's words, 'infamy'. Gould argued that the Treaty was 'an outstanding audacious statement of the bankers' ambition to achieve power'. But in the end, Smith carried the PLP vote overwhelmingly by 112 votes to forty-five. In March 1993, Smith backed this with the commitment that the next Labour government would bring the European convention on political and social rights into British law, thereby guaranteeing freedom of speech, a controversial issue in its own right.[42]

The Maastricht Treaty remained a running sore amongst Labour MPs, however, and it emerged as an issue again on Wednesday 10 March 1993 when Denzil Davies rejected the idea, under the Treaty, of member states not being able to run up a financial deficit of more than 3 per cent. Davies, supported by Austin Mitchell, argued that the Treaty would allow the Central Bank to rule the national economies. However, Smith won by ninety-four to thirty-five votes to support it. The only reservation was that the shadow Chancellor of the Exchequer, Gordon Brown, suggested that a future Labour government would not contemplate joining the single currency until five stringent economic tests were met. But alternative views had been expressed at least, with Peter Hain, a leading opponent of Maastricht, saying after the PLP's votes that 'we've lost, but at least we've been heard'.[43] Smith, having got his way, had George Robertson, the shadow Secretary of State for Scotland, harry the government over the bill. When the vote was taken, sixty-eight Labour MPs voted against the Maastricht Treaty, including Kate Hoey, a junior party spokesperson whom Smith sacked.

Smith's demonstrable control of the Labour Party depended upon one vital thing: his reduction of the power of the trade unions within the Labour Party. The overriding demonstration of his control was the securing of one member, one vote (OMOV) system at the Labour Party conference in Brighton in September 1993. The conference had already made it clear in 1990 that it would reduce the block vote at conferences from 90 per cent to 70 per cent, and this was implemented in 1992, at Smith's first conference as Labour leader. In making his bid for the Labour leadership on 14 April 1992, Smith argued that he would continue with the modernisation of the party, emphasising, 'I believe that we must continue to develop a wider democracy within the Party based, wherever appropriate, on the clear principle of one member one vote.'[44]

At the September 1993 Labour Party conference, the method of electing the Labour leader was altered to give equal weighting to the three parts of the electoral college – MPs/MEPs, trade unions and Constituency Labour Parties (CLPs) – and to change the system so both trade unions and the CLPs had to ballot their members before casting a vote.[45] This itself was not that problematic but the extension of OMOV to the selection of parliamentary candidates, which was designed to weaken the power of activists over their MPs, was divisive. The democratisation of the election procedure in the 1980s had empowered activists and trade unions at conferences to force the mandatory reselection of MPs, thus retaining some control over future Labour governments. Kinnock tried to reform the system in the mid-1980s and gradually won over the CLPs, but some key left-wing unions opposed and threatened to defeat the measure, and he was unable to win support for it at the 1992 Labour Party conference. John Edmonds, general secretary of the GMB Union, was strongly opposed to the changes and told his union's conference at Portsmouth in June 1993 that he 'will not compromise in the battle to retain the trade union block vote at Labour conferences'.[46] This was in response to Smith's appearance on Radio 4's *The World This Weekend* to put the case for change. The following day, Smith had Brown and Robin Cook start the campaign for OMOV by writing to each constituency party, who already had seen their vote share increase from 10 per cent to 30 per cent at the last conference.

A month before the Labour Party conference, Smith made a passionate speech at the TUC Conference on 7 September.[47] After offering a parody of Tory failures, Smith attempted to woo the TUC with his commitments to public services, which Smith asserted the Tories did not truly believe in, minimum wage legislation and the Maastricht Treaty – to ensure that the Social Chapter was accepted, giving the working people of Britain what the members of other states of Europe were receiving. Pursuing this commitment to industrial democracy, Smith emphasised that Labour was proposing a new Charter of Rights, which would 'give all workers basic employment rights which will come into force on the first day of a Labour government'.[48] Indeed, that meant equal rights for part-time and full-time, temporary and permanent workers, including protection against unfair dismissal and the right of all workers to join unions, which would have to be recognised by their employers. It was the type of message that the much-reduced membership of the TUC wished to hear.

Despite this, it was reported that Smith would face a humiliating defeat over the OMOV resolution. John Monks, the new TUC general secretary, felt that 'Labour must put more flesh on the bones and say what it stands for'.[49] The GMB was also to hold a fringe meeting at the Brighton Conference, which, according to the *Sunday Times*, '[threatened] to overshadow Smith's address to the conference'.[50] There was particular opposition from the National Union of Public Employees (NUPE), the Union of Communication Workers and the Transport and General Workers' Union about the part of the OMOV resolution that suggested that 5.5 million trade union members who paid a levy to the Labour Party would have to pay £3 extra to be able to vote on the selection of parliamentary candidates.[51] There was a widespread expectation that Smith would be humiliated and some feeling that Smith would have to go further than the 'one more heave' approach that OMOV represented, alongside the Bills of Rights, the Freedom of Information Bill, electoral reform, devolved power and electoral reform that Labour was offering for the next election.[52]

Nevertheless, in a master stroke, Smith linked OMOV and the £3 extra payment by trade unionists to vote with the implementation of a quota system for women where the seats were winnable. This meant that the Manufacturing, Science and Finance Union (MSF), which was strongly opposed to OMOV but held a commitment to all-women shortlists, abstained. This turned out to be vital: MSF held 4.5 per cent of the vote and the winning margin for OMOV was only 3.1 per cent.[53]

John Prescott's rousing speech in favour of OMOV, which Smith stated was 'brilliant', may also have helped in this narrow victory. Prescott declared himself a traditionalist, emphasising that trade unions which had a 30 or 40 per cent block vote could get 100 per cent if all their members paid £3 extra to vote. He stressed that the OMOV resolution was not an attempt to reduce the powers of the unions:

'Can you have any doubts about his [Smith's] commitment to strong trade union connection with the Labour Party?'[54] Indeed, he finished his speech by stressing that Smith believed 'in the relationship, and a strong one, between trade unions and the Labour Party'. 'He has put his head on the block. Now is our time to vote. Give us a bit of trust and let us vote to support him.'[55]

For Smith and the Labour Party, this win was transformative. From being a party dominated by the union barons casting block votes, Labour's public image turned overnight to one of being dominated by democratically arrived decisions, much in line with Smith's rhetoric on the future social democratic governance in Britain. This was, of course, only partly true because the trade unions would still control, by various means, up to 50 per cent of the conference vote and still directly elected twelve of the twenty-seven NEC members. It was acutely observed in *The Independent* that 'this marvellous wave of modernity looks more like a ripple'.[56] Still, Smith's victory was an impressive declaration of a more democratic Labour Party, which would elicit support from the trade union movement. Smith remained ever mindful of his support for the Labour government's Industrial Democracy White Paper in the 1970s, which advocated for trade union directors to be on the boards of large companies.[57]

Smith's continuing commitment to the unions was further revealed in his conversations and correspondence with Rodney Bickerstaffe, the general secretary of the National Union of Public Employees (1981–93) and UNISON (1996–2001). Bickerstaffe, who had been seen as one of the chief militants during the industrial action of the 1978–9 'Winter of Discontent', had become a close friend of Smith. Indeed, when asked on Smith's death about the relations between the trade unions and the Labour Party, he suggested they remained good and that the unions understood that the reforms in the Labour Party were about change rather than weakening them. Bickerstaffe added that Smith was a man one could trust: 'What you saw is what you got … one word to say about him was decency.' Indeed, he was 'a great lost leader' and though he had died, his legacy would last on 'through the eyes of the people he helped'.[58] This view is endorsed by the fact that immediately after the vote on OMOV, Smith had gone into meetings with the trade union leaders and particularly with John Edmonds of the GMB, aiming to maintain the close relationship between the Labour Party and the trade unions.

It is often overlooked that the OMOV victory also endeared Smith and Labour to the female electorate since it had gained the right of all-women shortlists for up to half of all winnable seats. Angela Eagle, Val Foley and Liz Davies were particularly vehement in their support of this controversial decision, which helped to increase the amount of Labour women MPs to 101 at the 1997 general election.[59]

The victory of OMOV has, of course, raised the question of the extent to which Smith carried on his mission to reform Labour. It has been suggested that Smith could be linked with the growth of New Labour in initiating the reforming agenda, but the balance of opinion is now that his reforming ambitions were very moderate, designed to improve Labour's chances of winning the next general election. Indeed, Roy Hattersley suggests that Smith was determined to reform the Labour Party but that 'he wanted to bring old principles up to date, not to replace them. He looked for intellectual improvement not ideological alternatives'.[60] Christopher J. Wilkinson has broadly agreed with this interpretation of his actions, suggesting that Smith was essentially committed to moderation by using his great communication skills to unify the party while reforming it.[61] Ultimately, modernisation and reform were to be within the context of an established Labour tradition that would be recognisable to its members and the electorate.

PUBLIC COMMUNICATION SKILLS AND POLICY PLATFORMS

Smith was a skilled debater, and his qualities are evident through his parliamentary performances. Yet it has been said that he was never at ease at party conferences, and the journalist Anthony Howard has suggested that 'the platform was not his strength any more than the House of Commons was Neil Kinnock's'.[62] There may have been questions about the delivery of his speeches on the platform at conferences but those he gave to the TUC in September 1993 and to the Labour Party conference in October 1993 were full of witty asides and his performances were possibly more effective than often suggested. In both speeches, Smith presented powerful arguments about the inequalities of society, the failures of the economic and social policies of the Conservative government and how he would re-establish the democratic rights of citizens in Britain. These speeches may have lacked the full wit of parliamentary debate but were essential for his policies in the absence of a definitive Labour programme. And he was clearly successful in getting his message across, as the opinion polls and the local elections results revealed.

In the municipal elections of 1993 and 1994, the only elections we can use to measure Smith's impact, Labour made steady gains. In the May elections of both 1993 and 1994, Labour increased its electoral position. It raised its vote share to 39 per cent and won 111 extra seats in 1993 to increase its number of councillors to 9,213 and then won 40 per cent of the vote in 1994, winning forty-four more council seats and ending with 9,257 councillors.[63] In contrast, the Conservative Party lost 486 seats and lost 15 per cent of the vote in 1993 to reduce their total vote share to 31 per cent and 7,802 councillors in total. In 1994, the party lost another 516 seats, reducing them to 7,286 councillors and a mere 27 per cent of the vote.

In effect, this meant that Labour increased its overall vote share and representation at local elections at the expense of the Conservatives and that the Conservatives lost more than 1,000 seats and fell 17 points in the poll rating between 1992 and 1994. Imperfect as these results are, often determined by local circumstances as well as national events, they are broad indicators of how Smith's Labour Party was progressing and confirm that Smith's message was getting across to the electorate. One might add that the 1990s was the only time between 1973 and 2022 – a span of just under fifty years – when Labour has held more council seats in Britain than the Conservatives, and that rise in the proportion of Labour councillors and the decline of the Conservative Party councillors was most dramatic between 1992 and 1995.[64] From 1996 onwards, the Labour position weakened as the Conservative Party recovered.

This success was achieved without a clearly defined set of 'Smithian' Labour social policies. Smith's Commission on Social Justice was set up on the fiftieth anniversary of the Beveridge Report to act as an independent body, offering deep thinking on the issues of social policy and social insurance from which he might draw the policies for Labour at the next general election.[65] The idea for a commission came partly from Donald Dewar and the Institute for Public Policy Research (IPPR) think tank and their belief that Labour's fifty or so policy review committees would produce a policy review 'of a Heinz-57 variety' rather than a co-ordinated set of social policies for Britain.[66] It drew in a variety of independent experts, such as Professor David Marquand from Labour and then the SDP, but also included Patricia Hewitt, deputy director of the IPPR, and David Miliband, a rising star on Labour's political firmament.

Independent of – but associated with – Smith and Labour, the commission was to be part of the process by which Labour would exorcise the ghosts of the 1992 general election. It aimed to offer a set of policies which would rethink the welfare state by seeking the opinions of more than ninety organisations.[67] The commission produced some interim reports and pamphlets before publishing its final report *Social Justice: Strategies for National Renewal* on 24 October 1994, months after Smith's death. The report revisited Beveridge's five wants – namely want, idleness, ignorance, disease and squalor – and added in a sixth, discrimination. It argued for an 'investors' Britain', where economic investment would be combined with the ethics of community in a mixed economy of capitalism and community, rather than the 'deregulation Britain' of the Tories, which would only ensure that the rich got richer and the poor got poorer. Committed to investing in the country, the commission came up with an holistic programme of suggestions for investing in lifelong learning, offering training schemes and a future welfare state that was not just about offering benefits for the poor in an industrial society but would encourage self-improvement and well-paid jobs, declaring that 'it must be a hand up, not just a handout'.[68] The idea was to move men and women from welfare to work because it was felt that the benefit system would continue to keep the poor in poverty.

The report also suggested the need for a national minimum wage, and it felt that every working adult should have a second pension as well as an old-age pension.[69] All this was to operate within local democracy, which would produce a 'thriving civic culture' that meant devolution for Scotland and Wales and for the English regions, local authorities regaining powers from unelected quangos, and citizens' service for sixteen to 25-year-olds. It recognised that there were many issues to be addressed – high taxes for the poor and low taxes for the rich, discrimination in employment, unfair tax allowance – and stipulated that there needed to be a better balance in society, more emphasis upon fairness and citizenship within the context of economic growth. To achieve this, the commission suggested that there should be a 'learning bank' to aid lifelong learning, a National Community Reorganisation Agency, community development trusts, a National Regeneration Fund and an investment bank to promote economic growth in Britain within a growing world economy, in order to ensure a better balance of income and wealth distribution in British society.[70] In other words, there was to be a move away from Clement Attlee's universality of welfare to a mixed economy, which would encourage citizens to improve their skills, increase their financial rewards and move away from benefit dependency.

Smith died before the final report was published, but while he might have been concerned about how these policies could be

financed out of taxation, the strategy advocated was sufficiently mal-
leable for Smith to have stamped his own mark on these policies.
They largely equated to the views he had been expounding for many
years, and local election results and opinions suggest that they were
resonating with electors.

The Commission was largely sidelined on the death of Smith, and
its influence on New Labour was limited. In an interview, Blair stated,
'Hmm, some of it isn't New Labour enough. Some of it is bang-on.'[71]
The recommendations were undoubtedly not specific enough for the
New Labour policies that Blair envisaged, including tax credits to get
people off benefits, and there is quite clearly no straight line between
the policies of the commission and New Labour. Nevertheless, David
Miliband and Patricia Hewitt, members of the commission, were to
find themselves in Blair's Labour governments, and their experience
and commitment was carried into New Labour. The commission's
idea of a 'hand up rather than a handout' and the idea of a national
minimum hourly pay became elements of Labour's new approach
to welfare. Other aspects of the commission were to emerge in New
Labour policy, including emphasising the link between industry and
the welfare state and a commitment to Europe. However, there clearly
were areas where the views of Smith and his commission were not
taken up by New Labour. Indeed, Hattersley acted as a siren voice
on this issue, criticising New Labour for its desertion of policies to
deal with the poor and its blatant disregard of the need to redistribute
wealth in order to move towards equality in the new working alliance between government and industry that was envisaged by New
Labour.[72]

Few think that Smith would have been so bold as to change Clause IV of the Labour Party constitution – its commitment to public ownership – because while it was no longer relevant, having being abandoned by Labour in the 1970s, it was part of the Labour Party heritage.[73] Nevertheless, Blair's much wordier, new Clause IV might have reflected Smith's thoughts of 'a dynamic economy serving the public interest in which the enterprise of the market and the rigour of competition joined with the forces of partnership and cooperation.'[74]

CONCLUSION

Success in politics is always amorphous and often temporary, but in John Smith's case it is clear that within a few months of assuming the role of Labour leader he dramatically improved Labour's position in the opinion polls and in local elections, following Labour's disappointing general election result of 1992. His leadership was clearly aided by a faltering Tory administration, brutally associated with failure and sleaze and eviscerated by 'Black Wednesday' in September 1992. Yet it is also clear that Smith had already established himself as the ultimate democrat, committed to active citizenship, regional devolution and Scottish devolution even before he became Labour leader. Although his commitment to such changes and to a fairer society was never fully established in tangible policies because of his early death, his clear message as a national politician from the 1970s onwards was that he believed that citizens should be given the right of a national minimum wage, a better system of ensuring good living standards and a welfare system which was 'a hand up, not a handout'. His commitment to a fairer society and a Bill of Rights certainly appealed to the electorate in the face of extremes of inequality, which the Tories seemed to embody in their policies.

Smith's commitment to industrial democracy from the 1970s ensured that even his spat with the trade unions over OMOV did not damage his relations with the trade union leaders. Indeed, it appears that they came to believe that OMOV led to a change of style rather than a weakening of trade union political influence, as Bickerstaffe suggested in his homage to Smith on the day of his death. Smith's successes with OMOV and the creation of all-women parliamentary selection lists in winnable constituencies, plus his control over the PLP, created an image of a man in control of his party, which by the early and mid-1990s was clearly not the case with Major and his Conservative government.

A brilliant wit in Parliament and more than just a good platform speaker, Smith had a lot of things going for him and was clearly no makeshift leader. Even his political opponents admired his qualities. Bickerstaffe, in his tribute, reflected of him that 'he was not shifty' and stood for decency, adding that the style of Smith was that 'I am not a whizz kid. I am not a silly person'.[75] Honesty and integrity in politics are often perceived to be rare things but Smith had them in abundance and turned them into political success for Labour. Using his skills, traits and rise in the opinion polls, he was able to reform Old Labour in his period of office and did so based upon the citizenship values of Old Labour, which were far from being the basis of the New Labour movement – though undoubtedly Blair's New Labour movement benefitted from his successful leadership. In the end, John Smith's political success emerged from the unusual political circumstances of the early 1990s, his distinctive blend of Old Labour and moderate, almost right-wing, reformism and his own unifying presence as the tribune of the people.

2

JOHN SMITH AND IDEOLOGY

Kevin Hickson

'Politics ought to be a moral activity.'

JOHN SMITH, 20 MARCH 1993[1]

T HIS CHAPTER AIMS TO locate John Smith within the
longer traditions of democratic socialist (or social democratic) thought.* In so doing, it is important to identify some key characteristics of Smith's ideological views. On the one hand, Smith is
regarded as a man who was guided by firm principles, drawn from
his Christian background. At the same time, however, Smith is seen
as a pragmatist, willing to adapt to changing circumstances and electoral realities as Labour sought to find a way forward from its fourth

---

*   I use the terms interchangeably for purposes of this chapter.

general election defeat in a row. As the epigraph at the start of the chapter shows, for Smith, politics was rooted in a system of beliefs.

THE NATURE OF BRITISH SOCIALISM

The Labour Party, much like the Conservatives, is itself a broad coalition of people with divergent views brought together by the first past the post electoral system. What defines the right and left wings has changed over time, but broadly speaking, in terms of political economy, the left sees itself as more hostile to capitalism, wishing to see a much more significant extension of public ownership and state direction of the economy. The right has often been seen as more willing to compromise with the private sector.* The left is usually seen as more fundamentalist and the right as revisionist.

Those seeking to revise or modernise the Labour Party's programme have relied on a distinction between values and policies or 'ends' and 'means'. While the policies are seen as flexible and requiring regular updating, the values are held to be timeless. However, this seemingly neat distinction is problematic because twice since 1945 the ends/means distinction has been important. Labour Party revisionists in the 1950s and early 1960s – such as Hugh Gaitskell and his followers Douglas Jay and Tony Crosland – argued that the left of the party had become fixated on public ownership, which was a means and not even a particularly important one at that.† Instead, attention

---

* There have, of course, been other prominent divisions over issues such as Britain's relationship with the US and nuclear weapons.

† Crosland has received considerable academic interest, Jay much less so. Hence the reason for my research on Jay that will lead to the publication of a biography in due course.

should be placed on ethical principles such as equality and social justice, which could be achieved through alternative policies more effectively.* The left protested that public ownership was more akin to an
end goal, but the party moved away from seeing it as such, adopting a
policy that owed more to indicative planning and Keynesian economics. A similar controversy over ends and means came about in the
New Labour years, with more traditional-minded social democrats
such as Roy Hattersley arguing that the Blair government was failing
to tax the richest in society sufficiently. Modernisers responded that
this failed to take account of a more globalised economy in which
social democratic policies had to be revised. But for traditionalists,
the principle of greater equality of outcome could not be achieved
without it, making New Labour revisionist – not just of means but
also ends.

These debates are relevant when positioning John Smith within
the social democratic tradition. According to Mark Stuart, Smith
was initially influenced by Crosland.[2] Smith first became an MP in
1970, when Crosland was entering what would turn out to be the final
decade of his life. Crosland, by this stage, had already established
himself as the leading theorist within the Labour Party, having published *The Future of Socialism* in 1956. Smith was on friendly terms
with Crosland, and the two would sit together in the House of Commons tea rooms and bars. However, when Crosland stood for the
leadership in 1976, Smith immediately supported James Callaghan,
probably on the basis that he was most likely to win (which proved
to be a correct calculation). By the time Smith entered the Cabinet,

---

* For them, this largely consisted of the extension of taxes on wealth and reform of schools.

Crosland had died. Smith could be seen as a Croslandite, notwith-standing his support for Callaghan. Despite his pro-Europeanism, Smith was never a close associate of Roy Jenkins and it would seem that he never seriously contemplated joining the newly formed Social Democratic Party in 1981.[3] Given this connection between Crosland, the high priest of Revisionism, and the early political career of Smith, it makes sense to analyse the latter's ideology in terms of the ends/ means distinction.

THE ARTICULATION OF ENDS

Smith subscribed to an ethical approach to socialism. In this, he was entirely consistent with earlier leaders. The Labour Party had quickly abandoned the revolutionary route to socialism when it was formed. Despite the revival of interest in Marxism at times of economic crisis – most obviously in the 1930s and 1970s – the Labour Party remained wedded to the ethical or reformist approach to socialism. This ethical approach consisted of an attachment to the principles of equality, liberty and community. The moral foundations for such principles were within the traditions of Christianity and humanism.

In terms of equality, Smith clearly believed in something that went beyond equality of opportunity. In this, he was consistent with the thoughts of Crosland. Though equality of opportunity was desirable, it was an insufficient notion for socialists. Equality of opportunity failed to recognise that starting points were unequal. Differences in income and wealth, family upbringing and innate qualities meant that people did not all have the same starting point. Therefore, there needed to be a focus on equality of outcome. However, for Crosland, complete equality of outcome was inefficient and would lead to an overpowerful state and the loss of personal liberty. There had to be a way of reconciling these issues, and for Crosland this consisted of a strong notion of equality of opportunity, in which people were provided with resources to overcome disadvantages, and greater equality of outcome through redistribution funded by higher rates of economic growth. Economic expansion was essential for the realisation of this agenda, since the rich would not be willing to see a fall in their absolute standard of living. Growth would allow for the maintenance of the absolute position of the better off, while also seeing an improvement in the relative position of the worst off.[4] Crosland later linked this to Rawls's notion of democratic equality in which inequalities were only justified if they were to the advantage of the least advantaged.[5]

According to Smith, the extension of individual liberty was his core value: 'Freedom is our goal.'[6] In this, he was entirely consistent not just with Crosland but also with his immediate predecessor, Neil Kinnock. Crosland had argued that without greater equality, individuals could not be truly free. In contrast, the New Right had tried to claim liberty from the left by linking it directly to the free market. As the state could only function by imposing laws, regulations and taxation on private citizens and companies, it inevitably eroded their personal liberty. The expansion of the state since 1945 amounted to a loss of liberty. The only way in which such lost liberties could be restored was through a contraction of the state and the expansion of the market, in which people could choose for themselves. Liberty was seen in purely negative terms – freedom from constraint – and

Thatcher claimed to be setting the people free. Drawing on the ideas of the likes of the economist Friedrich Hayek, the positive conception of liberty (that people are only free if they have the resources to act) was dismissed.

A central objective of the social democratic left in the 1980s was to reclaim the idea of freedom from the New Right. Philosophers such as Raymond Plant provided the intellectual basis for the restoration of the positive case for liberty. By asking what is liberty for, Plant argued that it is necessary to have liberty in order to be able to do things.[7] The theoretical freedom of negative liberty only made sense if people also have the capacity to act, which brings us back to the positive conception of liberty – the freedom of X from Y in order to do Z. Without adequate resources in terms of a social security safety net, free health care, employment, educational opportunities and such like, freedom was meaningless for the less fortunate in society. His ideas were taken up by Kinnock, Hattersley in his book *Choose Freedom* and others.[8] It also informed the *Statement of Democratic Socialist Aims and Values*, published in 1988, which Hattersley intended would lay the ideological foundations for the forthcoming Policy Review announced by Kinnock.

Smith made it explicit that his understanding of freedom was this positive kind:

Not just the abstract and theoretical choices of Tory privatization – but the practical ability to make the choices that can lead to personal fulfilment: the ability to choose that comes from high class schools and hospitals, and from high wages and highly skilled jobs.[9]

Smith also placed considerable emphasis on the idea of community. This was most explicit in his Tawney Memorial Lecture in 1993.[10] We know that this speech was important to Smith since he spent a lot of time on it – too much according to some of those close to him such as Donald Dewar.[11] He wanted it to be a clear statement of his beliefs. The speech is interesting because it was an explicit statement of his Christianity. Smith was a deeply spiritual person and worshipped in church regularly. Starting off with the caveat that one could be a socialist and hold the same values without being a Christian and that equally not all Christians came to a socialist view of politics, he goes on to make an explicit link between his religious and political beliefs. Drawing on the ideas of William Temple, as well as R. H. Tawney, Smith argued that the New Right were incorrect to see individuals as essentially private and self-interested. They were also inherently social beings, 'living in families, in communities, in regions and in nations'.[12] Individuals only reached their fullest stage of development and self-awareness by coming together in society, where they had rights and responsibilities to others. The Biblical command to love your neighbour as yourself required society to care for its fellow citizens: 'In this vital way we can ally our Christian faith to our democratic socialist conviction.'[13]

This was a key change of thinking about socialist ends from Kinnock, his immediate predecessor, since considerable scepticism had been expressed towards the idea of community in the late 1980s, with emphasis being placed on the core idea of freedom instead. For instance, in the development of the *Statement of Democratic Socialist Aims and Values*, some had argued that too much emphasis had been placed on the idea of individual freedom.[14] This applied to some still associated with the left at that time – David Blunkett for example, who penned an alternative statement with Bernard Crick that stressed the importance of community as an ideal much more. Their meaning of community was vague, however, beyond an emphasis on restoring local democracy. But criticism was not limited to the left – in private, some on the right, including Smith, had expressed their reservations to Hattersley and Kinnock.[15] In the end, the document was not taken especially seriously and hardly attracted any attention at the Labour Party conference when it came time to consider it.

Smith argued that the Labour Party's political philosophy, derived from the thought of Temple, stood for 'service to family, to community and to nation'.[16] This was entirely consistent with traditional approaches to ideology within the Labour Party, drawing on Tawney and Crosland, firmly rejecting the ideas of the New Right and placing clear constraints on the role of the market while seeing the central state as the key vehicle for social and economic progress. In terms of 'ends', therefore, we can say that Smith had not revised the values of the traditional Labour Party.

THE EVOLUTION OF MEANS

In terms of his political ideas then, Smith seemed entirely comfortable in his faith in what may be considered traditional Labour values. This may explain why those who were keener for a clearer break with 'Old Labour' grew frustrated with Smith. The sociologist Anthony Giddens had argued in 1994 that fundamental political, social, cultural and economic changes had rendered the terms left and right obsolete, and those on the centre-left had to move away from traditional ways of thinking, going 'beyond' left and right and embracing what would become known as the Third Way, including a greater focus on individualism and a greater role for markets.[17] These ideas were much closer to the direction in which Blair wished to take the party.

However, it would be wrong to argue that Smith's thinking did not undergo significant evolution. Indeed, there were critical changes in Labour Party thinking more generally from the 1987 general election defeat through to the death of Smith in 1994 – in which Smith himself played a critical role, first as shadow Chancellor and then as Leader of the Opposition. This can be seen in three broad areas: economic policy, European integration and constitutional reform. Since the details of these policy areas are set out in greater depth in this volume by Wyn Grant, Richard Johnson and Jasper Miles respectively, I will only touch here on these developments in order to show how they relate to my overall argument about the changing nature of democratic socialism at this time.

In response to the 1979 general election defeat and the subsequent economic hardship and inequality that the Thatcher governments created, Labour at first moved to the left, beyond its traditional Keynesian approach, with its Alternative Economic Strategy (AES). The AES included large-scale public investment in industry, controls on the movement of capital, restrictions on imports and subsidies for exporters. The policy was deemed to have failed with the rejection of Labour in the 1983 general election. Labour then moved back towards a Keynesian approach. Smith was, at first, consistent with this approach. He had always been associated with the Labour right and had never supported the AES. Just before becoming shadow Chancellor, he articulated a classic Keynesian response to the economic conditions of the 1980s, rejecting the government's economic liberal strategy and arguing that full employment was a 'fundamental objective of a socially just society'.[18] Despite their differences, the AES and Labour Keynesianism shared similar attitudes towards the nation state. Central government could and should intervene to achieve economic progress, the main policy goal should be full employment and the core economic unit within the international economy was the nation state. Governments should have as much autonomy as was needed in order to achieve full employment and economic growth.

However, from the late 1980s, starting with Labour's Policy Review, there was a key shift in thinking on economic policy. This change can be summarised as a shift away from discretion towards a rules-based order. This is to say that in place of allowing the government as much discretion and policy autonomy as possible in order to achieve its objectives, the state should be constrained by institutional reform and an adherence to rules. There were several reasons for this. The first is that there was growing pessimism over the capacity of the central state to manage the economy in the way democratic socialists wished. Events such as the 1976 IMF crisis, which Smith had experienced as an MP, and the failed Mitterrand government's attempts to grow the economy in France in the early 1980s had shown the constraints under which national governments now operated. The events of Black Wednesday in 1992 also seemed to confirm that national governments could not 'buck the market'. In a sense, the British government had always been under such constraints, as seen by the devaluations under Clement Attlee and Harold Wilson, but the argument was that now governments were even more constrained because of the rise of globalisation.

Added to this was a second constraint, which some on the left thought that the Labour Party faced. This was a more directly electoral matter. Inflation had once again become a problem in the late 1980s and early 1990s. Labour had long been associated with the high inflation of the 1970s. In order to show that it could be trusted not to return to a high-inflation economy if returned to office at the next general election, it was felt that a clear anti-inflationary policy had to be adopted. Such a policy required some form of discipline upon government. The Thatcher governments had adopted monetary targets, and this policy seemed to offer an easy way to control inflation by controlling the money supply, but the policy proved much more difficult in practice. It was quietly abandoned by the Chancellor, Nigel Lawson, who started to shadow the Deutschmark instead. This led eventually to a major rift between Lawson and Thatcher, not least over the role of her senior economic advisor Alan Walters. At the very end of Thatcher's government, she was persuaded to take Britain into the Exchange Rate Mechanism (ERM). The fixed exchange rate would, its advocates believed, instil the anti-inflationary restraint on government policy. However, the forced withdrawal from the ERM in 1992 led to a search for another nominal anchor.

Gordon Brown, influenced by his economic advisor Ed Balls, came to favour independence for the Bank of England with a Monetary Policy Committee of independent experts setting interest rates instead of the Chancellor – supposedly taking this crucial economic policy measure out of politics. Smith was initially very reluctant to support this option, seeing political control over the bank as essentially a matter of democracy. However, his senior policy advisor, David Ward (see Chapter 13 in this volume) believes he may have come around to the idea in return for greater regulation of the City. Writing in 2005, Mark Stuart, Smith's biographer, argued that the decision to grant independence to the Bank had been a success.[19] And it appeared that way for some time while Britain enjoyed relatively low inflation. However, when inflation increased after Russia's invasion of Ukraine in 2022, interest rates were raised, and many people faced higher mortgage costs. The role of the Bank of England has come under more criticism since then, with some arguing that it should be taken back under government control.

These dilemmas were compounded by the shifting attitude of the Labour Party towards European integration. Historically, the party had been largely Eurosceptic, albeit containing some prominent pro-Europeans. However, from the mid to late 1980s this changed. In the 1983 general election, Labour pledged to withdraw from the 'capitalist club' if elected. By 1987, this had changed to renegotiating the terms of membership with withdrawal as a last resort. In the period after 1987, Labour's view became more positive. This coincided with Thatcher's turn in the opposite direction as signified by her speech at Bruges in 1988. Jacques Delors, as President of the European Commission, advocated a social policy dimension that seemed to some on the left to allow the kinds of things which Thatcher had sought to move away from in office, such as workers' rights, with the additional bonus that these would be enshrined in EU law and therefore could not be undone by a future right-wing government in Britain. Smith had always been strongly pro-European, going back to his early days as an MP, and both encouraged and supported this development in Labour's thinking on the issue. He had advocated entry into the ERM and as leader, moved the party further towards pro-Europeanism on matters including the ratification of the Maastricht Treaty and the Monetary Union. Single currency, he argued, 'would offer Britain some advantages'.[20] Britain must 'stand for a positive partnership and active participation in the Community' so as to get the most out of membership, learning from the past mistake of remaining aloof.[21] As Richard Johnson states in this volume, he was the most pro-European leader in the party's history.

The debates over economic policy and European integration were closely related. For those subscribing to a Keynesian viewpoint, the sovereignty of the nation should be protected. The government of the day should have sufficient room for manoeuvre to achieve its objectives, subject only to the democratic constraints of a sovereign House of Commons. Arguments over the declining capacity of nation states in an era of alleged globalisation were exaggerated, they believed. Within the shadow Cabinet, these arguments were made by Bryan Gould, with Labour Keynesians on the back benches, including Peter Shore and Austin Mitchell, also making forceful interventions. A Full Employment Forum was launched in July 1993 and criticisms of Smith's direction were repeatedly made in meetings of the Parliamentary Labour Party, but it is clear that this stance was losing ground within the party. A policy framework primarily concerned with controlling inflation had been adopted. New Labour's subsequent economic policy was even more strongly pro-market, with light-touch regulation of the City and a greater focus on the supply side of the economy. Similarly, the Labour Party remained an over-whelmingly pro-European party despite divisions over membership of the single currency. By the time of the 2016 Brexit referendum, the Labour Party was almost exclusively Remain.

The focus on constitutional reform was also a key development in the Labour Party at this time. The Labour Party had historically been suspicious of constitutional reform, seeing clear advantages in the Westminster Model of the constitution – namely that with unri-valled sovereignty residing in the House of Commons over the whole territorial area of the UK, it would be easier for Labour to introduce the social and economic reforms it wanted once it had secured a man-date. This attitude appeared justified by the experience of Labour in power 1945–51. Even though Labour was in opposition for thirteen years between 1951 and 1964, demand for reform of the British con-stitution was not a feature of either wing of the party in that period. When Labour did reform the constitution, it was either in the hope of fending off competition from other parties, such as happened over devolution which was seen as a way to defeat the Scottish National Party, or it was to make the passing of its legislation easier, such as with House of Lords reform. Broadly speaking, Labour had confi-dence in the existing constitutional arrangements.

However, with three successive election defeats and growing de-mands for constitutional reform from sections of the party in the late 1980s, pressure mounted on the leadership.[22] Smith had long supported devolution to Scotland. In office as leader, he showed his strong support for constitutional reform in other areas too including reform to the House of Lords, increased powers for local authorities, freedom of information, human rights laws and so on. On the issue of electoral reform, however, Smith remained sceptical. A committee had been established by Kinnock to examine changing the electoral system, chaired by Plant. Smith seemed lukewarm to its proposals – arguing with Plant over it – though he did agree to hold a referendum on the issue if elected to government.

CONCLUSION

Smith's ideological position can be summarised as being consistent with traditional Labour Party views on the ends of democratic socialism, with his attachment to equality defined as equality of opportunity and greater equality of outcome, the positive conception of liberty and a community in which everyone shares responsibility to the common good. However, when examining the political means or policies through which these values are put into practice, we can see major differences between traditional Labour stances and those adopted under Smith's leadership. The Labour Party moved from Keynesianism in its political economy to advocacy of a rules-based order in which control of inflation became the main aim of economic policy; from a predominantly Eurosceptic to pro-European position on the EU; and from defenders of the constitution to advocates for radical reform. Smith was not solely responsible for these developments – they had been occurring under his predecessor – but they went further under his leadership.

It has often been remarked that Smith was far more confident and at ease with himself than Kinnock had been as leader. He had an intellectual self-confidence, which his predecessor lacked. This may have come from his legal work and his debating skills; he was instinctively more at home in the House of Commons (though a less inspiring platform speaker than Kinnock). But it may also be because Smith was leader in changed circumstances. The weaknesses of neo-liberalism were now much more readily apparent. He noted that some of those who at one time had been amongst its strongest advocates were now singing a different tune and that things were moving in the direction of social democracy.[23] Speaking about the previous fourteen years of Conservative government in 1993, Smith proclaimed, 'Let us not deny the tide of opinion which I believe is beginning to flow towards a recognition of the value of society and away from the destructive individualism.'[24] He went on to add that 'the intellectual ground is moving steadily towards the democratic left'.[25]

Smith almost certainly would have won the next general election had he lived and would have had more confidence in traditional Labour values than New Labour did. Whether or not the new, more pluralistic policy framework would have been capable of realising traditional democratic socialist values is more open to debate.

3

OCCUPYING THE PALACE: JOHN SMITH AND PARLIAMENT

Philip Norton, Lord Norton of Louth

T HERE ARE THREE DIMENSIONS to a Member of Parliament using Parliament effectively to achieve political goals, whether those goals be holding office or achieving specific policy outcomes. John Smith, rather like one of his predecessors as Labour leader, James Callaghan, succeeded in all three. Each dimension entails the use of space within Parliament.

One, the most obvious, is public space, primarily the Chamber and committee rooms, where members deliberate on the record. Their behaviour is observable and recorded and entails public performance, encompassing both oration and debate.

The second is private space, where, like public space, there is a formally convened gathering with an agenda and presiding officer but where the behaviour occurs behind closed doors. This especially covers meetings of parliamentary parties, as well as groupings such as all-party groups and unofficial political groups.[1] The activity may be important, with significant consequences for the political system, but it is activity that is not measurable and not observable by the outsider.

The third is informal space, also not measurable and observable to the outsider, where there is no formally convened gathering, no agenda and no presiding officer.[2] Examples of this kind of space are the tea and dining rooms, corridors and other places where members meet and chat. Inhabiting this space is invaluable for those who wish to hold office and those who wish to continue to hold office, as well as those who wish to mobilise support for a particular policy goal. It is also valuable for information exchange. For a new member, meeting informally with fellow members is key to understanding the norms and processes of the institution.

John Smith succeeded in utilising all three forms – in large part because of his commitment to Parliament. Other than his wife, there were three loves in his life: the law, the Labour Party and Parliament. He trained as a lawyer and maintained his legal interests while still an MP, which gave him a career that he could fall back on and enabled him to maintain a degree of independence. His advocacy skills translated well to the parliamentary arena. Smith was a Labour loyalist, committed to the party, with no interest in breakaway movements. And he was a committed parliamentarian. His wife, Elizabeth Smith, recalled that 'he told me almost as soon as we had met that he was going to be an MP'.[3] He fought his first seat in 1961, at the age of twenty-three, and was elected to the House nine years later. When he fought East Fife for a second time in 1964, as Elizabeth noted, 'he was in his element, assured and natural, a born politician enjoying himself enormously'.[4]

Once elected in 1970, Smith demonstrated an independent approach. His maiden speech departed from the convention of political neutrality, using the opportunity to criticise government policy. Unusually, he also spoke again the day after his maiden speech. Smith also demonstrated his independence by vote: in 1971, he was one of sixty-nine Labour MPs to defy a three-line whip and vote for the motion approving the decision of principle for the UK to join the European Communities on the basis of the arrangements that had been negotiated.[5] It was a principled stance, as well as a brave one for a new MP. In the event, it was his only rebellion, but that is explicable in terms of the fact that he was not a backbencher for long.

His pro-European vote was not to hold back his political career. As soon as Labour gained office in February 1974, Smith was appointed parliamentary private secretary to the Secretary of State for Scotland (having turned down the post of Solicitor General for Scotland, believing he could get stuck in a rut of legal offices), and following the October 1974 general election, he joined the government as a junior minister. The following year he was advanced to Minister of State level, and he joined the Cabinet in 1978 at the age of forty. When Labour lost the 1979 general election, Smith had experienced five years of ministerial office.

Being a 'good' minister does not necessarily solely encompass performance in a department and at the dispatch box. Each may be necessary but they are not sufficient to maintain political support on one's own benches. The use of both private and informal space is critical to maintaining and enhancing support.

After 1979, Smith was on the opposition front bench continuously until he was elected leader of the Labour Party in 1992. Lacking the resources of government, the use of parliamentary space comes even more to the fore in opposition. He had to rely on limited research and administrative support, making his mark through public performance and maintaining support through meetings of the Parliamentary Labour Party (PLP) and mixing with colleagues. He combined his ability to listen and gain the confidence of others with his skills of advocacy, with the political historian Tudor Jones asserting that 'he was above all a unifier'.[6]

It was Smith's period as Leader of the Opposition that was to be his greatest success in Parliament, through a combination of the opportunity to engage with the Prime Minister at Prime Minister's Questions and the problems faced by government. The government was vulnerable to Smith's debating skills.

IN THE CHAMBER

As a minister Smith was competent, his advocacy and pragmatism enabling him to defend the government in a demanding political environment. The challenges were particularly strong over the issue of devolution. In many respects, getting the Scotland Bill through the Commons helped establish his reputation – according to broadcaster and journalist James Naughtie, it put an 'obvious shine ... on his parliamentary reputation – for months on end he was a fixture at the dispatch box'.[7] Throughout the lengthy debates in committee – the bill, as a constitutional measure, was taken on the floor of the House – Smith was regularly on his feet, defending the bill against critics in all parts of the House, including his own back benches. As

Naughtie states, 'Smith popped up and down like a jack-in-the-box lawyer in a big trial, hour after hour and day after day defending the rather imperfect scheme against all that could be thrown at it.'[8] He was widely recognised as having done a fine job at the dispatch box, demonstrating his skills in debating and his sensitivity to the points raised by members. His reward was advancement to the Cabinet.

Opposition was not a congenial position for Smith, in part because it was opposition and in large part because of the rifts in the Labour Party. He played his part as a member of the shadow Cabinet but was not a prominent figure in the split that led to the formation of the Social Democratic Party, and he kept a relatively low profile in the Commons. The new parliament of 1983 saw Labour badly reduced in its number of seats, but it created an opportunity for Smith to make a notable mark in the House. Smith felt more comfortable under the leadership of Neil Kinnock than Michael Foot, but what enabled him to make a mark in the House was nothing to do with what happened in opposition but rather what happened in government. There were two controversies that enabled Smith to deploy his debating talents, helping mark him out as a future party leader.

The Westland crisis of 1985–6, where the Secretary of State for Defence, Michael Heseltine, clashed with the Secretary of State for Trade and Industry, Leon Brittan – ultimately resulting in both resigning – created an opportunity for Smith to attack the government using not only his skills of advocacy but also his humour. His capacity to use humour was to be a notable feature of his debating skills. As Nigel Lawson was later to recall, 'John Smith, my Labour opposite number, was an effective parliamentary debater with a particular talent for mockery ... Smith's jokes, which were often very successful

– he has a good, dry sense of timing – were invariably better than his speeches, which were entirely predictable.'[9] Smith's attacks on the government over Westland established him as one of the opposition front bench's most effective performers. He was further able to consolidate his reputation when the government announced plans to sell off the state-owned British Leyland Corporation to foreign buyers. The negotiations over its sale proved controversial and protracted, which enabled Smith to exploit ministers' difficulties in Parliament, producing 'a series of outstanding Commons performances'.[10] He won *The Spectator*'s Parliamentarian of the Year Award in 1986, the accolade demonstrating his effectiveness in dealing with both crises.

Smith's command of detail and his capacity for forensic analysis – also demonstrated by his steering of the devolution legislation through the House – showed the debating skills of his party leaders to be lacking by comparison: specifically, Foot in the case of devolution and Kinnock in terms of Westland and British Leyland.[11] Kinnock in particular tended to go for the bigger picture and, as was the case with Westland, fluff the big occasions. Smith's biographer, Mark Stuart, examines this in his book: 'It remains an article of faith to some Labour backbench MPs that if only John Smith had led for the opposition instead of Neil Kinnock, Mrs Thatcher might have fallen.'[12]

The disarray in government was also to benefit Smith when he was promoted to shadow Chancellor in 1987. He was not always the most confident or effective of debater in dealing with economic issues, since economics was not his field, although he made some effective attacks on the government – not least in response to the 1988 Budget. His most effective challenge was over the difficulties the government faced when Nigel Lawson clashed with Prime Minister Margaret

Thatcher over her use of Sir Alan Walters as her economic advisor. According to Lawson, 'Once Walters was there, Smith was able to ignore the economic policy issues with which he felt so uncomfortable and concentrate exclusively on the evident split between Margaret and myself and in particular Walters' role in this: a soft target which made the going very much more difficult.'[13]

Smith also effectively used humour to exploit the rift. In opening an opposition day debate on 7 June 1989 on the government's economic policy, he effectively lampooned Thatcher's claim that Lawson was a good neighbour with a lively rendering of the eight lines of the theme song of the television programme *Neighbours*.[14] He returned to the attack in another opposition day debate on 24 October, goading Lawson with the role played by Walters and the need for Lawson to assert himself: 'He knows how, month after month, the unelected and unappointed alternative Chancellor in No. 10 has thwarted his policies and contradicted his purposes.'[15] It was time, Smith said, 'that he [Lawson] told the Prime Minister that the moment has come to end the confusion and disarray in the formulation and explanation of Government economic policy. It is time that he said, "Either back me or sack me."'[16]

Lawson resigned shortly afterwards. The events, as Gordon Brown noted in *John Smith: Life and Soul of the Party*, served to enhance Smith's reputation as a parliamentary performer.[17] He again won *The Spectator*'s Parliamentarian of the Year Award in 1989, in recognition of his performance.

After the 1992 election, with Smith now Labour leader and the Tories' majority much reduced, he was again able to exploit the government's problems, most notably following Black Wednesday in September 1992 when the UK withdrew ignominiously from the European Exchange Rate Mechanism and then again regarding the splits in the Conservative Party over the Maastricht Treaty.

Following Black Wednesday, the House of Commons was recalled. The government was very much on the defensive, and Smith was making his first appearance as leader. As Conservative MP Gyles Brandreth observed in his diaries, 'The PM survived, but he didn't do well. John Smith was magnificent: dry, droll, devastating ... A few brave souls intervened on Smith ... but he wasn't to be thrown. He was on a roll and it was masterful.'[18] Interventions played to Smith's strengths. As his fellow Scottish lawyer Derry Irvine recalled, 'No one could think faster on his feet. Under fire he never failed in counter attack.'[19] The government won the vote but had clearly lost the argument, with historian Anthony Seldon concluding that 'no one could doubt that the day was Labour's'.[20] As John Major himself conceded, 'My words made little difference – but John Smith's response did. It was a brilliant debating performance ... Presented with an open goal, he joyfully smashed the ball into the net.'[21]

The government's problems continued to play into Smith's hands. In parliamentary terms, 1993 proved a notable year for Smith. He was able to exploit splits in the government's ranks following the resignation of another Chancellor, Norman Lamont. Smith's barbs in response to the resignation speech proved effective, as did his performance the next day at Prime Minister's Questions. The effect on both occasions was captured by Brandreth:

Wednesday 9 June 1993. John Smith could hardly have asked for a sweeter curtain-raiser. He took full advantage of it. And when he got to his peroration – 'the stark reality of a discredited government presided over by a discredited Prime Minister' – how they roared.

Thursday 10 June 1993. PMQs were chaos … John Smith followed up with a triple whammy exploiting Norman's barbs from yesterday. The PM did his best, but he played straight into Smith's hand:

PM: As one of my predecessors might have said, we've had a little local difficulty. We shall get over it. I am going on with the work in hand.

Smith: Doesn't the Prime Minister understand that when he announced business as usual this morning he caused apprehension throughout the land?[22]

Smith also benefitted from one other innovation – the introduction of television cameras in the House of Commons. Broadcasting began in November 1989, so Smith's attacks on the government became a feature of news bulletins. Viewers could now see and not just hear him as he laid into the government.

Smith was able to deploy not only his debating skills but also his tactical skills in exploiting the government's splits over the Maastricht Bill, which would give effect to the provisions of the Maastricht Treaty in domestic law. 'John Smith', noted Charles Clarke, 'was politically astute and skilled at harrying the Conservatives and fomenting their divisions. His parliamentary tactics contributed significantly to the government's defeat over Maastricht.'[23] During the committee stage of the bill, a Labour amendment on membership of the European Union's Committee of the Regions was carried with the support of twenty-six Conservatives and eighteen Liberal Democrats, the effect of which was to prolong proceedings on the bill, necessitating a report stage. (Bills that are unamended in the Committee of the Whole House do not have a report stage.) Smith then attacked the government over the handling of the social chapter of the Maastricht Treaty.

To get the bill through, the government accepted a Labour amendment stipulating that the Act would not take effect until the House had come to a resolution on a motion moved by a minister concerning the adoption of the Social Chapter – the government had accepted it, recognising that it was likely to be carried anyway. When this was subsequently put to the House, the government's motion was lost by one vote. The next day, Friday 23 July, it was again put to the House, but this time the Prime Minister made it a vote of confidence. In the Friday debate, as Brandreth recorded, Major's speech 'was workmanlike, but lacklustre. John Smith, by contrast, sparkled. He was stylish, sarcastic and effective. I intervened on him, to no good purpose.'[24] As we shall see, Smith had to walk something of a tightrope between those of his MPs who viewed the treaty as the least-worst option and those who opposed further European integration. Smith's attempts to frustrate the government in the passage of the bill helped keep on board opponents of European integration, while his pro-European credentials meant that those who favoured the treaty were prepared to trust him.

Despite Labour's splits on the bill – sixty-six Labour MPs voted against the third reading and five voted for, with the official line being to abstain – Smith benefitted from being in opposition. The media focus was on the government and the trauma it faced in getting the bill through what proved to be a protracted process.

In harrying the government, Smith was most effective when exploiting its problems through speeches and exchanges with the Prime Minister at Prime Minister's Questions. He was not necessarily a good platform speaker. As one of his front bench colleagues David Blunkett put it, Smith 'was excellent in debate ... but no one would describe him as an orator'.[25] It was a point reiterated by Smith's close friend Murray Elder: 'Put him on a conference platform in a big hall with a prepared speech and he was much, much more dull.'[26] He thrived in the adversarial format of the House of Commons, enabling him to debate and bounce off the attacks of others.

WORKING WITHIN THE PARLIAMENTARY LABOUR PARTY

Party meetings can be extremely important as a means of enabling MPs to make their views known to party leaders, helping to absorb or sometimes escalate dissent. Public unity may be a product of differences already having been resolved behind closed doors. Meetings of the PLP are especially important because of the factional nature of the Labour Party and the status of the PLP within the party's constitution. When the PLP was formed, the constitution required Labour MPs to abide by the decisions of the parliamentary party in carrying out the aims of the constitution.

Unlike its Conservative counterpart, the 1922 Committee, membership of the PLP comprises all parliamentarians who take the party whip. This provides a benefit to the leader in that frontbenchers form part of the voting membership. It also means the party leader is a member and can attend – in the 1922 Committee, the Conservative leader is not a member and attends by invitation. However, because of the factional nature of the party, meetings can be less than harmonious. The weekly meeting of the PLP nonetheless provides an opportunity for the leader to rally the troops and, if necessary, seek to impose some discipline. As Mark Stuart asserts, some leaders have adopted a strict disciplinary approach, demanding loyalty, while others have taken a more liberal stance and some a mix of the two.[27]

Smith adopted a liberal approach, enabling issues to be discussed and voted on. He had learned from previous leaders, not least Callaghan, how to handle the PLP. In any event, being willing to hear from people with alternative views fitted his approach to resolving issues. Even if he wasn't in agreement, he was prepared to listen to the other side. As Stuart observes, 'Smith's leadership was an extension of his inclusive and engaging personality, generating an atmosphere where everyone was allowed to have their say, but woe betide anyone who transgressed once a policy had been agreed.'[28]

Debates and votes within the PLP helped absorb dissent, not least over the Maastricht Bill. Given that Labour was as divided on the measure as the Conservatives, the parliamentary party required deft handling to exhibit some degree of unity.[29] Dissidents were allowed to put forward proposed amendments to the bill. Smith took the line of supporting the Maastricht Treaty in principle but objecting to particular provisions and objecting to the government's approach to getting the bill through, leading at one point to the opposition withdrawing co-operation. This enabled him to keep on board both those who supported and those who strongly opposed greater European integration. Allowing votes in the PLP (again, a practice not followed in the 1922 Committee) provided a form of safety valve, enabling members to express themselves but then feel bound to the decisions taken by the parliamentary party.

In this way, Smith again benefitted from the political conditions as well as his own nature. The government was in obvious difficulties and trailing badly in the opinion polls. It was in Labour's own interests to rally behind the leader and to exploit the government's difficulties. Smith could have taken a more disciplinary approach, but it was not in his nature to do so. The contrast was stark with his successor, Tony Blair, who was more executive man than Parliament man. Smith took the view that it was sufficient to let the Conservatives lose the next election, which influenced his approach to party management. He did not need to drive the PLP to unite behind new policies. By contrast, Blair was the arch moderniser and not prone to adopt a liberal stance when it came to PLP meetings, as discussed by Patrick Seyd: 'Ensuring party unity was a major priority, and both the shadow cabinet and the PLP were run in a strictly controlled manner from 1994 onwards ... But the price of such strict discipline was a clampdown on discussion of important issues ... Even some moderates felt the clampdown was excessive.'[30]

There was also a marked contrast with Blair's successor, Gordon Brown. Brown was a micromanager, but Smith could delegate. He was prepared to trust colleagues and once they had produced a policy and he was content with it, he could move on.[31]

RUBBING SHOULDERS WITH COLLEAGUES

MPs spend much time in the Palace of Westminster mixing with one another in the dining and tea rooms, utilising the opportunity not just to socialise but also to gather information on events, as well as lobby their colleagues in support of particular campaigns.[32] For leading party figures, it is a means of being seen and mobilising support.

The value of utilising informal space is perhaps most starkly illustrated by the fate of those who have neglected it. Conservative leaders Edward Heath and Thatcher failed to mix regularly with backbenchers in the tea and smoking rooms, and when they were challenged for the leadership it helped seal their fates.[33] The same may be said of Theresa May and Boris Johnson. Each was brought down by their fellow party MPs. Callaghan was successful in his use of all three dimensions of space, being brought down by the electors and not by his own MPs.[34] Smith also used informal space to effect.

As Smith's biographer Andy McSmith recalls, 'One of John Smith's strengths was his ability to get on well with people with whom he had profound ideological differences.'[35] This capacity stood him in good stead as a minister under both Leader of the House Michael Foot and Secretary of State for Energy Tony Benn. As Kenneth Morgan observes, 'He and Foot struck up the best of relationships.'[36] Smith had clear differences with Benn, but they never descended into personal conflict or animosity. Indeed, it is notable that Benn voted for Smith in the 1992 Labour leadership election. Benn believed that Smith laid the foundations for bringing left and right together.[37] This ability to get on well with others facilitated his use of informal space in Westminster.

Smith was well liked both within his party and across the House. Far from neglecting the Palace of Westminster, he spent long hours there. According to one MP, he would arrive there for breakfast and stay until midnight.[38] He was, in James Naughtie's words, 'naturally gregarious' and so mixed easily in the bars and informal spaces of the

Palace.[39] Late-night sittings and waiting around for votes kept him in the House, but for him it was not something against which he chafed. As David Blunkett put it, 'He just enjoyed the camaraderie and drinking whisky.'[40] The fact that he was Leader of the Opposition and not Prime Minister facilitated spending time in the Palace. He had official duties as opposition leader, but his principal base was the House of Commons, not Downing Street.

This feature of his behaviour also derives from another key distinction. He was, in the words of Bruce Grocott, one of his parliamentary colleagues, an 'out-of-London MP': 'His home was emphatically in Edinburgh.'[41] While in London, he immersed himself in Parliament. At that time, what the same MP referred to as 'expats' dominated the parliamentary party. Again, the contrast with some of his predecessors and especially his successor is notable. Blair, who like most post-war Labour leaders was not an 'expat', was not one to spend time rubbing shoulders with Labour MPs in the smoking room and tea room. Smith was traditional Labour in his approach not only to issues but also to bonding with fellow members, whereas his successor was New Labour and determined to take the party in a new direction.

CONCLUSION

Smith was, in the words of his parliamentary colleague Ann Taylor, 'the epitome of House of Commons man.'[42] He devoted time to the institution and mixed easily with fellow members, with Lord Grocott adding that 'he was at home in the House'.[43] It engaged both his debating skills and his conviviality. Rather than leaving to make more money pursuing his legal career, he remained loyal to party and Parliament.

Smith succeeded in Parliament not only because of his advocacy skills, honed in Glasgow University's debating club as well as in the law courts, but also because of circumstance. He was shadow to Leon Brittan at the time of the Westland crisis. He took over as Labour leader just as the Conservative government under Major was about to undergo a tumultuous time through international and domestic crises and party splits. Smith was able to exploit the situation through his quick wit and debating skills. Had he been in a situation in which he relied predominantly on set-piece speeches, he would likely have come across as a worthy speaker but not an inspiring one. As it was, his interventions and sharp attacks on government made him an effective Leader of the Opposition. Despite occasional hiccoughs both as shadow Chancellor and party leader, he was able to put the government on the ropes – a fact recognised by those on the government's benches. He benefitted from the presence of television cameras, the immediacy of television adding to the drama and effect of his interventions. He also benefitted from leading a party that had suffered four consecutive general election defeats and recognised the need to unite to win.

His effectiveness was clearly demonstrated in the weeks before his death. As Brandreth recorded on 24 March 1994: 'A bumpy ride for the boss at PMQs. He had to ... rebuff John Smith who (frankly) got it spot-on ... We did our yobbish best to barrack Smith, boorishly shouting him down as best we could ... but he wasn't thrown. He's impressive.'[44]

And on 29 March: 'Smith repeatedly put same question to Major ... The PM flannelled. John Smith repeated the question. The PM flannelled some more. For the third time, Smith repeated the question ... The PM was quite white, his mouth was dry and his hands shook as he held his folder. The other side jeered.'[45]

His role as a parliamentarian was perfectly captured by Prime Minister John Major, in paying tribute to him on the day that he died:

John Smith was one of the outstanding parliamentarians of modern politics. He was skilled in the procedures of this House, skilled in upholding its traditions, a fair-minded but, I can say as well as any Member in the House, tough fighter for what he believed in and, above all, he was outstanding in parliamentary debate.[46]

4

ONE MORE HEAVE? OPINION POLLS AND ELECTIONS DURING JOHN SMITH'S LEADERSHIP

Mark Garnett and David Denver

W HATEVER ITS EFFECTS ON the Labour Party and the country as a whole, John Smith's sudden death in May 1994 opened rich seams for political speculators. Was he really on track to become Prime Minister after the next election, or was he doomed to share the fates of James Callaghan, Michael Foot and the dual loser, Neil Kinnock? Positive answers came from some unexpected sources, including *The Sun* newspaper. Notoriously, however, some of his colleagues were unconvinced by Smith's election-winning calibre, insisting that Labour could not 'seal the deal' with British voters unless it made more radical changes to the party's organisation and policy platform in line with Kinnock's programme of 'modernisation'.

It would be very helpful if this difference of opinion could be settled by an appeal to 'objective' evidence. However, Smith's detractors

67

were not in the benefit-of-the-doubt business, and one senses that they would have refused to believe positive opinion polls or the implications of victories in by-elections and other contests, even if Smith had survived until the eve of the 1997 general election. As it was, he died before the mid-point of what was always likely to be a protracted parliament. The Conservative government was already in serious trouble, and if Smith really believed that Labour had only to wait while its opponents dug themselves into ever-deeper holes, then his judgement turned out to be sound. Nevertheless, Labour's capacity to secure electoral defeat left no room for complacency – Tony Blair himself remained nervous of his party's prospects right up until polling day. Thus, for Smith and his admirers, the best possible verdict to be derived from opinion polls and real-life electoral contests up to the time of his death would be 'so far, so good', making a Labour victory under Smith's leadership a 'what might have been, which probably would have been but, then again, might not have been'.

THE EVIDENCE OF OPINION POLLS

An overall assessment of polling data during Smith's leadership provides a strongly positive picture of the Labour Party's prospects. For the first few months after the 1992 general election – which had given them a lead of 7.5 percentage points in the popular vote – the Conservatives continued to be more popular than Labour (see Figure 1). After Smith's accession, however, Labour's position improved steadily and in November – two months after the UK's ignominious departure from the European Exchange Rate Mechanism (ERM) – the party's lead over its main rivals stood at 17 points.

After that devastating blow to the Conservatives' reputation for economic competence, the party floundered. Labour continued to record large leads (peaking, during Smith's time as leader, at more than 20 points in March 1994), but the party's actual level of support was somewhat dampened during 1993 and early 1994 by one of the periodic upsurges in the popularity of the Liberal Democrats under Paddy Ashdown. This died away with the advent of Tony Blair, however, so although the Conservatives inched painfully upwards, Labour's leads over them became even larger. Although Blair is (properly) credited with achieving quite spectacular opinion poll leads for his party, it is worth emphasising that, under Smith, Labour led the Conservatives for twenty-one consecutive months and that in the fourteen months preceding his death, the lead was in double figures. By any standard, this was a very solid performance.

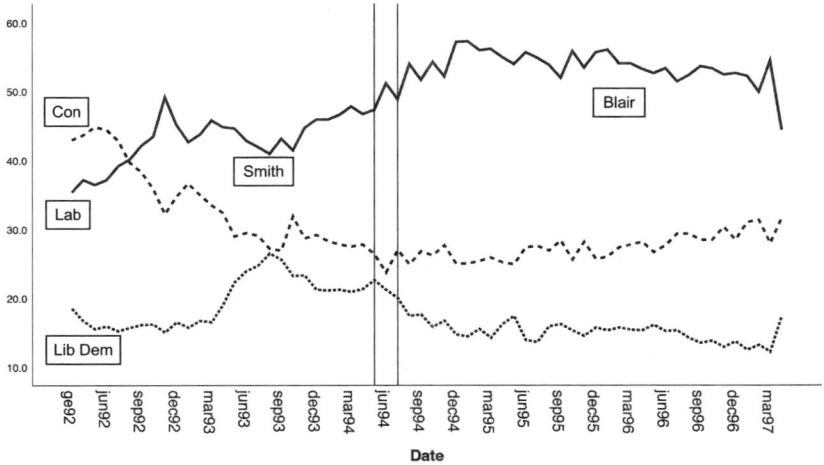

Figure 1: Voting intentions 1992–7

The graph is based on the monthly averages of all published polls. The general election results of 1992 and 1997 (Great Britain only) are the starting and finishing points.

On the face of it, this evidence supports the 'so far, so good' assessment of Smith's leadership. However, party analysts with a natural fear of false dawns were more impressed by private, qualitative polls, which suggested that voters were unconvinced by Labour – that, rather than indicating positive feelings towards the opposition, survey respondents were merely, as Andy McSmith put it, 'telling pollsters they would vote Labour because they wanted to vent their dissatisfaction with the Tories'.[1] In June 1993, Philip Gould, who continued to offer advice despite the fact that his Shadow Communications Agency had been dropped by Smith, warned that the party 'had not gained sufficiently from the demise of the Conservatives', adding that it was 'not trusted', even 'not relevant'.[2]

Given their tendency to admire Kinnock – and to resent the evidence that Labour would have fared better in the 1992 general election if Smith had been leading the party – 'modernisers' like Gould took an understandable interest in public assessments of the new leader. From their perspective, the changes required to make Labour electable could only be sold to a recalcitrant party by an individual with exceptional drive, charisma and overwhelming public approval. According to Gould, despite Smith's manifold virtues, he fell short in all of these respects. The public refused to recognise his positive qualities because it continued to distrust the party he led. This, Gould thought, was a problem that 'undermines all Labour Leaders'.[3] What he meant was that public distrust would continue to undermine Labour leaders unless, unlike Smith himself, they were fully committed to the kind of change which would make Labour into a sort of British facsimile of Bill Clinton's Democrats.

The relevant polling data are sufficient to explain why, on Gould's own testimony, Smith politely ignored his unsolicited promptings: he

appeared, after all, to have been a greater asset to Labour than his predecessor. At that time, Gallup regularly asked respondents whether they
thought the incumbent was proving to be 'a good Leader' or 'not a good
Leader' of the Opposition. Figure 2 shows the net level of public approval (percentage saying good leader, percentage saying not good) from
October 1983 to the 1992 general election for Kinnock, and for Smith
while he was leader. The former fell into negative territory by the middle
of 1984 and only occasionally thereafter recorded a positive score. In the
five years from 1987 to 1992, he had a (small) positive rating on only four
occasions and slumped to -36 in December 1988. In contrast, Smith's figures were overwhelmingly positive, the only exception being in July 1993,
around the time of Gould's doom-laden memo quoted in the previous
paragraph, when he registered -1. Evidently, public distrust of Labour
was much less of a drawback to Smith than it had been for Kinnock.

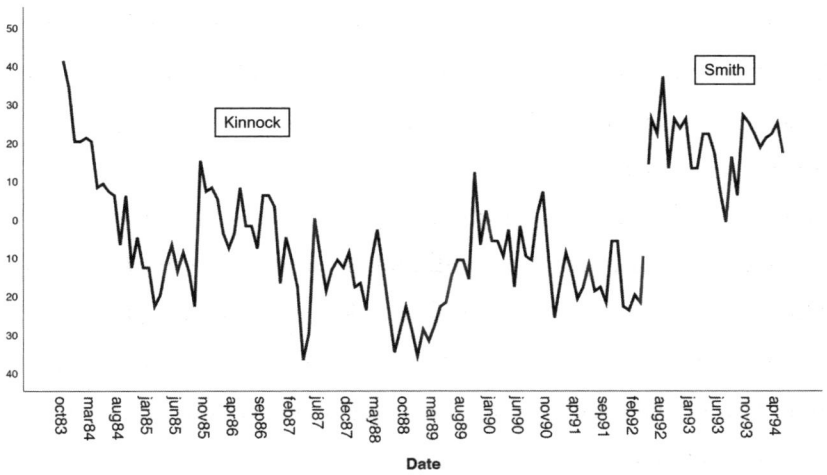

Figure 2: Net evaluations of Neil Kinnock and John Smith as opposition leaders

The data are from Gallup and show the percentage saying the person concerned was a good
leader minus the percentage saying they were not a good leader.

The same message was conveyed in responses to YouGov's question relating to the best person to be Prime Minister (see Figure 3). Although Smith trailed John Major in this respect until Black Wednesday, his lead from then on was never seriously threatened, even during the Ashdown 'surge'. In April 1994, he was 17 points ahead of Ashdown and had a lead of 21 over Major. It could be argued, then, that the 'so far so good' verdict applies as much to public perceptions of Smith's leadership as to the relative popularity of his party. On the other hand, the headline figures conceal reasons for caution. The public's preference for Smith over Major as Prime Minister was clearly affected by plummeting support for the Conservatives; the highest figure recorded in Smith's favour (November 1992) was 38 per cent, which was smaller than the proportion (40 per cent) who had considered Major the best option just before Black Wednesday. As noted above, a significant portion of the discontent with the Conservatives appears to have been channelled into support for the Liberal Democrats and the more flamboyant Ashdown. Nonetheless, the evidence suggests that Ashdown's appeal was beginning to tail off during the early part of 1994.

The polling evidence relating to Smith's perceived personal qualities was equally ambivalent. Although Smith's ratings over the range of attributes selected by Ipsos Mori – 'good in a crisis', 'understands world problems', 'down to earth' etc. – improved during his leadership, the relevant figures were not noticeably better than those which Kinnock had attracted. The general trend was for positive impressions to increase in the immediate wake of Black Wednesday and subsequently either to plateau or gently subside.

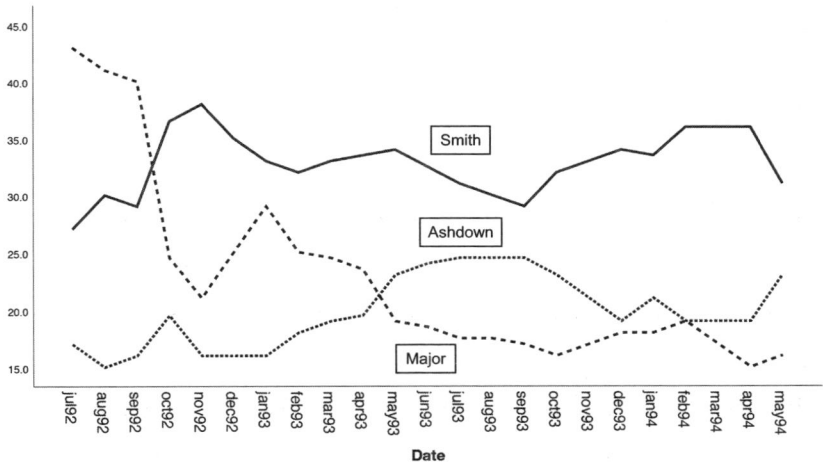

Figure 3: Best person for Prime Minister (July 1992 to May 1994)

Source: YouGov

The surveys also suggested that by the time of his death, a larger proportion of voters had decided that Smith 'talked down to people' and
was 'narrow minded'. The politician whose epitaph was 'An honest
man's the noblest work of God' must have been disappointed that, in
February 1994, only 20 per cent of respondents regarded him as 'more
honest than most politicians'. This was a mere 5 points higher than
the rating at the start of his leadership; in the intervening months,
the public estimation of 'most politicians' had been degraded by a
succession of scandals which should have made Smith – a family man
whose public persona radiated rectitude – seem like a shining exception. Either he had not perfected his pose as a sympathetic bank
manager or the public had begun to suspect the integrity of anyone
who could be associated with the over-bloated British financial
sector.

ELECTORAL EVIDENCE

Since Smith did not live long enough to lead his party in a general election campaign, one might turn to the results of parliamentary by-elections for more concrete evidence of his appeal to the electorate than is afforded by opinion polls. However, there were only three of these contests during his leadership – Newbury in May 1993, Christchurch in July 1993 and Rotherham in May 1994, just a few days before Smith's death – and they are far from a representative sample of British constituencies. The outcomes are shown in Table 1.

In each case, Labour's share of the vote fell compared to its performance in the 1992 general election. Rather than turning to the main party of opposition as a means of punishing an unpopular government, constituents in the southern English seats of Newbury and Christchurch rallied behind the Liberal Democrats, whose candidates won more than 60 per cent of the vote in both by-elections. Although Labour held Rotherham comfortably, the Liberal Democrat vote share in that demographically and politically different South Yorkshire seat rose by 17.4 points compared to 1992.

Table 1: Parliamentary by-elections, 1993–4

Newbury, May 1993

	1992 percentage	By-election percentage	Change
Con	55.9	26.9	-29.0
Lab	6.0	2.0	-4.0
Lib Dem	37.3	65.1	+27.8
Other	0.8	6.0	+5.2

Christchurch, July 1993

	1992 percentage	By-election percentage	Change
Con	63.5	31.4	-32.1
Lab	12.1	2.7	-9.4
Lib Dem	23.6	62.2	+38.6
Other	0.8	3.7	+2.9

Rotherham, May 1994

	1992 percentage	By-election percentage	Change
Con	23.7	9.9	-13.8
Lab	63.9	55.6	-8.3
Lib Dem	12.3	29.7	+17.4
Other	0.0	4.8	+4.8

Superficially, these data seem unpropitious for those who think that Smith put Labour on course for a return to office. However, Newbury and Christchurch were clearly hopeless targets for Labour. Not even the modernising magus Blair could conjure up a host of Labour supporters in either constituency at the 1997 general election; for anti-Conservative voters, the Liberal Democrats continued to be the logical choice four years after the respective by-elections. The Rotherham result of May 1994 may have been somewhat more disquieting for Smith. In a seat that Labour was never likely to lose, the turnout fell by 28 points compared to 1992. The 55.6 per cent of the vote secured by the winning candidate, Denis MacShane, was little better than the Labour candidate had received in the disastrous general election of 1983. The unconstructive mood of those who did bother to attend the poll is testified by the fact that Screaming Lord Sutch of the Monster Raving Loony Party notched up more than a thousand votes, in what turned out to be his best ever electoral performance.

Local elections provide another source of information about Smith's public appeal. Although the numbers and types of local authorities involved vary from year to year, these elections obviously encompass a much wider range of locations than parliamentary by-elections. Moreover, academic specialists have developed ways of estimating 'national equivalent vote shares' for each set of local elections – i.e. the shares that each party would have obtained had voting taken place across the whole country. Figure 4 shows the figures for elections from 1984 to 1996. As can be seen in the graph, under Kinnock Labour had very good results in 1989 and 1990 but fell back in 1991 and trailed the Conservatives by 16 points in 1992. Under Smith, Labour regained the lead in 1993 and improved still further in 1994 when the local elections took place on the same day as the Rotherham by-election. Even so, the level of support obtained by the party did not quite match the peaks registered under Kinnock.

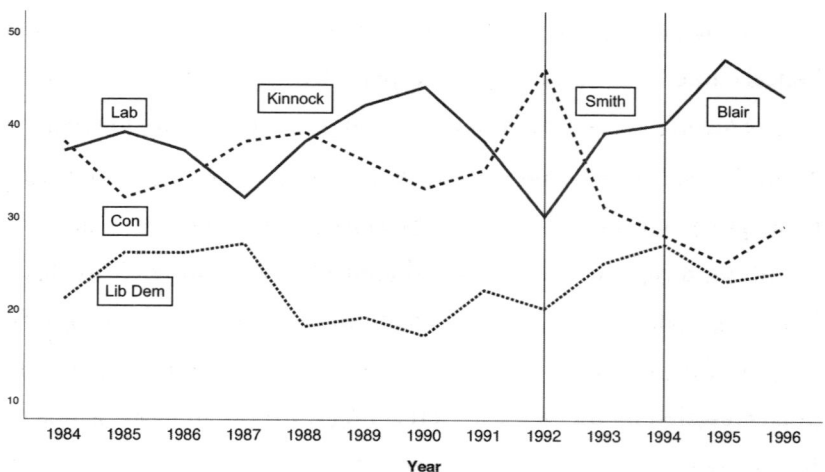

Figure 4: National equivalent vote in local elections, 1984–96

Source: C. Rallings and M. Thrasher, *British Electoral Facts*, Total Politics, 2006, p.229

In terms of seats won, Labour registered relatively modest gains in 1993 and 1994. In 1993, the party gained 111 seats and in 1994, forty-four additional councillors. In both cases, however, the party was defending the strong positions that had been achieved in the previous corresponding contests in 1989 and 1990. The big gainers in both 1993 and 1994 were the Liberal Democrats, whose vote share had been 19 per cent in 1989 and 17 per cent in 1990 but rose to 25 per cent in 1993 and 27 per cent in 1994.

On these figures, then, the report card for John Smith's Labour Party once again could not have featured a more favourable judgement than 'satisfactory'. It had consolidated a very healthy position in local government, which had been attained in previous elections when the Conservatives had been campaigning under the formidable self-inflicted handicap of the community charge or 'poll tax'. By 1993, that electoral albatross had been shooed away by the Major government. However, it had been replaced by a myriad of different reasons for voter dissatisfaction, which (like Black Wednesday) might not have been so closely related to local government but were no less newsworthy for that. For Smith's critics, 'consolidation' in this context was not enough: after all, Labour had outpolled the Conservatives in the 1991 local contests (if narrowly), only to lose the general election in the following year.

Philip Gould was prepared to concede that 'John's death had a profound effect on the British electorate' and even made voters feel differently about the Labour Party.[4] For normal people, however, the reaction to Smith's death is best regarded as an example of people not knowing what they had until it was gone. Presumably, Gould, from the peculiar perspective of an aspiring New Labour apparatchik, thought that by dying relatively young, Smith had performed his only significant service to his party, making the public inflate a limited leader into 'the greatest Prime Minister Britain never had'. Arguably, however, John Smith did not even secure Labour an electoral dividend in death. In the European Parliament elections held in June 1994, the party's vote share rose by less than 4 percentage points compared to the last result achieved under Kinnock in 1989 (see Table 2). Labour's lead over the Conservatives, at more than 16 points, was certainly a handsome one. However, once again, the chief beneficiaries of government unpopularity appear to have been the Liberal Democrats, whose share of the vote rose by more than 10 points.

Table 2: Results of European Parliament elections, 1989 and 1994 (Great Britain only)

	1989		1994	
	Vote share percentage	Seats	Vote share percentage	Seats
Con	34.7	32	27.9	18
Lab	40.1	45	44.2	62
Lib Dem	6.2	0	16.7	2
Green	14.9	0	3.2	0
Other	4.1	1	8.0	2

Although Labour won sixty-two of eighty-seven UK seats in the European parliament, the modest rise in vote share took some of the gloss from its performance, and although the party's proportion of the vote in Great Britain (44.2 per cent) was similar to the figure it recorded in the landslide 1997 general election, the turnout in 1994 was just 36.4 per cent.

On the same day as the European elections, a by-election was held in Smith's former seat of Monklands East. After a campaign overshadowed by allegations of corrupt practices involving the local Labour

Party – rather than Smith himself – the former leader's close ally Helen Liddell prevailed by less than 2,000 votes; Smith's majority in the 1992 general election had been nearly 16,000. The surge in support for the Scottish National Party, whose candidate's share of the vote increased by more than 25 points compared to 1992, was even more ominous for the future of the Labour Party than the Liberal Democrat revival under Ashdown, which was confirmed on the same evening by victory in a by-election held in the southern English seat of Eastleigh. In 1992, Labour had not been far behind the Liberal Democrats in that constituency, and in the 1994 by-election its share of the vote increased by almost 7 points. However, the overwhelming majority of Conservative defectors evidently preferred the Liberal Democrats to Labour, comfortably overturning a 1992 Tory majority of almost 18,000. The voters of Eastleigh, it might be presumed, had thought seriously about the various ways of registering a protest against a Conservative government now mired in 'sleaze' of various kinds and suffering through divisions over Europe and a newly acquired reputation for economic incompetence. Amongst the inevitable frivolous candidates who lost their deposits at Eastleigh, Screaming Lord Sutch trailed Nigel Farage of the United Kingdom Independence Party by 169 votes.

CONCLUSIONS

The claim that a Labour general election victory under John Smith would have been inevitable – that the party merely had to keep its nose clean and wait until a divided and discredited Major government ran out of time – was never put to the test. However, few of Smith's supporters have ever been misguided enough to make that claim; to do so would be to make no allowance for the inherent uncertainties involved in party competition under free and fair elections. For example, Michael Heseltine might have been drafted in as an emergency replacement for John Major if Smith had not succumbed so suddenly to the kind of heart problems that had affected Heseltine himself. Certainly, Smith's advocates do not argue that his leadership was 'transformative' of Labour's prospects; rather, they reflect Smith's own view that Labour was, on the balance of probability, likely to win next time if it stuck to its traditional principles but presented them more effectively and made necessary organisational changes in a manner that avoided internecine conflict.

For Gould, 'it was clear that, despite reasonable polling leads, Labour was not on course to win' under Smith.[5] The modernisers believed that Smith was guilty of complacency at best. Labour could only be sure of returning to office under a leader who truly believed in their 'project'. Whatever his other qualities – the ones which, Gould argues, made him a venerated figure once he had died but fell below the requirements for a successful living leader – Smith was an unbeliever whose deviation from the true faith was confirmed by his disobliging habit of sidelining Kinnock's key advisors.

While this negative verdict is not susceptible to conclusive disproof, the data examined in this chapter suggest that it is highly improbable. Its most glaring, basic flaw is the implicit denial of one of the oldest of all political dictums – that opposition parties don't win general elections, but governments can (and do) lose them. Modernisers scoured snapshots of public opinion for any evidence that Labour's support was 'soft', without considering that votes cast with the chief purpose of removing an unpopular government are no less valuable than those that reflect passionate positive feelings.

The modernisers would have a point if the Conservative malaise triggered by Black Wednesday had shown any signs of being a short- (or even medium-) term 'blip'. However, Britain's departure from the ERM in the first months of Smith's leadership was toxic for the Tories to an extent that effectively deflected public attention from the fact that Smith was committed to the same policy. While the full extent of Conservative disarray after Black Wednesday could not be foreseen, 'Europe' had been a running sore since Thatcher's Bruges Speech in 1988, and even if the Conservatives had somehow avoided fratricide on that issue, many of the scandals that contributed to the public feeling that it was 'time for a change' had actually been heaped up during the years of supposed Thatcherite 'hegemony' between 1979 and 1990. Major, arguably, merely reaped the rancid harvests that his predecessor had sown.

Modernisers might like to think that the substitution of Blair for Smith placed Major under intolerable electoral pressure, preventing the Conservatives from launching an effective fight-back. However, Major was not the kind of politician who could ever have 'spun' his way through the post-Thatcherite minefield. Smith's forensic approach to Prime Minister's Questions was not always effective, but it caused Major at least as much discomfiture as Blair ever managed with his snappy soundbites and in set-piece debates. The Smith–Major battle was invariably a morale-sapping mismatch whose effects contributed to the feeling (as John Redwood's Conservative Party leadership campaign slogan of 1995 claimed) that the Conservatives had 'no chance' unless they changed their leader.

The evidence of opinion polling and 'real' votes during Smith's short spell of leadership could be used to suggest that he was insufficiently apprised of the threat posed by the Liberal Democrats to Labour's chances of securing an overall parliamentary majority. This danger might have been pre-empted by the negotiation of an electoral pact with Ashdown's party, but Smith had no interest in any deal.[6] As such, he invited a repetition of the scenario of the 1980s, when the voting intentions of an anti-Conservative majority had been thwarted by the operations of the simple plurality voting system, which, despite considerable private reservations, Smith was reluctant to reform.[7]

For proponents of electoral reform in Britain, Smith's hesitant approach implies a woeful lack of political imagination, derived from the same 'tribal' attitude to his party's traditions that overtried the patience of Labour modernisers. However, Smith's attitude to the Liberal Democrat challenge and his ambivalence about electoral reform could just as easily have arisen from a flexible interpretation of trends within the increasingly volatile British electorate. The three by-elections held under his leadership in particular suggested a remarkable degree of tactical voting under the existing first past the post system: even if Liberal Democrat supporters had turned out in force at Rotherham, they were able to do so without inhibition since there was no chance that their choices would facilitate victory for the Conservative candidate. From Smith's perspective, if anti-government tactical voting at this relatively sophisticated level was replicated in a general election, it would help to ensure that Labour won enough seats to form a majority government, and, given their demonstrable ability to win seats in areas which Labour could never hope to reach, the Liberal Democrats might even replace the Conservatives as the main party of opposition to a future Smith-led government. Arguably, the substitution of Smith for Kinnock had made tactical voting less hazardous for risk-averse citizens; the Conservative argument that a vote for the Liberal Democrats would help Labour to regain office was sure to sound less bone-chilling when the prospective Prime Minister was Smith rather than Kinnock.

At the risk of straying into the realms of speculation – and into territory which more properly belongs in other chapters – Labour's overall record in terms of measures of public opinion under John Smith seems to satisfy the party leader's own criteria for successful leadership. Namely, this was the belief that a workable parliamentary majority was all that the party needed to achieve, not only to break its run of demoralising electoral defeats but, more importantly, to roll back some of the most damaging effects of Thatcherism. Although Smith did not accept the 'one more heave' approach attributed to him by his critics, there was, going by this view, no need for the Labour Party to transform itself into a 'catch-all' vote-winning ma- chine on the lines envisaged by the modernisers. A landslide victory secured on such terms would be tantamount to a defeat – the falsest of dawns for Labour and for members of the public who wanted something different after eighteen years of neo-liberal rule. Leaving aside the benefit of hindsight, which strongly suggests that the Con- servatives were doomed to defeat whether or not Smith had lived, the safest conclusion to be drawn from the public reaction to his leader- ship of the Labour Party is that, at worst, it would have resulted in the kind of modest overall parliamentary majority that a veteran of the precarious positions of the Wilson and Callaghan governments in the 1970s would have found quite satisfactory.

PART II

POLICIES

5

ECONOMIC POLICY

Wyn Grant

IT IS TEMPTING, AND not altogether inappropriate, to view
the economic policy legacy of John Smith in relation to contemporary debates in the Labour Party. The economic landscape is once
again challenging, but how cautious should Labour be in terms of
macroeconomic policy, public expenditure and taxation?

There is no doubt that Smith inspires great affection and loyalty
amongst those who worked with him. They consider that in many
ways his policies have been misrepresented by Labour modernisers,
who sought to extract from his tenure as shadow Chancellor and
leader the lesson that Labour should avoid high rates of personal
taxation. Something of a myth developed that he was responsible
for Labour losing the 1992 general election with his shadow Budget,
although the evidence base for that claim is weak.

It is important to consider Smith's values because they had a considerable influence on his approach to economic policy. David Ward, Smith's former head of policy, testifies that he 'was a man with remarkable inner self-confidence':[1] 'He was sure in his beliefs – informed by a Presbyterian faith and imbued by an upbringing in Scotland's Western Highlands – and blessed with a loving and devoted family. In short, he was very secure in himself and that was felt strongly in his politics.'[2]

In an age when many politicians seem to be headline- and popularity-seeking opportunists, or at best competent technocrats, it is refreshing to encounter a politician of integrity who sought to put his values into practice. However, there is a possible downside. Could someone with Smith's background fully understand the preferences of a swing voter living in south-east England? This was essentially the issue that arose in the controversy over his 1992 shadow Budget. While he was not as dismissive of focus groups as some claimed, according to Ward 'he was more influenced by his own encounters with ordinary people, especially those attending his own constituency surgery in Monklands East'.[3] He would certainly have encountered many examples of various forms of deprivation, reinforcing his commitment to social justice, but a constituency in Scotland's Central Belt was not representative of Scotland as a whole, let alone the UK. This potential criticism was taken up by his Conservative opponent as Chancellor, Norman Lamont: 'I always suspected that economically he was something of a flat earther, out of touch with realities in most of the country and overly influenced by conditions in his Lanarkshire constituency.'[4] Even so, one British politics expert I consulted thought that his image was the reassuring one of a competent bank manager (such people still existed then). Indeed, with John

Major as Prime Minister, the political contest could be portrayed as one between two bank managers. However, perhaps Smith was the kind of manager who explained that your mortgage interest rate was going up faster than your savings rate. It was indeed challenging for him to empathise with swing voters in southern England.

This is not the place for a comparison between the Church of England, increasingly divided into divergent sects, and the Church of Scotland . It is worth pointing out, according to James Naughtie, that 'at its best … the Kirk is engaged in talking about the real world more than in theological hair-splitting'.[5] Smith 'grew up in [the Kirk], and especially in his later years found it a helpful companion'.[6] Spirituality was important to Smith, symbolised by his burial on the island of Iona. He went there the summer before his death and each day he joined the community for prayer in the sacred Abbey Church.[7] For him, religion was a highly personal matter, worshipping on his own without the family to which he was close. According to Smith's biographer Mark Stuart, 'John drew on the ideas of Archbishop William Temple, who believed in the notion of Christian fellowship, that people had an obligation or a duty to one another.'[8] This led to a repudiation of individualism and a belief that people were social animals bound together by mutual commitments. It is the antithesis of the admittedly somewhat misquoted notion of Margaret Thatcher that there is no such thing as society. Without a strong society, a flourishing economy is not possible.

Smith had a strong belief in social justice. This is something of a 'hurrah' phrase – no one is likely to declare themselves in favour of social injustice. Fervent defenders of a market economy are prone to argue that a rising tide lifts all boats, with trickle-down benefits reaching the least well off. In broad terms, the concept of social justice could be said to be informed by a broadly Rawlsian notion that policy should seek as a priority to improve the situation and opportunities of the less well off in society. According to Stuart, Smith was able to call in aid 'the early writings of Adam Smith, including his *Theory of Moral Sentiments*, where he argued that however selfish a man might be, there were some principles in his nature that interested him in the fortunes of others'.[9] He 'provided to the Labour Party the combination of social justice on the one hand and economic efficiency on the other: you had to create the wealth before you set about wealth redistribution'.[10] In summary, the influence of his values on economic policy was that there was a moral basis for state intervention, but it shouldn't be taken to the point where it undermined enterprise, individual aspiration and effort.

THE MODERNISERS' NARRATIVE

The Labour modernisers who succeeded Smith as leader have – if they have not airbrushed him out of the party's history – treated him as an example of what to avoid, a critique centred on a particular account of his shadow Budget in 1992. Tony Blair was more critical and dismissive of Smith than Gordon Brown, reflecting their different backgrounds, perspectives and policy emphases – though this is not to say that Brown, who was a moderniser rather than a traditionalist, had no criticisms of the stance taken by Smith. Blair came to see Smith as one of yesterday's men, particularly in terms of Smith's retaining close links with the trade unions. As far as Blair was concerned, in the 1992 campaign 'his proposed tax rises for those earning £30,000 and above were great for the party faithful but plainly problematic for the public'.[11] Some of Blair's allies, notably Peter Mandelson, went further in wiping Smith out from party history as part of a problematic past with a new era starting in 1994.

It is necessary to examine the tensions within the Labour Party over economic policy after the 1987 defeat to understand the context of the 1992 shadow Budget. Having turned down the post of Solicitor General for Scotland in February 1974, which he feared could become a political cul-de-sac, Smith became parliamentary under-secretary at the Department of Energy after the narrow October 1974 general election victory, subsequently becoming Minister of State at the age of thirty-seven. He enjoyed this role and 'would remain a believer in certain strategic industries remaining in state control because such undertakings required long-term planning'.[12] This was not a New Labour view, nor one held in the contemporary Labour Party.

Smith was elected to the shadow Cabinet every year from 1979 to 1992. In 1983, he was promoted from shadow Secretary of State for Energy to shadow Secretary of State for Employment. In 1984, Neil Kinnock appointed him to the more important trade and industry portfolio. In this post, according to Stuart, 'he settled on a consistent theme that would characterise his economic beliefs for the rest of his political career: that an efficient economy and a fair society were not mutually exclusive pursuits'.[13] Smith's public prominence was still relatively low at this point, but the Westland affair gave him the chance to display his skills as a crisp debater, which contrasted with Kinnock's poor performance against Thatcher in the crucial Commons debate. One of his contemporaries recalled in a personal communication:

> I heard him debate for Glasgow in a heat of *The Observer* Mace. He was superlative and won *The Observer* Mace. I had been school debating champion but never debated again. I realised I would never reach anything like that level. When I heard him in *The Observer* Mace round it was one of the most exciting experiences of my life.[14]

In June 1987, Smith became shadow Chancellor, somewhat to the irritation of Bryan Gould who had polled higher in the shadow Cabinet elections but had to be content with being shadow Secretary of State for Trade and Industry. The Conservatives were enjoying what turned out to be an illusory Nigel Lawson boom with tax cuts focused on the better off. Smith was able to point out that the boom was not underpinned by industrial investment and the tax cuts were both unfair and inefficient. Unfortunately, in October 1988 he suffered his first heart attack and Gordon Brown substituted for him. After his return to his duties in January 1989, his task was made easier by a Conservative government whose economic policies and personnel were starting to fall apart. Major differences started to appear between Lawson as Chancellor and Thatcher as Prime Minister, exacerbated by the role of her special economics advisor, Sir Alan Walters. Thatcher claimed not to know that Lawson was shadowing the Deutschmark until she read about it in the *Financial Times*. Smith was able to mock the pair in the House of Commons (see Lord Norton's chapter in this volume). William Hague has 'recently admitted that Smith was so funny that "he had our own side cracking up when we weren't supposed to be"'.[15]

Although the Conservatives were increasingly offering an open goal on economic policy, Smith knew it was insufficient to demonstrate that they were incapable of managing the economy, something which in any case didn't become fully apparent until the ERM crisis in 1992, after they were re-elected. Labour had to have its own credible alternative offer and developing it was not helped by cool personal relations between Smith and Kinnock and tensions over policy with Gould. Gould was chairing the Productive Economy Group in the policy development process and Smith chaired the Economic Equality Group. Gould's group was really concerned with the supply side and Smith's with macroeconomic policy. Unemployment reduction targets present in the 1983 and 1987 manifestos were abandoned, and the reduction of inflation became the priority: 'Public spending commitments were limited, in line with the goal of stabilising public spending as a share of GDP.'[16]

Inevitably, the work of the two groups overlapped and tensions arose from the different perspectives of the two chairs. David Butler and Dennis Kavanagh, in their history of the 1992 election, state:

> Mr Smith felt that Mr Gould's work on industrial policy strayed too often into economic policy and contradicted the market friendly message he was trying to convey. Compared to Smith, Gould favoured a more interventionist role in the economy and in the City and he was more sceptical about the European Community.[17]

Smith had indeed embarked on what would be called a 'prawn cocktail offensive' in the financial services sector, dining with senior executives at the likes of the then-extant Lehman Brothers and Goldman

Sachs. This was intended as an exercise in reassurance, and one indication that it worked was the *Financial Times* advocating a vote for Labour in 1992. As Smith explained at the time, 'I am not in the business of seeking the City's endorsement. Our policies are for society and not for the City. I do not want to make enemies of them but I am not going round hawking for approval.'[18] This was followed up by an international extension of the prawn cocktail circuit, with a very successful visit to Washington DC. His praise of the dynamism and efficiency of markets was well received, as was his pledge not to spend more than the economy could afford. There was also very favourable coverage in the British media. A poll in *The Economist* found that 57 per cent of City economists 'believed that Labour would either be good for the economy or make no difference'.[19]

In November 1989, Gould was shunted off to be shadow Secretary of State for the Environment and Gordon Brown brought in to the trade and industry portfolio. Smith had little time for Gould, who eventually resigned from the shadow Cabinet in a high dudgeon and a blaze of publicity on the eve of the 1992 Labour Party conference. In January 1990, the three teams concerned with economic policy – there had also been one headed by Blair on employment – were merged into a single Economic Policy Sub-Committee chaired by Smith, which met fortnightly. It soon got into a fight with Gould over what should replace the unpopular local rating system in which householders paid a local tax based on the imputed and largely artificial rental value of their property. Smith, aided by his growing group of expert economists, ditched Gould's scheme and replaced it with something more credible. Gould, once again, had to retreat with his tail between his legs as Smith underlined his command of Labour economic policy.

Kinnock backed Smith in this battle, but the relationship between them remained strained, as demonstrated by the infamous Luigi's restaurant affair. In an effort to improve relations with the press, Kinnock had been holding private dinners with them, including one at Luigi's restaurant in London's West End on 14 January 1992. No decision had then been taken by Labour on a proposed increase in national insurance contributions, but Kinnock chose to discuss an earlier policy document with the journalists present, which stated that any increase would be phased in. This proposed increase had not been pursued in more recent policy documents. According to Butler and Kavanagh, 'John Smith reacted frostily when news of the dinner conversation leaked. He suspected he was being "bounced" into phasing, because Mr Kinnock was reacting to an adverse opinion poll, and he and his team resisted.'[20]

Stuart, Smith's biographer, offers three possible interpretations of the Luigi restaurant episode. One explanation is that an astute *Financial Times* journalist trapped the Labour leader into saying more than he intended to reveal. Given that Kinnock could be garrulous at times, this is at least plausible. A second explanation is that Kinnock backed phasing in and wanted it to be policy, backed up by a letter that Kinnock wrote to Smith on the morning of the 14th. Stuart concludes that 'Kinnock did not mean to say what he said to the journalists, although he strongly supported the concept of phasing-in the national insurance increases'.[21]

In fact, as per the third explanation, it seems to have been more a case of a spinning error rather than a conspiracy. As Naughtie explains, 'The version of the story that most now believe is that in a taxi going back to the Commons [Kinnock's] press secretary, Julie Hall, elaborated to some of those who had been at the dinner, and gave the impression that there was indeed a change of policy.'[22] Within a few days, the story was all over the papers. Smith and Kinnock agreed a line of not ruling anything in or ruling anything out: 'One effect of Luigi-gate was that any nuances of difference on tax between Labour shadow cabinet members were now blown up into blazing rows.'[23] Thus, when Smith's usual supporter Roy Hattersley told lobby journalists that he had pressed Smith to introduce the increases in one go, this immediately became a blazing row between the two allies.

All this might seem like a trivial incident, a misunderstanding over some pasta. In fact, 'the Luigi's incident was a symptom of the difficulties at the top of the party about taxation and spending and, specifically, between Mr Kinnock and Mr Smith'.[24] This was not the first time that Kinnock had floated ideas that undermined the calculations of Smith's Treasury team. Kinnock was inclined to come up with ideas that might look superficially attractive but in fact were generally regarded as not very practical. The Treasury has always opposed hypothecation, the assignment of tax revenues for a particular purpose, but this did not stop Kinnock floating the idea in relation to the NHS, which Smith saw as having the effect of reducing a Chancellor's autonomy in relation to tax policy.

DID THE SHADOW BUDGET LOSE THE ELECTION FOR LABOUR?

On 16 March 1992, John Smith presented his shadow Budget with great ceremony and a touch of political theatre, although at least he avoided holding a dummy red box aloft – avoiding a mistake made by the Liberal Democrats towards the end of the coalition government when they used one in their party colours. Presented at the suitably grand Institute of Civil Engineers, the shadow team then walked round to the Treasury for photographs on the steps, which Lamont 'saw as the first hint of the triumphalism that was to do Labour much harm'.[25]

Lamont had wrong-footed Labour in his Budget of 10 March. Rather than cutting the standard rate of income tax by 1p in the pound, as anticipated, he had introduced a new 20 per cent tax band, which benefitted the least well off. Lamont recalls, 'When I announced the lower rate band, I could see frantic conversations taking place between Neil Kinnock and John Smith who were plainly very discomfited and confused.'[26] Reversing the 20 per cent band would hit those on relatively low earnings, but it would reduce Labour's room for manoeuvre to help middle-income earners:

> The real problem was that while the poorest in society gained quite a bit under Smith's budget, those earning between £7,000 to £20,000 gained very little … while it could be argued that a small but electorally vital group of middle-income earners were clobbered quite hard by the removal of the upper limit on national insurance contributions.[27]

The initial reaction to the shadow Budget was quite positive. It eclipsed the launch of the Liberal Democrat manifesto that day in terms of media coverage, much to their chagrin. Smith got the better of Lamont in a television debate in the evening. Lamont thought he had done quite well, despite some wild gesticulating, but 'others …

told me that I hadn't done well and they must have been right'.[28] It took Lamont four days to come up with some kind of coherent reply to Smith's proposals, although he blamed the delay on officials. Eventually, according to Stuart, 'the Tories, not knowing how to respond properly, chose to run the campaign they were going to run with anyway, as though Smith had never delivered a detailed account of Labour's tax and spending plans'.[29] Major, in his autobiography, argues that Smith's 'proposals fell apart under examination'.[30]

Ward's analysis of the 1992 shadow Budget uses myth as a central concept, in particular quoting election studies expert Paul Whiteley's argument that the so-called 'tax bombshell' was an 'urban myth'.[31] This myth that Smith's shadow Budget cost Labour the election has persisted, as Butler and Kavanagh have asserted: 'The favoured target for blame became John Smith's tax package. The claim that 8 out of ten families would be better off under this budget had not been believed, for some 50 per cent of voters feared that they would pay more tax under Labour.'[32] The false Conservative claim that Labour's spending plans would cost £38 billion probably did even more damage. Kinnock believed that Smith should have outlined his tax plans much earlier in the run-up to the elections while attacking the government's economic record.

Always looking for a window of political opportunity, when Ken Livingstone stood 'against Smith in April 1992 for the Labour leadership he cited the fact that taxing so heavily over £20,000 was particularly harsh for people living in London, faced with higher than average house prices and a higher cost of living in general'.[33] There may have been something in the argument that Smith got enveloped in the kind of swirling mist that could arise on one of his Munros, (the Scottish peaks he loved to climb), as Stuart explains: 'A member of Smith's Treasury team feels that £20,080, while a large amount in Smith's constituency, was not in the South-East, and John did not fully appreciate that.'[34] However, a reductionist explanation of the 1992 general election result is not possible because there were many different and sometimes contradictory factors influencing voters' decisions.

Some analysts have focused on Kinnock's triumphalist behaviour at the pre-election Sheffield rally. The image of a Welsh boyo celebrating a victory at his rugby club hardly enhanced his stature as a future Prime Minister, but it is questionable whether it shifted many votes.

One outstanding feature of the 1992 election was the failure of the opinion polls to predict the result. They showed a consistent Labour lead, hence intensifying how much of a blow the actual result was. There seems to be no single explanation of the failure. There is some evidence of a late swing, confirmed by the exit polls, with Conservative voters in particular deciding at the last moment, but it was not of a magnitude to explain the discrepancy. Heath, Jowell and Curtice found 'very little evidence' to back the argument that voters had second thoughts about letting Labour back in because of the prospect of a cut in their disposable income.[35] Those survey respondents who said they would vote Labour and then failed to do so were 'not particularly adverse to high taxation, rather they seemed people who had relatively little faith in Labour's ability to improve services like health and education'.[36]

The broader difficulty is that because of the way macroeconomic policy was drafted within the Labour Party, it was 'neither fully thought through or coherently expressed'.[37] The shadow Budget 'did not cost Labour the election in 1992, but it clearly failed to achieve its objectives'.[38] The Labour stance was defensive yet failed to deal with the Conservative 'tax bombshell' narrative. Labour was 'constrained by a macroeconomic strategy that was extremely cautious' and that has implications for current policy, which will be returned to in the conclusion.[39]

SMITH AS LEADER

In the words of Gordon Brown, 'National economic decline under the Tories became John's main theme, which he hammered home in early speeches as Leader. Jobs, investment, training, the minimum wage and employment rights – these were the issues on which he focused his arguments.'[40] These were worthy and important topics but perhaps not ones to excite the electorate or to motivate activists. Indeed, the way in which Smith's message was delivered could be seen as too moralistic, even didactic. 'The impressionist Rory Bremner created a caricature of Smith in a pulpit, all beetling brows and stern gaze, delivering a sermon,' according to Naughtie.[41]

After Smith became leader, the Conservatives presented Labour with an open goal with their humiliating exit from the Exchange Rate Mechanism (ERM). The Conservatives lost their reputation for economic competence, something that persisted until the 1997 general election. Labour and Smith had, of course, advocated ERM membership as a means of restraining inflation, but this did not stop Smith attacking Major.

Smith had already adjusted his policy on the ERM towards a revaluation of the Deutschmark within the mechanism. This would have the same effect as a devaluation but avoided the word itself, which was an issue for Labour given its role in two previous devaluations of the pound. However, this led to tensions with Brown who favoured no change of policy, concerned about Labour's historic reputation as the party of devaluation. He admits, 'I stood out against this longer than I should have.'[42]

Lamont asserts that 'if John Smith ... had been Chancellor the result would have been exactly the same'.[43] And it was the case that Germany was preoccupied with its own domestic inflationary problems resulting from reunification and was not predisposed to be helpful to other countries in the ERM. In particular, they were reluctant to make any concessions on their domestic interest rates. However, Lamont did not handle the crucial ECOFIN meeting at Bath well. Major states that 'the Germans had obviously deeply resented Norman Lamont's style of chairmanship at the Bath summit'. One of the interpreters 'ripped into Norman's handling of the meeting. It was, she claimed, very bad, had raised tempers, and had seemed like special pleading by Britain dressed up as concern for the French.'[44] Smith had a strong commitment to Europe, unlike Lamont, and was capable of being emollient while firm and reducing tension with a joke. He could well have produced a favourable outcome, unlike Lamont.

Smith's critics argue that there was too little policy development in his time as leader. He was confident of winning the next election and did not want to create too many hostages to fortune. This has been examined by Ward: 'He was fully aware that Labour's tax and welfare policies ... would need to be reviewed and insulated from future Tory exaggerated "tax bombshell" attacks.' He therefore set up a Commission on Social Justice to come up with new ideas on how to create a fairer tax and benefits system. The drawback of bodies of this kind is that they provide a means for delaying difficult decisions rather than identifying feasible solutions. The initial interim reports were 'very slim documents, merely outlining broad principles, rather than going into great detail'.[45] However, this was what Smith wanted as he was concerned that specific policies at that stage of the electoral cycle would be too risky. As his last speech, made the day before he died, made clear, he had an overall conception of the role of government in the economy: 'It must not be a Government which imagines that it can decide everything for business or decide everything for people. It is above all an enabling Government.'[46] This was close to traditional continental conceptions of social democracy, in terms of as much market as possible, as much state as necessary, but with a requirement that business 'must respect the social rights of our people'.[47] This anticipates the current emphasis on business acting in accordance with ESG principles (environment, social and governance).

Smith's speech at the Trades Union Congress in September 1993 defended the role of trade unions, reiterated the commitment to full employment and proposed new protections for both full-time and part-time workers. According to Ward, 'Both Brown and Blair disliked the speech – worrying that it was heralding a return to union "beer and sandwiches" at Number 10.'[48] In the wake of Black Wednesday, Smith developed an interest in financial regulation. This allowed Rory Bremner to portray Smith as a regulator, the man from OFGOV. That echoed 'the murmur that was beginning to circulate in the Party, that Labour was in danger of seeming too complacent, not fiery enough; to be too established in the style of an Opposition that perhaps expected to stay there'.[49]

It is very difficult to separate any assessment of Smith as a leader from subsequent events, in particular the electoral success of New Labour and the progress it made in terms of domestic policy, albeit in a very favourable international economic environment. One view would be that Smith was rather old-fashioned, a decent and moral individual inspired by a desire for social justice while recognising that one needed a successful economy to provide support for the less fortunate in society. The dilemma about the balance between taxation and public expenditure remains, even for Conservative governments. For a variety of reasons, governments are more fiscally constrained than they were in the past, but this does not mean that Labour cannot differentiate itself from the Conservatives on fiscal policy. It should not be a justification for interpreting Smith's legacy through a New Labour lens as a reason for excessive caution.

CONCLUSION: THE RISKS OF PRUDENCE

There are few politicians of whom I can remember where I was and what I was doing when they died. President Kennedy is one; John Smith is another. There is no doubt that he was respected and liked across the political spectrum. If he had become Prime Minister, he would have been a different leader to Blair. For example, he was doubtful if he would have adhered to Conservative public expenditure plans for the first two years in office (indeed, the Conservatives wouldn't have done so themselves). He thought that the better off should make a contribution through higher levels of taxation. It can be argued that Blair had a better sense of how to reassure voters that their individual aspirations for a better life would be empowered rather than damaged by Labour.

One lesson that has lodged itself in the Labour Party's collective memory has been the myth of the shadow Budget. It is thought to demonstrate that the party must be very cautious about any proposal to increase taxation. However, the Smith legacy is more complex than that. Reassuring the international financial community and the City of London that Labour offered a safe pair of hands 'tended to squeeze out anything too radical or distinctive, diminishing any positive sense of what the Labour Party stood for … Labour risked being portrayed as a pale imitation of the Conservatives.'[50] All the available evidence suggests that the shadow Budget was not a decisive factor in Labour's defeat in 1992.

Labour runs that same risk today under Keir Starmer. Of course, any new Labour government would have a difficult economic inheritance: low growth, poor productivity and historically high levels of taxation. It is not unreasonable to reassure business that there would be a more constructive relationship and less erratic policymaking than under Boris Johnson or Liz Truss. However, Labour has to offer something beyond a more competent version of the Conservatives. Policy commitments are continually being diluted. A policy that has become emblematic of this tendency is the refusal to contemplate removing the Conservative government's two-child benefit cap. Potential Labour voters faced with an offer of prudence and business as usual may decide to vote for the Greens or not vote at all.

6

SOCIAL POLICY

Ben Williams

HAVING ASCENDED TO LABOUR'S leadership in the devastating aftermath of the party's fourth consecutive general election defeat in 1992, the social policy landscape facing John Smith appeared initially bleak amidst the harsh context of ongoing voter rejection. Nevertheless, viewed from another perspective, there was some underlying potential for a more convincing policy reset within this specific sphere, which had not wholly been the case previously, entailing further innovation and reform and the possibility of a future Labour administration delivering quality social services and presiding over the broader modernisation of the welfare state. This underlying sense of opportunity was particularly resonant given recurring observations that, despite the Conservatives' repeated electoral success, social policy had been an area that continued to be neglected by the party in office since 1979.[1] Even though John Major had attempted to re-engage with social issues from 1990, successive electoral victories had been secured by a broader public perception of comparatively greater Conservative economic focus and competence.[2] This imbalanced policy perception was of particular frustration to Labour frontbenchers by the early 1990s, as considerable time and energy had been exerted on social policy over the previous decade, and while it was historically an area of durable strength for the party, the social policy agenda had struggled to make the positive political impact required.

Smith's leadership therefore had to deal with the legacy of Neil Kinnock's relatively expansive social policy package that had seemingly been electorally unpopular at the 1992 general election. Kinnock's egalitarian instincts were frustrated by the fact that in both 1987 and 1992 he failed to present his fairly ambitious social policy goals in a formula that could persuade the electorate that such an agenda could be affordably delivered: 'Labour's capacity to convince the electorate of the affordability of its social policy goals was evidently never convincingly achieved.'[3] On this premise, Smith's leadership had the advantage that it could learn from such errors of the past: namely that to secure a better public reaction in the social policy realm, there had to be stronger foundations behind the various social policies affecting welfare and social security, health, and housing in terms of them being both credibly funded and practically deliverable. This was a critical lesson for Labour if it was to achieve future political and electoral progress; yet to the younger modernisers, Smith often appeared reluctant to wholly learn from it. Within such a context, here we seek to assess how social policy evolved and developed during Smith's relatively short (just under two years) tenure as Labour Party leader and what particular foundations were subsequently laid in this policy area for the New Labour era (in both opposition and government) that followed.

JOHN SMITH'S SOCIAL POLICY OUTLOOK

With regards to the broader policy agenda approach that was pursued during Smith's leadership from mid-1992, the general debate at the time – and since – has tended to revolve around to what extent he was inclined to merely moderate and tweak Kinnock's policy legacy and broadly continue with the trajectory of Kinnock's political narrative (aligned with the 'one more heave' mindset).[4] Would Smith adhere to much of the 1992 manifesto package, or was he willing to embrace further policy innovation, new ideas and even radical reform? In social policy terms, Smith had loyally endorsed Kinnock's fairly generous 1992 social and welfare agenda and had indeed crafted a somewhat notorious Budget to fund it.[5] Kinnock had pledged improved levels of public funding for specific social policy areas such as health, pensions and public housing provision, which was somewhat in defiance of the prevailing Conservative narrative. While Smith was traditionally more aligned with the Old Labour right (moderates) compared to Kinnock's left-wing heritage, both men were of a generation strongly attached to the original universalist (and costly) principles of the post-war welfare state.

There were fluid internal Labour dynamics during the early 1990s, as new factional positions emerged and politicians moved and responded in varying directions to a further electoral loss. Within such a context, a key early test for Smith was to see if he would revert to conventional Labour thinking in this specific policy sphere or actively engage with the emerging ideas of the fledgling 'New Labour' mindset and its younger generation of politicians with more flexible political perspectives. In this context, Smith's social policy outlook could be said to have been initially ambivalent in that it was both backward and forward looking: influenced by and associated or aligned with what had gone before, yet gradually acknowledging the need to re-shape the party's broader policy narrative if he wanted to become Prime Minister.

Smith's natural inclinations could be said to have stemmed from the Labour Party's approach to social policy formulation for much of its history. Its egalitarian emphasis has been aligned with 'the tradition of social administration associated with T. H. Marshall and Richard Titmuss, which saw universal benefits and services as a tangible expression of equal social citizenship'.[6] This positive emphasis on universal welfare as a vehicle towards greater equality dated back to a previous and idealised era of the welfare state as it was conceived in its contemporary guise in the 1940s, but the financial and demographic strains it was experiencing by the 1990s were nothing new. Indeed, the 1960s saw the introduction of supplementary benefits and the formation of pressure groups such as the Child Poverty Action Group, which suggested that universalism was not effectively delivering even then.

While the Callaghan government of 1976–9, in which Smith served, managed to restrict the gap between rich and poor during the 1970s, it escalated out of control under the Thatcher premiership during the 1980s.[7] Any incoming Labour government knew that it would face a more unequal socio-economic landscape than ever. Labour's reformers therefore argued that within an environment of diminishing financial and material resources, and amidst the culture of a post-Thatcher smaller state, there was limited evidence that an adherence to reinvigorated universalism could close this gap or indeed that there was a broader political appetite for such an approach. On this premise, the moderniser position was that maybe a more conditional, streamlined and targeted welfare approach for those most in socio-economic need was the way forward.

From an early stage of his leadership, many contemporaries came to perceive Smith as being more entrenched within the conventional Old Labour mindset, which was often resistant to reform and change, both in terms of internal party organisation and external policy-making. This perspective of the leader was possibly re-enforced by Smith's own fears that the wider party was unwilling to follow such a revised and ultra-modernised approach as espoused by some, amidst particular fears that it would alienate the party's left. There were claims from contemporary observers that 'he [Smith] feared nothing more than a divided party'.[8] His most ardent allies therefore saw him as a safer pair of hands and a more unifying figure than his often abrasive and polarising predecessor, Kinnock. Smith's more consensual approach may have been linked to the fact that he was one of the few Labour frontbenchers with experience of holding ministerial office – during the divisive and turbulent 1970s – and would have been aware of the pitfalls and uncertainties of governance when pursuing potentially controversial policy agendas with a fragmented parliamentary group and amidst often uncertain economic and political conditions.

Some specific evidence of Smith's apparently cautious approach has been recalled by several political contemporaries from this period. His shadow Cabinet colleague Jack Straw recollected that Smith angrily warned him in early 1993 about 'stirring up a hornets' nest' with regards to Straw's interests in reforming Labour's symbolic Clause IV, which Blair of course later did in 1995.[9] Similarly, the arch-moderniser and Labour pollster Philip Gould recalls that, in his view, Smith's instinct was for 'consolidation, not modernisation', having previously 'expressed his reservations about the [Labour] modernisation process' under Kinnock.[10] Another high-profile moderniser, Peter Mandelson, has claimed that in party terms, Smith 'was essentially conservative, reluctant to embark on fundamental reform ... who would not try to change the party further'.[11]

All three of these individuals had found themselves quickly pushed out to the fringes of influence by Smith, after being more central and involved within the Kinnock team. To this younger generation of more impatient modernisers, Smith disappointed from the outset. This was linked to their shared emphasis on continued modernisation being essential if the party was to become more electable and consequently able to both formulate and deliver achievable social (and other) policies suited for the twenty-first century in line with Labour's traditions. However, Smith seemed less convinced by such moderniser remedies. The essential Labour moderniser view of this period was that without ongoing reform, the party remained at great risk of further general election defeats, with its very existence and viability possibly under threat 'unless Labour's modernisation accelerated'.[12] In this way, the pace and nature of change was certainly a root cause of such intra-party tensions.

THE LEGACY OF THE 1992
SHADOW BUDGET

It has also been claimed by some academic and political sources that while there were certainly internal party pressures from an early stage of Smith's leadership that demanded a new direction in social policy formulation, there was also a personal and maybe even a self-centred element that influenced his specific involvement in this evolving process. This stemmed from the perspective that in his role as shadow Chancellor between 1987 and 1992, Smith was ultimately responsible for the party's economic programme and consequently stood accused by some internal critics of having played a high-profile negative role in the disastrous 1992 electoral setback. He therefore now wished to transcend and redeem his own personal degree of culpability for its outcome. This arose from the growing and recurring criticism from figures such as Mandelson that Smith's 'tax and spend' shadow Budget, as presented during the 1992 campaign, had been responsible for 'alienating voters of almost every class and background'.[13]

In order to suppress such simmering internal unrest and to consolidate his own leadership position going forward, it has been suggested that Smith became keen to 'bury' and detach himself from the memory of Labour's 1992 shadow Budget, which 'was viewed as a big reason for [Labour's] general election defeat for which, as Shadow Chancellor, Smith was responsible' and which somewhat ironically was 'an attempt to show greater fiscal responsibility' by the provision of 'details of how Labour would fund proposals for benefit increases'.[14] The damning allegation was that Smith's financial recklessness had ultimately cost Labour the most recent general election, and this narrative incorporated a prominent social policy element, stemming from what was perhaps Smith's honest calculation when seeking to sufficiently finance the party's 'plans for pension and child benefits' in particular.[15] Smith's subsequent post-1992 internalised manoeuvring implies that the recalibration of social (and welfare) policy was occurring as a response to what was increasingly viewed as a strategic electoral blunder during the 1992 campaign. It was from this context that Smith came to accept the need for some significant movement on such social policy matters, albeit for possibly more personalised reasons – in response to this damaging criticism – and still more slowly than some would have liked.

THE COMMISSION ON SOCIAL JUSTICE

To reflect this increased willingness – for whatever motives – to engage with the evolution of Labour's social policy, Smith, as promised during his leadership campaign, established a grandiose-sounding Commission on Social Justice. This was formally put in place from 17 December 1992, with the launch attended by Smith, his deputy Margaret Beckett and the various members of the commission, who in their part-time and unpaid roles were charged with the challenging remit of refreshing and reformulating social policy in the build-up to the next general election.[16] A key figure in laying the groundwork for this formal process was Donald Dewar, a fellow Scot and a Smith ally, who had been appointed shadow Secretary of State for Social Security when Smith became leader in July 1992. It would be Dewar's departmental policy programme that would be most impacted by the commission's eventual welfare-related recommendations.

This initiative can be seen as ongoing consolidation of the legacy of the wide-ranging post-1987 policy review instigated by Kinnock. The specific context for the commission and its very title was that over previous years, the concept of 'social justice' had become increasingly prevalent as a broadly 'progressive' term that favoured and was associated with the egalitarianism of the political left, stemming from the argument that the Thatcherite New Right economic agenda of the 1980s had created adverse social circumstances and 'injustice' for many. The commission would go on to define social justice as follows:

The equal worth of all citizens, their equal right to be able to meet their basic needs, the need to spread opportunities and life chances as widely as possible, and finally the requirement that we reduce and where possible eliminate unjustified inequalities. Social justice stands against fanatics of the free market economy; but it also demands and promotes economic success. The two go together.[17]

Smith himself started to more actively engage with such language and rhetoric, and in the autumn of 1992 he used the term five times in his annual leader's speech, alluding to the incoming commission and confidently declaring that 'the Labour Party was ... a force for social justice and for change'.[18] The following year, at his 1993 leader's conference speech, he proclaimed that the Labour Party needed to be 'bold in our ambitions ... bold in our unyielding commitment to social justice; bold in our vision of a truly free and democratic society'.[19]

Such expressive language provided the context for what ensued in more vigorous social policy terms. The date of the commission's launch was of significance as it marked 'the fiftieth anniversary of the Beveridge Report' with the Commission's output billed as a 'new Beveridge'.[20] This was a symbolic and focused comparison, not lost on those within the Labour hierarchy who felt that this was an appropriate moment to revisit the principles of this historic legacy in a more reformist and radical fashion. While the welfare state had always been viewed as a sacred tenet of Labour's political heritage, this had consequently created a degree of conservatism within elements of the party – on both its traditional left and right – that resisted questioning its ongoing cost, structure and viability. Consequently, the Conservatives, notably during their Thatcherite hegemony, were able to effectively attack the 'perceived profligacy and impracticality of such alternative policies from the political Left'.[21] Such a debate has been a recurring one that has continued over subsequent decades.[22]

The new wave of party modernisers had pragmatically concluded that previous and repeated electoral failures indicated that a revitalised approach and reformist attitude to welfare and social policy was essential for the party to pursue (in order to outflank the Conservatives in both electoral and policy terms). Due to demographic change and rising costs, the welfare state could no longer be merely viewed as 'a passive provider of benefits, but as an enabler'.[23] On this premise, the commission was promoted at the time as the leadership's 'big idea' that offered a 'radical rethink' for the future of the struggling and over-burdened welfare state:

> With its remit running across the whole of the tax and benefits system, including the possibility of integrating them, as well as employment,

education, training, housing and childcare, the commission has more room for manoeuvre than any politically backed study since Beveridge.[24]

The recently established and pro-Labour think tank the Institute of Public Policy Research (IPPR), founded in 1988, was subsequently brought on board to work closely on the commission and to solidify the gradual formulation and co-ordination of its proposals. Its role was seen as vital, with its emergence coming to symbolise 'the renewal of thinking for the left' according to contemporary observations.[25] Key figures in this aspect of the process were future Labour Cabinet ministers Patricia Hewitt and David Miliband, both of whom were employed by the IPPR – Hewitt as its deputy director.[26] Miliband would become the commission's secretary upon its creation.

Chairing the commission would be Gordon Borrie, someone without any evident experience in social policy, but who was an 'old friend of Smith's, a lawyer and former Director General of the Office of Fair Trading'.[27] While undoubtedly having an impressive professional background, whether this gave him the required skills for this particular role is open to debate. In theory, he was officially independent but had pro-Labour leanings and was a former Labour parliamentary candidate.[28] Some may allude to a potentially nepotistic appointment, but he was clearly someone whom both Smith and Dewar felt they could trust to preside over this delicate but highly significant political matter. In terms of the practicalities of this position, Borrie headed a body of sixteen commissioners in total, pledging to pursue a 'wide-ranging review', and ostensibly 'nothing was off-limits – even the future of universality'.[29] The commissioners subsequently engaged in 'outreach' visits to eighty different organisations across eleven specific areas of the country between February 1993 and April 1994,[30] as well as receiving between 450 to 500 submissions from across a wide range of society, including 'academics, charities, politicians, trade unions, businesses and members of the public'.[31]

SOCIAL POLICY RECOMMENDATIONS AND OUTCOMES

A key aim of the commission was to uncover longer-term and well-researched social policy solutions rather than quick fixes, to reflect the changing world in 'economic, social and political terms' over the previous three decades in particular.[32] It would therefore focus on 'a strategy and programme of policy changes over 15 years', implying a multi-term Labour government, with the ultimate aim of addressing the demands of the impending new century that lay ahead.[33] However, Borrie asserted that it was not necessarily the basis of any future Labour manifesto.[34] This sentiment seemingly reflected the views of Smith, with the various policy documents that ensued focusing on 'broad principles, rather than going into great detail'.[35] This suggested that lessons had been learned from the 1992 campaign, notably financial ones via the formative 'prudence' of Smith's shadow Chancellor Gordon Brown.[36] At this relatively early stage of Smith's leadership, it was noted by Borrie that Smith particularly 'feared the political dangers ... in appearing to commit the Party to specific policies'.[37] A succession of thirteen proposed policy papers and discussion documents consequently emerged over the next eighteen months, stemming from sixteen full commission meetings.[38] They covered an extensive range of policy such as general social security reform and the ongoing viability of universalised welfare provision, as well as more specific issues such as occupational pensions, restructured taxation levels, taxation of some benefits, learning and skills provision and local government services.

In hindsight, this wide-ranging process can now be viewed as pivotal to ongoing attempts to bolster and revitalise the party's existing social policy agenda in the build-up to the next general election, which Smith obviously expected to lead the party into. As already noted, Labour's broader social policy offer had already been considerably revamped prior to 1992, with further changes dating back to major policy reviews during the late 1980s.[39] Consequently, much of the previous 'Old Labour' socialist tendencies had been diluted, although not completely removed. The commission's outcomes therefore broadly aspired to continue Labour's social policy evolution while also reflecting one of Smith's most cherished beliefs, namely that 'social justice and economic efficiency could go hand in hand', regardless of the contrary narrative that the Conservatives had established during the 1980s.[40]

Within such a context, the further evolution of yet another variant of the party's social policy agenda could be, as previously alluded to, linked to internal pressures imposed on the Smith leadership from younger shadow Cabinet ministers like Brown, Blair and Straw. They were impatient for government, wanting quicker and more observable policy and image change, aligned within the broader narrative of a modernised approach. The modernisers and Smith's critics within Labour (not always the same people) felt that various commission recommendations were inadequate, while Smith himself seemed to lack a clear vision. There remained some within the party who feared that reform need not be so radical, but to the modernising tendency more was still needed, with concerns expressed that the commission's 'large and diverse membership' – including academics, religious leaders, journalists, business figures, welfare experts and economists – was potentially a problem, as 'it looked for compromises', which ultimately meant that it failed to provide an outcome as coherent, radical or focused as Beveridge had done back in 1942.[41]

Others felt it was potentially hampered from the outset by Smith's expressed political instincts towards a generous welfare settlement, which could be said to have steered its outcomes. In particular, his 'renewed commitment to the remaining universal benefits' led to contemporary observations of subsequent 'difficulty the party may have in adopting any radical changes proposed by the commission'.[42] The commission's conclusions also failed to wholly address the critical issues of 1992 – namely, whether such social policies were affordable. Despite this, such moderniser advocacy for developing a more enabling, efficient, dynamic and proactive welfare state would subsequently be consolidated by Labour throughout the 1990s and eventually put into practice during the Blair government from 1997. Smith's prevailing traditionalist caution and affinity to (expensive) universalism would therefore be later replaced by Blair's less sentimental and more pragmatic view of the welfare state.

The major issue, however, is that Smith died before any such specific policies arising from the commission were confirmed. So, while there has been much speculation, nobody knows precisely what his final agenda was in the spheres of child benefit, health care, unemployment and housing – to name but a few core social policies – and to what degree a markedly different direction would evolve from the positions outlined within the 1992 manifesto. This situation can, of course, be linked to and explained by the timing and evolution of the parliamentary cycle, with the early phase usually for policy formulation, and the second half of a parliament when 'the policies of the opposition [are] sold to the wider electorate'.[43] Smith was experiencing the first phase (1992–4) at the time of his death but was, of course, denied the critical second part of this cycle. In July 1994, just two months after Smith's untimely death, the Commission on Social Justice published its final paper, *Act Local: Social Justice from the Bottom Up* by David Donnison. As a concluding proposal, it marked a posthumous tribute to the legacy of Smith and his focused efforts over previous years within this policy area, with an assumption that associated policies would follow. The very same month, Blair was overwhelmingly elected by Labour members as Smith's successor, and the era of New Labour was truly underway, with a more rapid pace of social policy modernisation set to follow.

The key duopoly of Blair and his shadow Chancellor Brown, who continued in the role served under Smith, were said to have respected the commission's work and some of its recommendations for social policy developments for a future Labour administration – although Brown more so than Blair, according to Borrie.[44] Indeed, there is some evidence that notable New Labour welfare policies such as tax credits, the minimum wage and welfare benefits having conditionality linked to employment outcomes arose in some form from this process. In addition, influential figures involved in the commission such as David Miliband would go on to head up Blair's policy unit during his first term in Downing Street.

Nevertheless, the broader attitude of Blair to the commission and its legacy 'was not about how far he agreed or disagreed, used or did not use their ideas, but that it was Smith's Commission, not his'.[45] Blair felt that as party leader, he should not be wholly committed to it or indeed restricted by its recommendations. However, the commission and its findings could be viewed as 'symbolic' and original due to its engagement with dynamic and contemporary political themes, fresh concepts and new ideas. In addition, by its process of wider public engagement and the rigour of its diverse social policy menu, it could be said to have positively 'signalled change to the electorate' in terms of Labour's electoral appeal.[46] Yet, in various aspects, Blair and his allies seemingly viewed the various commission recommendations as not sufficiently radical, with one observation being that it was 'good on analysis, less good on prescription', particularly in terms of practically delivering a functioning and affordable welfare state that was suitable for a new century.[47]

LESSONS FOR NEW LABOUR

As Smith's successor, Blair presided over the formal publication of the Commission for Social Justice's final recommendations and report in October 1994.[48] However, just five months after Smith's death, the goalposts had seemingly already moved in a relatively short space of time. In the period 1994–7, Blair's leadership in opposition escalated the pace of social (and broader) policy development even further, becoming more sharply focused on aligning with a public mood that was often critical of the perceived cost, dependency and waste within the welfare system, in the pursuit of Labour returning to power after such a long exile. In his more open-minded, impatient and pragmatic approach, Blair went beyond the ethos and proposals that stemmed from the commission, consequently loosening the party's former ideological adherence to relatively generous welfare universalism and therefore re-aligning Labour's social policy in a more substantial manner compared to Smith's more tentative inclinations. For reasons of both cost and efficiency, Blair steadily moved in the direction of more explicitly streamlined welfare conditionality; the targeting of resources; benefits linked to labour market and employment outcomes; private finance initiatives, notably for the NHS; and curtailment of some elements of escalating social policy expenditure – all of which would later materialise in office after 1997.

The Blair–Brown leadership axis also sought to avoid the mistakes of Smith's 1992 Budget by pledging to adhere to existing Conservative spending plans for the first two years in office.[49] This had significant implications, and indeed limitations, for the scope and ambition of social policy in the early years of a future Labour government and potentially extinguished some of Smith's more expansive policy preferences. However, Blair may have overreached his 'strategic positioning' and pushed things slightly too far, given that the party mainstream wanted to retain Labour's more traditional values on welfare and social policy. This was notably evident when Blair challenged Minister of State for Welfare Reform Frank Field to provocatively 'think the unthinkable' regarding the welfare state's inexorably escalating cost, only to hit a wall of internal party resistance and practical obstacles.[50] Field was a welfare radical, someone with a deep-rooted background in the issue and director of the Child Poverty Action Group (1969–79), as well as being chair of the Commons Social Security Select Committee between 1990 and 1997. Field advocated a more proactive welfare state with emphasis on individual responsibility and the securing of genuine employment opportunity rather than long-term receipt of benefits. This would transcend a form of 'welfare dependency' which he viewed as a damaging side-effect of historically generous welfare provision. Field wrote a book in 1995 called *Making Welfare Work*, which provided a flavour of the more targeted, employment-driven and cost-effective social policy agenda that Blair embraced more enthusiastically than Smith.[51] On this issue, he therefore had Blair's attention.

CONCLUSION: SMITH'S SOCIAL POLICY LEGACY

Due to his premature and untimely death, it remains a matter of some conjecture as to specifically what a John Smith-led government's social policy agenda would have looked like. Some contemporaries have confidently claimed that it would not have been too different from what Blair pursued in office after 1997.[52] Both were leaders with similar Christian imperatives regarding the humane and civilising role of welfare support, but hindsight suggests that Blair was never fully convinced by Smith's slower pace of travel while part of his shadow Cabinet. This was evident from late 1994, when Blair instigated a strategic detachment from some potentially costly recommendations of Smith's Commission for Social Justice – namely universalism – which suggested that its legacy and 'influence were already on the wane' less than six months after Smith's sudden death.[53] Indeed, Borrie reportedly observed that once in office after 1997, Blair's government did not view his report as a 'valuable resource'.[54]

Nevertheless, the commission had sparked significant debate about new ideas and triggered policymaking momentum for Labour in opposition, which can be viewed as a positive legacy. However, somewhat adversely, resistance did emerge from within the party to what some perceived as excessive meddling by New Labour with the core principles of the post-war universalised welfare state. This became evident in the form of a series of significant parliamentary rebellions from mainly left-wing backbench Labour MPs against various welfare reforms and cutbacks during Blair's first term in office. Thus, the internal divisions that Smith had been so keen to avoid did come to fruition under Blair's more abrasive and radical strategy – but he could afford to ride them out due to his huge parliamentary majority.

On this basis, we can conclude that Blair transcended Smith's more unifying, traditionalist and consensual agenda in the social policy domain, provoking and confronting the party's conventional instincts in order to pursue a more radical direction, which resulted in more explicit change within this policy sphere. This was aligned with the post-Thatcher public mood and longer-term social changes, with Blair seeking to cautiously assuage previous electoral concerns about Labour regarding the scale and extent of welfare service delivery and affordability. This ultimately struck a chord of heightened appeal for New Labour with a more welfare-sceptic Middle England audience from 1997 onwards, paving the way for the emergence of a more explicitly 'Blairite' social policy agenda within the first decade of the twenty-first century. However, given the anti-Conservative public mood by the mid-1990s, such radicalism may not have been wholly necessary, and Smith's own approach may well have had similar electoral potency.

John Smith was by no means hostile to policy modernisation, and according to one contemporary, he 'was determined to modernise his party. But he wanted to bring the old principles up to date, not replace them.'[55] What he would have done differently to the Blair administration within such core social policy issues therefore remains subject to speculative and hypothetical political debate, but based on the evidence outlined within this chapter, it seems unlikely that he would have been so bold.

7

SCOTTISH HEART, ENGLISH HEAD: LABOUR'S EDUCATION POLICY, 1992–4

Joseph Tiplady

'Disciplina, fide, perseverantia.'

DUNOON GRAMMAR SCHOOL MOTTO

IN AN INTERVIEW ON BBC One's political programme *On the Record* in 1993, John Smith said, 'As Neil Kinnock wisely observed, it is education and training that are the commanding heights of the modern economy.'[1] This phrase was taken from a landmark speech made earlier the same day to Labour's local government conference in which Smith sought to bolster his modernising credentials by renouncing Labour Party shibboleths, amongst them Clause IV and nationalisation.[2] Contemporary historians have advanced the popular narrative that Smith's leadership maintained the momentum of the modernisation and change programme that had been initiated by Kinnock. However, in the development of the Labour Party's education policy the case for modernisation is much weaker. While Smith and his shadow Secretary of State for Education, Ann Taylor, accepted the revisions to the broad approach to education bequeathed to them by Kinnock, Smith's policy agenda would see a return to the status quo in Labour Party policy: comprehensivisation and a close relationship with the teaching unions. Influenced by his own personal biography and the other political actors involved in the policymaking process, this culminated in the sole education policy paper of Smith's leadership, published shortly after his death, *Opening Doors to a Learning Society*.[3]

This chapter will trace the development of education policy during the tenure of Smith as leader of the Labour Party from 1992 to 1994. Despite Smith's short tenure as leader, the two-year period of his leadership made a significant contribution to the continued development of the party's approach to education. These contributions came from both internal and external sources. Internally, the party sought to undertake a serious consultation process to produce policy. Externally, the Labour Party benefitted from an intellectual climate on the centre-left that was proactively seeking to develop and reinvigorate ideas in education, most notably in publications by the Institute for Public Policy Research (IPPR).

POLITICAL ACTORS

The political actors central to directing and influencing the Labour Party's education policy in this period were John Smith as leader and Ann Taylor as shadow Secretary of State for Education. A third notable actor, albeit to a lesser extent, was education academic Professor Sally Tomlinson, who was an advisor to Taylor throughout this period.[4] All three had an influential role in guiding the policymaking of the Labour Party during this short period.

In the case of education, Smith's own upbringing and formative experiences of schooling in Scotland were influential in shaping his views. Smith was raised in a Scottish Presbyterian family with a father who became headmaster at Ardrishaig Primary School in his early infancy. Due to his father's occupation, Smith would grow up in the headmaster's residence attached to the school, which he would also later attend. Early in his scholastic career, at junior school, Smith was involved in debating and contributed to the school magazine. At the age of fourteen, while some of Smith's peers left school, he continued his secondary education at Dunoon Grammar School.

Dunoon was founded in 1641, with a strong Presbyterian religious character. Although Dunoon was a non-selective state school, it had several characteristics more akin to an English grammar than it did to its comprehensive counterparts.[5] Dunoon organised pupils into groups by academic ability for core subjects, such as English and maths. Similar to the multi-lateral schools envisioned by post-war advocates of education reform, it divided pupils into academic and vocational streams with lessons taking place on the same school estate. This was effectively an internal selection of pupils for an academic or vocational course of study: Latin for the former and manual work for the latter.[6] The exterior and interior of the school's buildings also signalled its long history and status as the region's most significant educational institution. The imposing buildings of recognisable architectural styles from previous centuries and an interior furnished with valuable and hardwearing materials differentiated it from its secondary modern peers.

Smith's upbringing, in a household where education was highly valued, and the formative experience of education under the tutelage of both his own father and then at the historic Dunoon Grammar had a direct influence on Smith's view of education. This in turn would influence the policies of the Labour Party under his leadership. In this way, Smith was a strong advocate for comprehensive education, while being highly sceptical of public schools and selection. The central claim in his praise of the comprehensive school was grounded in social equality. That such schools accept pupils regardless of their personal characteristics, background or household income was viewed as a core strength. In contrast, Smith's sceptical view of public schools and selection lay in the perceived divisions they sowed within society by erecting barriers between pupils based on academic attainment or through wealth. It is noteworthy that Smith aired such views from early in his career as a parliamentarian, arguing against public schools and selection as an issue of social justice, which undermined equality.[7]

These views were further influenced by Smith's close friendship with one of his parliamentary colleagues: Tony Crosland. Crosland, as an author, had identified reform to the education system as the main method of ameliorating social inequality. Later, as Secretary of State for Education and Science, he initiated the comprehensivisation of the secondary school system in England and Wales when he issued Circular 10/65, which requested that Local Education Authorities (LEAs) reorganise their schools along comprehensive lines.

As other authors have outlined Smith was an admirer and friend to Crosland, although this did not extend to him being a Croslandite.[8] Smith's personal friendship with the influential Labour thinker and his emphasis on comprehensive schools seems to have reinforced the views that Smith had arrived with in Parliament.

The evidence for Smith as a moderniser is often given as his support for and the confirmation of the changes Kinnock made to the Labour Party's ideational underpinning and policy agenda. However, this framing is not consistent with his approach to education. Smith's vision of education, as demonstrated above, was more aligned with the ethical socialists of the late nineteenth and early twentieth centuries, such as the Workers' Educational Association, who argued for a broad highway along which pupils would travel to educational attainment. This was in contrast to the vision of Sydney Webb and other members of the Fabian Society, who advocated a meritocratic approach, often described as a ladder of opportunity, which only those capable students would be able to ascend.

The second most significant political actor during this period was shadow Education Secretary Ann Taylor. Born in Motherwell, Scotland, Taylor was raised in Bolton, Lancashire. She attended the Bolton School, an independent day school, on a scholarship and would go on to study at the universities of Bradford and Sheffield, becoming an Open University lecturer before her election to parliament.[9] First elected to Parliament to represent the constituency of Bolton West at the October 1974 general election, by 1992 Taylor was a political veteran. She had served in government and in opposition, holding several shadow ministerial roles under consecutive leaders of the Labour Party. Taylor's first political role was parliamentary private secretary to Fred Mulley during his tenures as Education and then Defence Secretary, before becoming an assistant whip between 1977 and 1979 in the last Labour government under Prime Minister James Callaghan. Following Callaghan's defeat in 1979, as Leader of the Opposition he appointed Taylor to be a spokesperson for education, deputising to shadow Education Secretary Neil Kinnock.[10] On the election of Michael Foot as leader of the Labour Party, Taylor was moved to an environment brief, before losing her seat at the 1983 general election.[11]

Following her election for Dewsbury in 1987, Taylor occupied a number of shadow ministerial roles before making a concerted effort to secure a place in the shadow Cabinet. On her election in 1987, Kinnock, now Labour leader, swiftly appointed Taylor to a shadow Home Affairs portfolio before she was shuffled to a junior brief to oppose water privatisation in the environment team.[12] In the latter stages of Kinnock's leadership, Taylor challenged for a place in the shadow Cabinet. In the 1989 shadow Cabinet elections she finished as first runner-up with 100 votes. At the time, there was an expectation that she would supplant then shadow Education Secretary, Jack Straw, but he received 104 votes, keeping his place.[*13] In 1990, she retained this level of support, placing twelfth, and received extra responsibility in her shadow Environment brief as a result.[14] This was the beginning of an upward trajectory for Taylor, as she placed ninth with 126 votes in 1991 and eleventh with a peak of 129 in 1992.[15] According to Taylor, Smith, the new Labour leader, offered her a choice of shadow portfolios, of which she chose the shadow education brief.[16] Taylor's

---

* Jack Straw was Labour Member of Parliament for Blackburn between 1979 and 2015. He served as Kinnock's shadow Secretary of State for Education for four years between 1987 and 1992.

shadow education team included Jeff Rooker, Tony Lloyd and Win Griffiths, a former teacher.[17] In brief, Labour's shadow education team was led by a former lecturer and experienced parliamentarian, who was well versed in the mechanics of the legislative and executive branches, with a long-term interest in education and strong political ambition.

One further individual played an influential role on education policy during this period, Professor Sally Tomlinson, a highly respected and widely published academic. For the majority of her career, she has taught and researched in the higher education sector and has held several professorial chairs at major universities. Pre-eminent in her field, Tomlinson specialises in education, educational policy and related subjects, such as ethnicity and race. From the late 1980s onwards, Tomlinson became involved in politics, participating in an advisory body to then shadow Education Secretary Jack Straw between 1989 and 1992. She then became an advisor to Straw's successor, Ann Taylor, with whom between 1992 and 1994, she shaped the green paper, *Opening Doors to a Learning Society*.[18]

OPENING DOORS TO A LEARNING SOCIETY

Following the Labour Party's defeat at the 1992 general election and the subsequent leadership election, Smith and Taylor wasted no time in changing the party's policies. In her first interview as shadow Education Secretary in September 1992, only two months into Smith's leadership, Taylor spoke directly about the changes to the party's approach to education and distancing herself from the policies adopted during Kinnock's leadership.[19] This included bringing schools that had greater autonomy, such as Grant Maintained (GM) schools and City Technology Colleges (CTC), back under the control of LEAs and a return to a more sceptical view of the role of public schools. Similarly, there was a re-establishment of a more cordial relationship with the teaching unions. In this interview, Taylor's comments demonstrate that the Labour Party's approach to education under Smith would be conservative. Rather than a modernising agenda underpinned by a revisionist social democratic approach, Smith oversaw a return to the status quo. This was associated with an interpretation of education that sought greater social equality, which would be achieved through policies to complete the comprehensivisation of the school system and support for the education trade unions.

While *Opening Doors* has been described as an 'Old Labour' policy document, including by one of its contributors, Tomlinson, this terminology is inaccurate.[20] The term 'Old Labour' was coined by Tony Blair and New Labour as a rhetorical device to draw a distinction between the party's past and present and to disassociate themselves from the failure of previous governments. It also served to simplify the diverse ideational traditions present within the Labour Party, ranging from the Old Right and Old Left to the Centre and New Left.[21]

After eighteen months of wide-ranging consultation, the Labour Party published its only major education policy document under Smith's leadership, *Opening Doors to a Learning Society*. It begins with an opening statement from Smith, which set out his vision for education in broad terms and succinctly explained why the Conservative government's approach must be rejected. In this statement,

Smith asserts that 'in the modern world a good education is the indispensable key to personal fulfilment for the individual, to economic success for the nation, and to the creation of a more just and cohesive society'.[22] This is followed by a paragraph in which he explicitly rejects the Conservative government's agenda of consumerism, centralisation of power and choice within education, in addition to the continuous changes in education policy itself. In Taylor's opening statement, she makes clear that this document was intended to act as a catalyst rather than an end in itself. In a similar vein to Callaghan's 'great debate' on education policy following his Ruskin College speech in 1976, *Opening Doors* was to act as a starting point, initiating a broader discourse on education. The Labour Party wanted to facilitate responses from a broad cross-section of those individuals and organisations involved in, or with an interest in, education through public participation in seminars and meetings to ensure support as broad as possible for the proposed policies.

Rather than a conventional policy document, setting out a political party's policies or broader agenda, the green paper introduced five principles and values that would guide education policymaking. These principles were: access for all, quality and equity, continuity, accountability, and partnership. The use of 'learning society' in the paper's title emphasised the role for education to play in shaping and preparing individuals to take their place in society as well-rounded and respectful citizens. In setting out access for all, Labour's definition bears greater resemblance to the 'broad highway' model as advocated by ethical socialists. The principle of quality and equity speaks to the Labour Party's overriding education priority in the twentieth century: the structure of the education system. The summary of the document explicitly links quality and the comprehensive provision of education, as the party sought to mitigate disadvantage within the school gates, while CTCs and GM schools are highlighted as exacerbating an already unequal school system. The principle of continuity can be defined as the party supporting lifelong learning and making educational opportunities available to the greatest extent possible. In terms of accountability, Labour sought to reduce the statutory powers of the Education Secretary and related quangos and to establish greater rigour in government decision-making and spending. Finally, Labour sought to redress the balance between central and local government in education by having the former set a broad framework for education, while the latter oversaw its delivery.

The paper then sets out a belief in equality, inclusion and the removal of unnecessary barriers and subsequently relates a coherent set of values to a broad range of issues, from a national curriculum to the teaching profession itself and assessment and examinations. In this, *Opening Doors* reaffirms the approach set out by Taylor in her September 1992 interview. This can be seen clearly in the statements made on some of the most contentious issues for the Labour Party in education. Amongst the most significant of these are school league tables, the role of LEAs and the marketisation of education. Taking them in turn, school league tables had been an issue for the party since at least Giles Radice's time as shadow Education Secretary.* As part of a broader ideational shift in the party's approach to education, Radice attempted to change the party's understanding of education

---

* Giles Radice was Labour Member of Parliament for Chester-le-Street between 1973 and 1983 and for North Durham between 1983 and 2001. He served as Kinnock's shadow Education Secretary for four years between 1983 and 1987.

as a public service. This meant the Labour Party representing the interests of the wider education community, including parents and pupils, rather than just the teaching unions.[23] In 1994, this approach was rejected, with league tables being particularly disliked by the teaching unions. With the Labour Party seeking a closer relationship with them, it criticised league tables for oversimplifying the appraisal of schools and adopted a pragmatic line about their replacement, only providing vague proposals on the information about schools that would be provided to parents and pupils.[24]

The latter two issues in education can be treated as a single issue, as one flows from the other. Two central policies were introduced by the Conservative governments of Margaret Thatcher in the years immediately prior to the publication of *Opening Doors*. First, the introduction of greater autonomy for schools by placing them outside of the control of LEAs. This facilitated the second, which saw an element of choice and competition introduced within the school system. These policy changes resulted in the introduction of new types of secondary school, including CTCs and the GM schools. These two issues served to further highlight the changes that had been made to the Labour Party's education policy under Smith and Taylor. Where Radice and his successor as shadow Education Secretary, Jack Straw, had shifted the party to a broader understanding of equality that considered the quality and standards in schools to be as important, if not more so, than the structure of the school system in the pursuit of a more equal society, the priorities were reversed for Smith and Taylor. The response to the introduction of a quasi-market for Smith and Taylor was straight-forward. Despite the popularity and political salience of these schools and education more broadly with the aspirant middle classes, they were primarily viewed as an affront to greater social equality and a barrier to achieving the comprehensivisation of the secondary school system. Both issues served to reinforce that the Labour Party's approach to education under Smith and Taylor was small 'c' conservative and a reversion to the status quo. Although they broadly accepted the changes made, such as the inclusion of quality and standards as a politically salient issue, during this period the policy priorities reverted to those primarily concerned with the structure of the school system and a closer relationship with the teaching unions.

A source of considerable tension in education policy during Smith's leadership of the Labour Party was the internal discourse over the funding and financing of the expansion of the higher education sector. Early in Smith's leadership, Jeff Rooker, the shadow Minister of State for Further and Higher Education, suggested students from more privileged backgrounds could pay tuition fees.[25] The following year, in 1993, the higher education section of an early version of *Opening Doors*, which considered policy proposals for reform including a 'graduate tax', was removed by the Joint Policy Committee (JPC).[26] This was supported by Taylor, who was against such a policy.[27] The extent of Smith's institutional control over the policymaking process as chair of the JPC, a body comprised of members of the shadow Cabinet and the National Executive Committee and which was responsible for overseeing all policy documents, meant the leader of the party held significant influence over any proposals that were considered by the JPC, including attempts to shift the party's approach to higher education policy.[28] The consideration of alternative policies for the funding and financing of higher education was effectively subdued for the duration of Smith's leadership. Consequently, Rooker was sacked in a reshuffle.[29] This episode demonstrates that, under Smith, the Labour Party had adopted a cautious approach and held a preference for the status quo across education policy. In this, Smith and Taylor were aligned as they shared a more traditional view of education and were influenced by their relationship with the education establishment.

MODERNISING EDUCATION

From the late 1980s onwards, one of the factors that became increasingly important in influencing the Labour Party's contemporary education agenda was the intellectual climate and discourse on issues in education and the resulting publications. This was an intense period of activity, in which the intellectual discourse on the centre-left was seeking to develop and modernise both the underpinning ideas and the policies of politically salient domestic issues, including those in education. Publications from think tanks such as the IPPR, authored by practitioners, researchers, and academics, would contribute to this climate in which new ideas and old beliefs would be similarly challenged.

The establishment of the IPPR in 1988 by Clive Hollick and John Eatwell would make a considerable contribution with the frequent publication of research reports and policy papers. These included papers from David Miliband, such as *A British 'Baccalaureat'*, *Learning By Right*, and *Markets, Politics and Education* as part of the Education & Training series.[30] There were also papers by respected and influential academics including Sally Tomlinson, who authored *Educational Reform and its Consequences* and contributed to *Education: A Different Vision*.[31] Similarly, other prominent figures published with IPPR, such as Michael Barber who, together with Tim Brighouse, authored *Partners in Change: Enhancing the Teaching Profession*.[32] Barber would go on to make several influential contributions to this discourse, including his 1995 Greenwich Lecture, *The Dark Side of the Moon: Imagining an End to Failure in Urban Education*, two further publications in 1996, an inaugural professorial lecture at the Institute of Education entitled 'How to do the Impossible' and his book, *The Learning Game*.[33] The networking of these individuals, creating an informal peer-review process, led to more robust arguments in these publications, as highlighted by Barber who recalls the strength of Miliband's comments on an early draft of his IPPR publication, co-authored with Tim Brighouse.[34]

Smith and Taylor trusted and utilised the IPPR, most notably basing the Commission on Social Justice (CSJ) there, but maintained an arm's-length relationship with the organisation. This arrangement allowed the Labour leadership to oversee the CSJ's work and facilitated plausible deniability if anything too radical was proposed.[35] Given the absence of the IPPR's ideas on education being incorporated into Labour policy under Smith and Taylor, it can be assumed that they similarly utilised this relationship to reject alternative policy proposals.

CONCLUSION

Despite the popular narrative of Smith being a moderniser, this is demonstrably not the case in education policy during his tenure as leader of the Labour Party. The foremost influence on his view of education was his upbringing and formative experiences of education in Scotland. On entering Parliament, these views were reinforced by his friendship with Crosland. Similarly, although Taylor was perceived as being on the centre-right of the party, her views on the major issues in education did not align with this characterisation. Together, Smith and Taylor accepted the broad changes to education policy they had inherited from Kinnock. However, as evidenced by Taylor's interview early in Smith's leadership, she considered the end to be greater social equality, which would be achieved through the comprehensivisation of the secondary school system, a hostile view of public schools and closer ties with the teaching unions. Later, in *Opening Doors*, this approach would be confirmed as official party policy, as Labour's agenda in education sought to re-establish LEA control of schools and the abolition of league tables. Finally, there was a growing intellectual climate and discourse that sought to reinvigorate the Labour Party's ideas and policies on education with a diversity of views and resulted in a wealth of publications on the topic.

This rich font of ideas offered an alternative policy prospectus that could have been drawn upon to develop a more nuanced approach to the perceived inequalities of the education system. However, Smith and Taylor's decision-making oversaw the reinstatement of the status quo in Labour policy with an agenda that prioritised the structure of England and Wales's secondary school system over the quality and standards agenda and gave precedence to a close relationship with the teaching unions over parents and pupils.

8

JOHN SMITH AND THE BRITISH CONSTITUTION: A COMMITTED REFORMER?

Jasper Miles

T HE CENTRALITY OF CONSTITUTIONAL reform to the New Labour agenda did not simply emerge in 1997. Instead, it was the culmination of a long process dating back to the 1970s and 1980s, in which the Labour Party shifted its thinking on the constitution. Various factors drove the changing view of the constitution, including electoral pressures, concerns of Conservative hegemony, societal changes and an opening up of thinking beyond 'Labourism' to include liberalism, feminism and other critical perspectives. Before this point, critics accused Labour of being a 'constitutionally conservative' party, wedded to the Westminster system and the British political tradition. When the party did engage with constitutional reform, it was often done to defeat an electoral opponent, such as

Attlee's House of Lords reform or the Callaghan government's devolution proposals. However, by the late 1980s a more fundamental shift in thinking had occurred. Labour questioned and then moved away from a conservative view of constitutional politics, accepting much of the pluralist critique.

Here, John Smith played a key role, building on Neil Kinnock's policy changes. Smith was closely associated with the devolution referendums in the 1970s and had been a longstanding critic of an unelected House of Lords. Therefore, by the time he became leader, he had developed a reputation as someone critical of the workings of the British constitution. In a speech made early on during his leadership, he affirmed:

> It is clear to me that we need to re-examine the relationship between individuals in our society and the institutions that purport to represent them. I will argue that, in our over-centralised democracy, it is not only the style of government but also its structure that has led to this over-centralisation. And I will propose that we need a new system of government, appropriate to a modern European state, which puts the citizen at the centre of the picture and which has levels of government that are sensitive to individual needs and aspirations ... all is not well with the governance of this country'.[1]

This extract captures the significance of constitutional reform to Smith's political agenda, which is reflected in the existing literature. For instance, according to John Morrison, those who worked alongside Smith considered him as 'partly an old-fashioned centraliser'. However, his 'radical attitude to constitutional orthodoxy reflected his education in the continental tradition of Scots law. He was also anti-London in the sense of being a man from the periphery'.[2] Anthony Barnett writes that 'Smith was attracted to the European model of consensual rule-based power'.[3] For Andy McSmith, one of Smith's biographers, he 'was close to being a card-carrying moderniser'.[4] Reflecting on Smith's leadership, Gordon Brown argues that Smith saw 'democratic renewal as central to his vision of a future Britain, an important element of a John Smith Government' and while portrayed as 'staid and traditional, was actually a proponent of radical constitutional change'.[5]

Consequently, this chapter aims to build on the existing accounts in three ways. First, we discuss Labour's journey to constitutional reform, introducing the tensions between the traditionalists and the pluralists. As such, this section charts Labour's interest in constitutional matters and then fleshes out three competing approaches towards the constitution – pluralist, traditional and Marxist. Second, the chapter will explore Smith's constitutional reform agenda. This section will centre on a document titled *A New Agenda for Democracy: Labour's Proposals for Constitutional Reform*, published in 1993. The document and some notable speeches capture the extent of constitutional reform under a future Smith government. From there, it will become clear that Smith was firmly in the pluralist and decentralist camps: he proposed a radical critique of the British constitution. However, he was less keen on proportional representation (PR) and there is conjecture over his view of codification. Neil Pye's chapter charts Smith's approach to devolution, meaning that this chapter does not discuss that topic in any meaningful way. Third, we consider the legacy of Smith's constitutional reform agenda, comparing his approach to New Labour and whether he supported codification. To finish, the chapter proposes further research into whether significant constitutional reforms have been in the interests of the Labour Party.

LABOUR'S ROAD TO CONSTITUTIONAL REFORM

Labour's interest in constitutional reform has fluctuated since the party's inception. Initially, the party embraced home rule and electoral reform, albeit with strong reservations towards the latter from leading figures such as Ramsay MacDonald, with the party only formally committed to electoral reform for brief periods. This began to change in the 1920s as the party enjoyed greater electoral success and two spells in office as minority governments, firstly in 1924 and then 1929–31. The party's electoral meltdown in 1931 and weak showing in 1935 did little to revive interest in constitutional reform. Indeed, the prevailing view within the Labour Party had come to see the workings of the constitution and the institutions of the British state as compatible with the introduction of social reform. Labour's wartime experience as part of the National Government, their winning of a parliamentary majority in 1945 and the social reforms of the Attlee governments convinced the party of the merits of the British constitution. Critics of the working of the British constitution and Labour's acceptance of Britain's constitutional arrangements were confined to the fringes of British politics.

However, the governing difficulties of the 1970s and the broader changes within the British party system emboldened the critics within and without the party. After all, it was no longer clear, according to reformers, that Britain's governing institutions were fit for purpose or fulfilling their supposed advantages. Figures such as Roy Jenkins and John Mackintosh led the intellectual arguments within Labour. The former articulated the need for a written constitution and PR in a noteworthy speech titled 'Home Thoughts from Abroad'. The latter published several texts emphasising the necessity of the transfer of power away from the centre. Labour MP Peter Shore challenged this view, arguing that Britain's constitutional settlement had served the country well and allowed for peaceful change across British society.

Following defeat in 1979, interest in constitutional reform subsided as the party focused on internal democracy and mechanisms. The internal divisions and concerns over policy and entryism led to the Social Democratic Party (SDP) breakaway in 1981. Those that formed the SDP generally favoured constitutional reform and were, therefore, guilty by association. This was particularly so for PR, which many within Labour thought was a strategy to completely break the party and ensure that their new rivals had a permanent stage on British politics. The heavy defeat in 1983, the first of Thatcher's landslide victories, was blamed on policy – 'the longest suicide note in history' – and the workings of the first past the post (FPTP) system hindered the SDP, ensuring that Labour clearly remained the main opposition party.

Interest in constitutional matters gathered pace after 1987. The party considered it had run a successful election campaign, yet it resulted in marginal gains. Therefore, weak electoral prospects in the face of a dominant Conservative Party prompted some to look again at the workings of the constitution. But interest in reform went beyond fears of Conservative hegemony. The policies of the Thatcher governments, inspired by the ideas and thinkers of the New Right, had undermined the planks of social democracy introduced by the Attlee governments. Yet this had been achieved on a vote share in the mid to low forties. Indeed, even if Labour performed well at the next election, it was possible they would require the support of the Liberal Democrats. This encouraged thoughts of a progressive alliance between non-conservative forces, bound together by a commitment to constitutional reform. Elsewhere, the intellectual climate had changed. In the immediate post-war years, academics, intellectuals and commentators had taken a largely positive view of Britain's political tradition and settlement. However, by the 1970s onwards, a more critical take had emerged and by the 1990s found expression in the works of Paul Hirst and Will Hutton. Pressure groups formed, such as the Labour Campaign for Electoral Reform and Charter 88, which advocated for a written constitution. In addition, pressure for reform grew in Scotland, with a Scottish Constitutional Convention arguing for home rule.

Therefore, an initially reluctant leadership – especially Roy Hattersley – had by the 1992 general election committed themselves to a substantial list of constitutional reforms. This included reform of the House of Lords via removing hereditary peers, ultimately leading to an elected second chamber; the introduction of a Freedom of Information Act; and a Charter of Rights. Moreover, there was a manifesto commitment to introduce a Scottish Assembly within the first year of a Labour government, and the manifesto also mooted the idea of a Welsh Assembly. As for PR, the Plant Report would continue to assess the workings, arguments and theories of different systems in relation to the different institutions proposed by Labour's constitutional reform agenda. Kinnock also suggested opening the working group's membership to those outside of the party, including the Liberal Democrats. However, a fourth successive electoral defeat and the Smith leadership would take Labour's constitutional radicalism a step further. Smith ignored Hattersley's concern that Labour's electoral chances in 1992 had been hampered by a heavy focus on constitutional matters in the days leading up to polling day.

Before we consider Smith's constitutional reform agenda, it is important to try and make sense of Labour's approach to constitutional reform throughout the twentieth and twenty-first centuries. One method is to identify the different traditions and approaches towards constitutional reform within, and at times, without the party. One of the issues facing the Labour Party is that it has rarely, if ever, enjoyed a unified view of the state, arguably reflecting Tony Crosland's comment on the aversion of intellectual thinking within the party. For him, the party 'always preserved a marked anti-doctrinal and anti-theoretical bias'.[6] The extent to which this is accurate is debatable.[7] Yet, regarding the constitution and wider British state, we can see different traditions within the party and Labour movement competing for influence and dominance. In addition, it is essential to note that approaches to the constitution do not fit neatly into the left–right spectrum.

First, there are the traditionalists, or to use another term, 'elitists'.[8] This group adheres to a top-down view of politics, democracy and social democracy, in which social reform can be enacted from the centre through the workings of the constitution and the institutions of the British state. For much of the Labour Party's history, the leadership, often drawn from the centre or right of the party, have subscribed to this approach, sceptical of any reforms that would limit a Labour government: for instance, an elected second chamber, proportional representation, a written constitution or a more pronounced role for the judiciary, all of which would undermine the capacity of the centre to govern. Consequently, they are 'elitist' insofar as they accept and, in some cases, celebrate the Westminster model and the British political tradition, both professing to a narrow view of politics conducted at the centre. Notably, this traditional approach is also evident on the left of the party. Tony Benn was attached to parliamentary sovereignty because it guaranteed national independence and democratic accountability, preserving hopes of a democratic socialist Great Britain.[9] Recently, the Labour-supporting academic Richard Johnson has sought to revive the 'Old Labour' view of the British constitution. He has emphasised the case for a political constitution, warning the party of the dangers of reforms that would constrain the power of a majority Labour government.[10] As such, this grouping has a benign view of the British constitution and state, believing that through a parliamentary majority, a Labour government can utilise the apparatus of the state and introduce social reform.

Second, there are the pluralists, for whom power and decision-making should be transferred away from the centre, upwards towards supranational bodies, outwards towards non-governmental bodies and downwards to sub-national parliaments. In addition, the remaining power of the centre should be constrained by a written constitution, proportional representation and an elected second chamber. Such a view has found support within and without the party from its inception, but the statist view of socialism as previously outlined came to dominate by the mid-twentieth century.

However, for reasons already stated, a pluralist conception of socialism and democracy then came to the fore. From within, the Labour MP Robin Cook wrote early during Smith's leadership that 'under a system in which the largest party takes all, Labour as the second largest party is left with nothing'. The Conservative government's actions had flattened 'all centres of opposition which had hitherto provided the opportunities for pluralism in public life that parliament denied'.[11] From without, Hutton argued that these constitutional reforms were not ends in themselves. Instead, 'they are means of attacking the economics and politics of exclusion upon which the British state is founded'. In turn, they will create a 'democracy which permits institutional creativity and widespread engagement by all of society – and challenges the aloof executive discretion upon which British government is organised'.[12] Yet, the implications of such a change go beyond the workings of the British state and transform the Labour Party, away from 'Labourism' towards a truly progressive force – according to its proponents, towards a healthier, more engaged and representative system and a Labour Party fully committed to democracy.

Third, there is Marxism, which has rarely held influence within Labour. This view critiques Labour's acceptance of what it sees as a capitalist democracy and offers an alternative to the present arrangements. Interestingly, there is some overlap with the pluralists, insofar as both are critical of Labour's constitutional orthodoxy, which posits that social democracy, or perhaps more accurately 'labourism', can be introduced through existing machinery. Indeed, both ascribe a role to extra-parliamentary groups to bring about reform. Yet, whereas for the pluralists the existing arrangements are undemocratic, for the Marxists they maintain class relations and inequality. As such, the Marxists critique Labour's acceptance of British capitalist democracy. Here, the critique often stems from outside of the party. For instance, the academic Ralph Miliband noted that the party was often defensive, always prepared to retreat, never challenging capitalist power. Indeed, when the conflict between capital and socialism became too sharp, the party would side with capital.[13] Elsewhere, the writer Tom Nairn spoke about Labour's 'mystical faith in the superiority of British society and the British constitution' as central to the tenets of labourism.[14] This idea is rooted in 'exceptionalism', in which the British and the British state are inspired by a higher moral purpose and historical experiences unavailable to continental countries.

This view has rarely found much favour within the Labour Party but has found favour with academics, critics and commentators outside of the party. Instead, the discussion and debate within the party have tended to be between the traditionalists and the pluralists – the former dominant for much of the twentieth century, in which they accepted the Westminster model of government. However, the pluralists challenged this view from the 1980s onwards. As will become clear, Smith was firmly in the pluralist tradition, favouring decentralisation and the dispersal of power, thus taking the Labour Party further down the road of constitutional radicalism. He made high-profile speeches on constitutional reform in late 1992 and throughout 1993. The ideas within these speeches were fleshed out in *A New Agenda for Democracy: Labour's Proposals for Constitutional Reform*, presented as a National Executive Committee statement to the 1993 Labour Party conference by Tony Blair, then shadow home affairs spokeperson. Here, we take a closer look at the arguments and ideas underpinning Smith's constitutional reform agenda.

SMITH'S CONSTITUTIONAL REFORM AGENDA

According to Mark Stuart, one of Smith's biographers, Smith had a strategy for the first two years as Labour leader, with the first year focusing on constitutional change.[15] Indeed, Smith moved quickly on constitutional matters. In the leadership campaign he had spoken of a new constitution for a new century. He claimed Britain was 'alone among the major Western European nations in not laying down the basic rights of our citizens and in not giving them direct means of asserting these through the courts'.[16] In his first Labour Party conference speech as leader in 1992, he alluded to democratic government, strengthening local democracy and decentralising power.[17]

Three factors convinced Smith of the necessity of new governing structures. First, successive Conservative governments had centralised power, often at the expense of local governments. Second, the European dimension. Third, the changing of perceptions more widely, as individuals viewed themselves less as subjects and more as citizens. Moreover, the Labour Party was the 'natural party of constitutional reform'. After all, the party and wider movement came into existence to bring about change and 'to reform a system that assured the supremacy of a ruling elite and the tyranny of private capital'.[18] Smith continued to develop these ideas throughout 1993.

In a wide-ranging speech titled 'The Standards and Practice of Government', delivered in January 1993, Smith criticised the over-centralisation of British government, something that had been accelerated in recent decades. As such, there were too few checks against the arbitrary use of power. Smith outlined several solutions, including strengthening the power of Parliament over the executive, devolving power to the nations and regions of Britain and reviving local government. A Bill of Rights, freedom of information and a culture of openness would protect individual rights from both the state and private power. This would result in a 'mature democracy in which there is wide participation, keen debate and open decision-making', ensuring 'accountable and responsive government'. He concluded that the purpose was to 'fashion a new constitution for a new century'.[19]

Smith developed these points during a key speech titled 'A Citizens' Democracy', delivered to Charter 88 on 1 March 1993. Charter 88 had become the UK's leading and most influential constitutional reform pressure group by this point. Anthony Barnett, then director of Charter 88, recounts how the speech came to be delivered. Smith had discussed with David Ward, then Smith's head of policy, that constitutional reform had voter appeal and this required a set-piece speech. Ward suggested Charter 88, expecting Smith to reject this as too bold, but Smith agreed. Ward wrote to Barnett that Smith 'knew very well that Charter 88 had played a decisive role in constitutional reform and that you would represent a critical and possibly sceptical audience. But that appealed to him. It [showed] his inner self confidence and commitment'.[20] Moreover, Smith was at ease with the press attending and with a post-speech question-and-answer session.

Smith argued in favour of replacing the 'out-of-date idea of an all-powerful nation state with a new and dynamic framework of government'. Britain would then become a 'modern European state', based on 'subsidiarity' and empowering 'municipal, regional, national and European decision-making'. He rejected the view that constitutional reform was of interest only to the chattering classes and a distraction from bread-and-butter issues. Instead, he had observed a deep sense of frustration with the present system, arguing that existing structures and institutions were failing to represent the people. As a result, there was now disenchantment and cynicism in the political system, putting at risk the future health of British democracy. He continued, attacking the 'relentless centralisation of power' under the Conservatives which had taken power from local authorities and shifted it upwards towards central government. Consequently, this had made Westminster 'dictatorial and remote'.[21]

What was needed was a 'new constitutional settlement, a new deal between the people and the state that puts the citizen centre stage'. At its heart was an array of reforms: human rights and the incorporation of the European Convention into British law, availability of legal aid to all, ending government secrecy through a right to know and Freedom of Information Act, an independent statistics office to end 'government deception' and laws against corporate cover-up to ensure that 'the cobwebs of unnecessary secrecy around the British boardroom are blown away'. This new deal would see a 'fundamental shift in the balance of power between the citizen and the state – a shift away from an overpowering state to a citizen's democracy where people have the rights and powers and where they are served by accountable and responsive government'.[22] After the speech, during the question-and-answer session, Smith said, 'We do have an elective dictatorship. I myself used to believe in the mysteries of the British constitution. My experience over the last ten to twelve years, like many people, has caused me to change my mind quite fundamentally on that.'[23]

Such ideas inspired *A New Agenda for Democracy: Labour's Proposals for Constitutional Reform*. Its introduction further expanded Labour's reasoning and justification for a 'new constitutional settlement'. The aim was to create a revitalised democracy, protecting citizens from the abuse of power. Moreover, it was important for the Labour Party to take the lead, retrieving the true ideological basis of democratic socialism – 'action by the community for the benefit of the individual' – something that goes beyond traditional forms of central government intervention. 'Government itself is a powerful interest that requires to be checked and controlled', fundamentally redressing the power in favour of the citizen from the state. This new settlement, claimed the report, should be affected in two ways. First, by promoting greater participation by people in developing the country's democracy, encouraging an active notion of citizenship. Second, by prioritising checks and balances and limiting the executive, reflecting 'the more pluralist, more decentralised, more devolved government which the people of our country want to see'.[24]

The report concentrated on a variety of constitutional issues beyond local and regional government, building on what Smith had outlined in previous speeches. For instance, the report advocated the incorporation of the European Convention of Human Rights into British law, with an eye on formulating a UK Bill of Rights, and the creation of a Human Rights Commission. It also affirmed the importance of formally enshrining rights in law, protecting individuals against state power. A future UK Bill of Rights, deliberated by an all-party commission, would require entrenchment, the recognition of social and economic rights and complement legislation regarding other areas, such as gender and race. The report further argued in favour of curtailing prerogative powers, such as signing international treaties or declaring war. Instead, Parliament should have the formal right to consent, enhancing control, accountability and scrutiny. Reform of Parliament centred on reform of the second chamber by removing the hereditary peers and replacing the House of Lords with an elected second chamber. The Plant Working Party on Electoral Systems recommended a party list electoral system with twelve regional constituencies.[25]

The report also recommended strengthening departmental select committees and reducing the power of ministerial patronage. Elsewhere, it proposed a Judicial Appointments and Training Commission. The commission's responsibilities would include devising a more rational career pattern for judges, judicial training, monitoring the careers of existing and aspirant judges, considering policy, reviewing cases and formulating guidelines for its staff. Lastly, the case for open government was framed around a Freedom of Information Act, albeit with some limitations; reform of the Official Secrets Act; reform of the way personal information was held; and accountability of the security services and the private sector.[26]

Interestingly, and perhaps surprisingly given Smith's pluralist turn, he remained sceptical about a move away from FPTP towards an alternative electoral system. For constitutional reformers, FPTP is seen as one of, if not *the* central plank of the British constitution, and only an alternative system, preferably some form of PR, will open British politics. However, Smith's view is unclear, certainly when compared to his firm position on other constitutional matters. McSmith cites an occasion in 1991 when Smith and then leader of the Liberal Democrats Paddy Ashdown discussed options for PR and particular institutions. Ashdown argues that Smith was willing to concede PR for the House of Commons, but Smith's version was that 'we did not talk specifics'.[27]

During the leadership contest, Smith insisted on the preservation of the constituency system: 'I am therefore not favourably inclined to the [single transferable vote] system of large multi-member constituencies but recognise that such a link could be retained in an added member system.'[28] As leader, he made public statements deferring the matter until the Plant Working Party had published its findings. Yet, Smith had argued with Raymond Plant, chair of the working party, at the 1992 party conference over whether they should deliver firm recommendations or conclusions of BBC-like impartiality. In May 1993, Smith released a press statement affirming that most voters vote for the creation of a government, something not relevant for other institutions. He rejected the mixed-member system, a variation of the German model, as it would create two classes of MP, dilute the constituency link and make coalition government the most likely outcome. The mixed-member system was Plant's preferred choice, although when his working party came to vote, he voted for the supplementary vote system for fear of the working party coming out in favour of the status quo. For Smith, the constitutional significance of reforming the Westminster electoral system necessitated a referendum.

This has resulted in some conjecture as to whether Smith did or did not favour reform. McSmith, writing shortly after Smith's death, argues he was willing to accept the German model but kept this in reserve in the case of a hung parliament.[29] Stuart wrote that electoral reform was the exception to the constitutional radicalism of Smith.[30] Barnett claims that Smith was not convinced of the need for PR – a consequence of his attachment to the constituency system.[31] Due to his contrasting statements, it is therefore challenging to locate Smith into a particular position on electoral reform at Westminster. Perhaps, then, he falls into the sceptical camp, accepting that FPTP is imperfect but asserting that the arguments for reform are not as clear cut nor as strong as proponents insist and that the arguments favouring FPTP are stronger than critics maintain. In addition, while much – but not all – of the party were willing to accept his constitutional reform agenda, electoral reform at Westminster was a different matter. The party and wider movement were divided. It is conceivable that Smith wanted to avoid further division over a subject matter that he was neither passionate nor intellectually convinced about and was willing to accept a referendum as a compromise. Murray Elder, then one of Smith's closest aides, implied that in a referendum, Smith would have continued to support FPTP at Westminster.[32]

Smith's scepticism towards reforming the Westminster electoral system drew criticism from *The Guardian*. The newspaper asserted that his statement was not at all encouraging for a future realignment of British politics, indicating that 'he is not seriously interested in a more pluralist political system'. The editorial continued:

> He identifies himself inescapably with the bedrock culture which sees no need for Labour to attempt to be a different kind of party. He depicts himself deaf to new ideas. Perhaps this is unfair. If so, the onus is very much on Mr Smith to show us otherwise, soon, and often.[33]

Of course, this was unfair. Regardless of Smith's position on electoral reform, he had driven the intellectual, moral and political arguments in favour of a new constitutional settlement to be delivered by a future Labour government freed from its constitutional orthodoxy: reform and renewal of local government; freedom of information; substantially altering relations between Westminster, local and regional government and the European Community; reform of Parliament; and reform of the judiciary. As Mark Evans notes, Smith's constitutional reform agenda went a considerable way towards meeting the demands of Charter 88. Their Manchester Declaration had emphasised that existing bodies of the state must be made more democratic, and shared power must replace 'the absolute sovereignty of parliament', encouraging participation and entrenching rights so we cease to be subjects and become citizens.[34]

As we have seen, the Labour Party embraced different ideas and thinking throughout its history. By the 1990s, the party had accepted various aspects of liberalism – political, social and economic – and re-engaged with Labour's pluralist and decentralist tradition, challenging the more statist view which had dominated since the mid-twentieth century. Under Smith's leadership, the Labour Party became a different party.

CONCLUSION: LEGACY

What are we to make of Smith's understanding of the constitution and the implications of how his leadership shaped the party's approach towards the constitution? In one sense, he gave impetus to the constitutional reform agenda through his personal beliefs and commitment to democratic reforms. Lord Norton notes that parliamentary reform often requires a 'change champion', a senior figure committed to reform.[35] The same principle applies here: a senior figure within the Labour Party personally willing to push it towards a more radical view of the constitution. As Morrison writes, 'Smith brought constitutional reform to the centre of Labour's agenda,' and his leadership was 'the high point of the constitutional reform lobby's influence over Labour'.[36] Indeed, it would not be an exaggeration to claim that Smith, of all Labour's post-war leaders, was most at ease with widespread constitutional reform. Consequently, he has a very favourable reputation amongst advocates of constitutional reform. Much like Roy Jenkins is the favoured choice of pro-Europeans within and without the Labour Party, Smith is the favoured choice of constitutional reformers, perceived not as a mere reformer but a *democrat*, closely aligned to the academic and intellectual notions of decentralisation, democracy and pluralism.

The differences between Smith and those that rose to prominence under New Labour help clarify this distinction between radical and reformer. Smith was a constitutional radical or a democrat, aligning himself with European-style democracies. He argued for the transformation of the British constitution and state, for a fundamental change in the relationship between citizens and the state. Despite New Labour implementing much of Smith's agenda, they are best considered reformers. They accepted that the British constitution, and Britain more generally, required updating. However, they fell short of transforming the idea of parliamentary sovereignty and, according to critics, kept the central planks of the Westminster system intact.

This distinction begs the question of the endpoint of Smith's constitutional reform agenda. Was it a 'new constitutional settlement' or a move towards a written constitution? After all, the latter was the objective of groups like Charter 88, supported by liberal-minded 'progressive' intellectuals in the media and academia. As with Smith's view of electoral reform, the answer is unclear. For Barnett, Smith had accepted the logic of a written constitution, which was his tradition, and he would have pursued it: 'A new constitutional settlement is a written constitution. If he had meant unwritten, he would have said so.' He later wrote that if Smith had become Prime Minister, Britain would by now have a written constitution, thanks to the democratic reform process he started. Elder's assessment differs, suggesting that Smith might not have implemented all parts of this package, especially around the judiciary and an elected second chamber, as it would have challenged the primacy of the House of Commons.[37] Moreover, *A New Agenda for Democracy* looked both ways. It rejected the claim that these reforms entailed a formal written constitution, but it was a 'step in that direction', with the option left open and to be revisited later.[38]

While Smith would have pursued an even more radical approach to constitutional reform than New Labour, it is difficult to say confidently that he favoured codification. He differed in important details with New Labour's approach and would, in all likelihood, have gone further in certain areas. Yet, his vision as outlined in his speeches refrained from explicit commitments to codification. Moreover, he would have faced similar internal and external pressures: high-profile Cabinet colleagues who did not share his zeal for constitutional reform, a parliamentary party and wider movement concerned about jobs, growth, schools and hospitals, constitutional overload at the expense of other pressing matters, a sceptical written press, political pressure from Labour's opponents and the limited electoral saliency with voters.

Regardless, and reflecting on the past twenty-five years of constitutional upheaval, it seems safe to say that we are now closer to a codified constitution than at any other time in our history. Smith played an important role in taking the UK down this road, all of which continues to have political, electoral and ideological implications for the Labour Party. The orthodox view in academic and intellectual circles purports that these reforms did not go far enough, and if only Labour would wholeheartedly embrace constitutional reform, then a progressive twenty-first century awaits. However, a critical take asking whether these reforms have delivered on their objectives, furthered the cause of social democracy in Britain and advanced the electoral interests of the Labour Party might temper such optimism. Such questions require further investigation, but one suspects that a critical examination would reveal evidence and ideas that constitutional radicals and reformers would not like to hear.

9

JOHN SMITH: DEVOLUTION AND NORTHERN IRELAND

Neil Pye

WHEN HE BECAME LEADER of the Labour Party, the issue of devolution was seen as being 'unfinished business' for John Smith.[1] This dated back to his experience as Minister of State at the Privy Council Office in James Callaghan's government, when Smith, who used advocacy and debating skills learned during his student days at the University of Glasgow to great effect, managed to steer two highly complex devolution bills for Scotland and Wales (which eventually became one bill) onto the statute book. This legislation could have led to the creation of a Scottish Parliament and Welsh Assembly had it not been undermined by wrecking measures. In the words of Smith, devolution during that period had effectively been 'opposed by blinkered unionists and blinkered separatists'.[2]

A motion introduced by George Cunningham rendered the March 1979 referendums for Scottish and Welsh devolution as a pointless exercise in democracy by stipulating that for the 'Yes' vote to succeed, it had to be supported by 40 per cent of the electorate. This made the prospect of devolved parliaments almost impossible to achieve.[3] Along with the backdrop of the disastrous 1978–9 Winter of Discontent, the failure of devolution sowed the seeds for the fall of Callaghan's government in May that year.[4] However, Smith was one of the few politicians who came out of this episode with any credit, and his first attempt at providing devolution acted as a template for many years to come, especially in terms of lessons that could be learned.[5]

Both in opposition and as a Labour leader, Smith was a staunch unionist. Unlike his close friends and colleagues Donald Dewar and John Mackintosh, who consistently campaigned for constitutional change and devolution throughout their political careers, Smith initially believed that home rule for Scotland would not work in terms of redistribution of wealth and that it would lead to separatism, which was the overriding goal of the Scottish National Party (SNP).[6] A prime ministerial document which summarised the attitudes of Labour Party MPs towards devolution from July 1974 identified Smith, along with Tam Dalyell and Robin Cook, as being 'opposed' to decentralisation.[7] However, when confronted with the reality of steering government policy through Parliament during the mid to late 1970s, John Smith's perspective underwent a conversion, and for which as his former head of policy, David Ward once put it, devolution had to be presented as a new deal for democracy and empowered citizenship.[8]

In terms of what Smith achieved during his short-lived leadership of the Labour Party, a key question, which this chapter will attempt to answer, is had he survived, how much would Smith's approach to devolution have differed from his successor as Labour leader, Tony Blair? On devolution and many other policies, Andy McSmith, Smith's biographer, has questioned – a question which has also interested the Labour Party – whether he was 'simply an unreconstructed 1970s right-wing Labourite' or, on the contrary, if 'he actually would have presided over a radical, reforming government' on such issues.[9]

Further, would Smith have held a referendum or simply argued that a Labour general election win was a sufficient mandate to establish a Scottish Parliament, Welsh Assembly and regional assemblies for England, along with other constitutional reforms such as a Bill of Rights? It is clear that during his leadership, Smith positioned Labour as being 'the natural party of constitutional reform', and his successor continued along that political trajectory throughout his premiership from 1997 to 2007, although on a limited basis compared to what Smith was proposing.[10]

Running parallel to the devolution debate was the Northern Ireland question. Under John Major's Conservative government, from April 1992 onwards, there were significant changes in policy towards Northern Ireland. Instead of the hard-line approach adopted by his predecessor as Prime Minister, Major ventured along the path of trying to secure a peace settlement to end the Troubles. Here we will examine whether Smith was more sympathetic to the Unionist cause in Northern Ireland than previous Labour leaders and question whether, if elected as a future Prime Minister, he would have solved the crisis in a similar way to Blair?

BACKGROUND

When Margaret Thatcher became Prime Minister in May 1979, the issue of devolution went into cold storage, and the Scotland and Wales Bill, which had caused so much turbulence for Callaghan's government, was repealed.[11] Throughout a long period of consecutive Tory governments from 1979 to 1997, both Thatcher and – to a lesser extent – Major had argued that the creation of Scottish and Welsh Parliaments would not only lead to the break-up of the UK's system of public expenditure but also place huge strain on the Union.[12] Reflecting on events that occurred later, including the 2014 Scottish independence referendum when David Cameron arguably gambled with the British constitution, their judgement proved correct.[13]

Throughout her premiership, Thatcher persistently identified unionism with Westminster-centrism and saw 'no virtue in subsidiarity to local councils or regional assemblies', showing contempt towards both.[14] However, the consequence of Thatcher's strategy and staunch defence of the Westminster and Whitehall way of governing the UK was the creation of a North–South divide and an overly centralised state, which is still a major issue for policymakers more than thirty years later.[15]

Under Thatcher's governments, the decline of traditional industries in northern Labour heartlands went hand in hand with the creation of an economy built around financial services, which were largely concentrated within the London and South-East corridor. This effectively pitched mainly Labour voters in the North against mainly Conservatives in the South.[16] This chasm within the UK meant that despite attempts by Thatcher to place devolution and constitutional change into cold storage, the issue would not go away and eventually resurfaced during the latter half of her leadership.

A critical turning point was the outcome of the June 1987 general election. Michael Ancram argues that it placed devolution 'firmly back on the political agenda', especially amongst Scottish voters. Despite the issue hardly being raised on doorsteps, the Labour Party won fifty out of seventy-two seats in Scotland. Fallout from the events of the 1979 devolution referendum, along with the early introduction of the poll tax in Scotland in 1989 – Scottish residents being effectively used as guinea pigs for this experiment – meant that the questions of devolution and independence were, according to Ancram, still 'deeply rooted in the editorial psyche of the Scottish media'. He stressed that it would take 'an unwise and foolhardy politician or political party' to ignore it.[17]

Despite the 1987 election being Thatcher's third successive general election victory, decline in support for the Conservatives in Scotland was so sharp that many Scottish voters felt like they were being run by a government based at Westminster alien to them. As a consequence, many different groups decided to come together and organise in an attempt to bring about change. The Scottish Constitutional Convention demanded a parliament in Edinburgh based upon Scottish claim of rights, and other organisations campaigned for other reforms to the constitution, as discussed in the previous chapter. It was in November 1988 that all of these distinctive voices were brought together under the umbrella of Charter 88, and as a consequence, demands for both electoral reform and a written constitution gained greater traction. As devolution and constitutional reform crept up the political agenda because of a trend towards regionalism and self-determination in

Europe, the fall of the Iron Curtain in 1989 created a new context for nationalism and greater participation within the UK.[18]

From a Labour Party perspective, it was against the backdrop of turmoil within its own ranks that, as chief spokesperson for Scottish affairs, Donald Dewar had managed to keep the flame of devolution 'flickering' and saw Smith's 'unfinished business' as a matter of duty.[19] While in opposition during the 1980s and 1990s, Labour had more time than ever to shape its policy proposals for devolution – unlike the 1970s, when its response to the question was rushed as a result of the rapid need to appease demands for control over oil revenues and independence made by the SNP and cultural claims for separation articulated by Plaid Cymru in Wales.[20] Former Lord Chancellor Derry Irvine has pointed out that during the 1970s, Labour in government had 'erred' when it was decided that every legislative power devolved to Scotland should have its small print 'meticulously specified'.[21] As Irvine put it, Scotland should have received a 'general power of legislative competence, subject to powers expressly reserved to the centre' such as 'defence, foreign affairs, the Constitution and the Crown', but instead the entire devolution debate ground into an impasse, which meant that progress was slow and always contentious.[22]

DEVOLVING FROM THE FRONT

When John Smith was elected as leader of the Labour Party in July 1992, one of the major problems which both his party and leadership faced, following the outcome of that year's general election, was the fact that the Conservatives had not only won a fourth successive national poll but had improved their position in Scotland. According to Major, for the first time in a decade, a Conservative government had placed the opposition parties 'on the back foot' when it came to devolution and constitutional matters.[23] Such was the discernible anger amongst Scottish Labour MPs at this state of affairs that a group of rebels staged an early challenge to Smith's leadership by joining an escalating cross-party home rule campaign called Scotland United, which was supported by sections of the SNP and Liberal Democrats.[24]

When shaping his shadow Cabinet, one of the first things that Smith did was to remove Dewar from the role of shadow Secretary of State for Scotland to shadow Secretary of State for Social Security, in order to oversee the direction of the Commission on Social Justice.[25] Given his expertise on Scottish matters, one suspects that Dewar would have been privately unhappy about being moved to steer a national policy. According to journalist Ewen MacAskill, he never really wanted to ply his trade anywhere but in Scotland.[26] But it was during his leadership that Smith took it upon himself to embark upon shaping devolution on his own terms and how he saw fit. In turn, he relied upon Dewar's valued political opinions, forming an inner circle with shadow Lord Chancellor Derry Irvine, whenever a second opinion on the legal framework was needed in order to shape devolution policy.[27]

Back in 1992, the issue of constitutional reform was in a muddle. The creation of a Scottish assembly with legislative and tax-raising powers would have left the position of Scottish MPs 'totally unclear'.[28] Furthermore, the position of Major's government was ambiguous insofar as its Northern Ireland policy was geared towards producing a local assembly, whereas this was being resisted in Scotland. Also, there were clear grievances amongst Scottish voters about governance arrangements. The continuing over-representation of Scottish MPs at Westminster and debates about the Barnett formula being too generous for Scotland were heavily contested issues amongst Tory MPs. For Major, rather than introduce a tax-raising assembly which would put the Union at risk, the introduction of regions throughout the entire UK was seen as a solution, strengthening the case for retaining district councils rather than counties.[29]

Throughout the 1980s, there was an upward shift of powers from local to central government. At the same time, the Thatcher government abolished metropolitan and county councils in Merseyside, Greater Manchester and Greater London in May 1986, partly because of ideological differences – especially in the case of the Greater London Council under its left-wing Labour leadership – but also because they were seen as a wasteful and unnecessary tier of government. This created a political void and 'missing middle tier' of governance, which led to action in Greater Manchester when both its city and district council leaders came together and focused on the bigger picture. By putting the city first through partnerships and collaboration with both central government and the private sector, rather than getting bogged down in conflict and confrontation – as happened in Militant-led Labour councils in Liverpool and Merseyside during the mid-1980s – this acted not only as a template for place leadership but also paved the way for the Association for Greater Manchester Authorities to emerge. Many years later, this developed into the Greater Manchester Combined Authority.

To briefly describe how the Barnett formula works, the UK government allocates funding grants to the devolved administrations in Scotland, Wales and Northern Ireland. The largest of those grants is the block grant, and the Barnett formula calculates how the block grant changes each year. This formula was first used for Scotland in 1978, introduced by and named after the then Labour Chief Secretary to the Treasury, Joel Barnett. It was extended to Northern Ireland in 1979 and to Wales in 1980 and was only meant to be used as a temporary measure to avoid annual negotiations on funding allocations between the UK's nations. According to Sarah Tudor, this formula was used to determine the level of UK government spending on public services in Scotland, Wales and Northern Ireland until 1999, when devolution in the UK was brought in under the then Labour government.[30]

Michael Quinlan, Permanent Under-Secretary of State for Defence, wrote in April 1992 that Scotland was an issue which had to be 'coped with' because of two factors. First, its 'justifiably distinct national consciousness' and second, its 'physical and psychological distance from London'. Quinlan noted that Scotland back then was 'a Labour country', which did not like Conservative governments, and highlighted that when the UK was not performing well economically, 'demerging in some degree or other' looked attractive. At the time of writing, Quinlan argued that Scotland already had 'a great deal of effective decentralisation', which was 'embodied in the Scottish Office's wide functions and manoeuvre room', along with 'more than its fair share of public resources' in comparison to the rest of the UK.[31] Smith contested this view, stating that despite the Scottish

Office being 'a powerful instrument of state' and 'a steady increase in administrative devolution over the last hundred years' occurring, there had been 'no devolution of political control over Scottish affairs to the Scottish people'.[32]

Smith's predecessor as Labour leader, Neil Kinnock, had opposed decentralisation over fears that it could potentially end up splitting the Scottish Labour Party, the Labour Party as a whole, and the UK into fragments. However, this was a risk that Smith was willing to take.[33] As Conservative one-party rule strengthened, Smith made the modernisation of the UK constitution one of his main priorities, which prompted attacks on the Tories over 'excessive secrecy' and 'neglect of individual rights'.[34] In one of his first speeches as leader, Smith was highly critical about the pattern of centralisation that had taken place in Britain since the Conservatives were elected to power in 1979:

> We are one of the most centralised states in Europe. Labour's mission must be to challenge that immense concentration of power in Whitehall and open up the process of government by decentralising decisions to the regions of England and devolving policy to the nations of Scotland and Wales. We must lead a renaissance of local government. Our task must be to restore to local authorities, not just the ability to provide decent local services, but the freedom to pioneer new ways of meeting local need. Local democracy must be encouraged as a creative innovative force for change, not constantly disciplined by the state as a threat to central power.[35]

During the early 1990s, there was an acceptance from certain figures – for example, Thatcher's former head of Number 10 Policy Unit,

Ferdinand Mount, author of *The British Constitution Now: Recovery or Decline?* – that under successive Conservative governments 'excessive centralism' had taken hold.[36] Lord Hailsham, who famously coined the term 'elective dictatorship', was a critical voice regarding the actions of his own party in power. The European Policy Forum, led by Graham Mather, published a report titled, *Accountability to the Public*, which argued that throughout the Thatcher era, non-elected elites had taken control of many public services. Further, Professor John Stewart from the University of Birmingham argued that 'a new magistracy' had been created, where unelected and unaccountable elites were found 'on the boards of health authorities and hospital trusts, training and enterprise councils, the boards of governors of grant-maintained schools, the governing bodies of colleges of further education and housing action trusts'.[37]

In September 1992, Smith used his very first Labour Party conference speech as leader to not only attack the Major government's record but also outline a vision about the need for 'active government' in order to lift the UK out of what he saw as being 'a spiral of decline'. For Smith, this involved greater accountability through collectively strengthening the rights of people at work. He stated, 'We believe the rights of workers are best advanced through the work of free and active trade unions, with whom we in our party are proud to be linked.' During this maiden speech as leader, Smith reaffirmed Labour's commitment to devolution, which included a Scottish Parliament, Welsh Assembly and power to English regions. His view was that instead of people thinking that they were moving forwards, they were 'struggling to stay in the same place', and he wanted to re-address that balance and create a fairer society.[38]

During the 1980s and early 1990s, along with Scotland and Wales, many English regions had suffered social, economic and political difficulties through the loss of heavy industries such as coal, steel and shipbuilding, which not only caused huge unemployment but also created many deprived areas and a 'brain drain' from those areas. London and the south-east acted as a magnet, and the power of the state and economic activity became more centralised than ever in this area, leading to the neglect of other places and regions across the country as they were starting to embark upon a process of deindustrialisation.[39]

In 1982, John Prescott identified a solution to the problem of governance in the form of regional assemblies, which stemmed from the *Alternative Regional Strategy* report drawn up that year.[40] The collegiate nature of Smith's leadership meant that Prescott won support for his ideas, namely that the creation of an elected regional assembly in a given place would assume strategic powers for a range of policy areas from health to culture and housing to transport, with the intention of giving a region not only a stronger voice but also greater control over its own affairs.[41]

However, it was not until 2004, ten years after Smith's passing, when the people of the north-east of England were given the chance to vote for their own regional assembly, which Greater London would gain too, only for it to be rejected. Reflecting on this policy initiative, John Prescott asserted, 'I was going to do it in the North East, North West and the whole North.' However, the policy was not adopted by Labour because 'most of our people, Tony [Blair] et cetera, weren't devolutionists'.[42] Had Smith been Prime Minister instead of Blair, it is suspected that he would have implemented the idea of regional assemblies, although quite possibly would have run into the same difficulties as Blair did. In the end, the policy initiative failed after what seemed like early promise, following a campaign involving a young Dominic Cummings, who described it as 'a training exercise for the EU referendum', and in turn, persuaded the people of the north east to reject the idea.[43]

Smith was also heavily critical of Major's administration for creating blurred lines between government acting in the national interest and, alternatively, in the interests of party politics. What Smith wanted, off the back of scandals such as the Matrix Churchill episode, was a wholesale clean-up of the entire political system. Speaking in January 1993, Smith stated that having the same political party in office for fourteen years had created a culture in government where abuses of power had become 'systemic' and a norm and demanded 'a published code of conduct', which could set out 'clearly and unambiguously' the respective roles and responsibilities of ministers':

> The over-centralisation of British government which has gone on apace over the last decade seriously accentuates the problem in our country, with too few checks and balances against the arbitrary use of power. We need to strengthen the power of Parliament over the Executive. We need to devolve power to the nations and regions of Britain. We need to revive and restore local government as a vibrant part of our democracy.[44]

Around the time when Smith made this speech, there were criticisms of his leadership amongst his own MPs that Labour was not only failing to make an impact on the electorate but also lacking new ideas, despite Smith's decent personal poll ratings. An internal battle started to emerge between what Alastair Campbell termed the 'frantics' – frantic because the party did not know what it stood for other than to oppose the government – which included Gordon Brown, Tony Blair, Jack Straw, Kim Howells and Frank Field and the 'longgamers', comprised of Smith, Margaret Beckett, John Prescott and Robin Cook, who felt that Labour had time on its side. They believed that rather than risk a Tory theft of ideas, 'one more heave' would eventually win power. At the time, Campbell pointed out that a party which sought to excite the public with constitutional changes was 'hardly likely to succeed when its own constitution was in a mess'.[45]

The internal struggle seemed to stir Smith into action, with some commentators and pundits arguing that while Tory ministers had used the Scott Inquiry to avoid questions over arms sales to Iraq, similarly Labour was using the vehicle of its Social Justice Commission to avoid debates about taxation and benefits.[46] In February 1993, Smith spelt out the sweeping constitutional reforms that he wanted to make and committed Labour to wholesale change for Britain if the party was returned to office. When outlining devolution policy, the Labour leader not only repeated pledges for devolution to Scotland and Wales but also argued that Britain should have a total of four layers of government consisting of Europe, Westminster, regions and local authorities.[47] The following month, Smith made what was the most significant speech of his leadership on devolution and constitutional issues at an event organised by Charter 88, in which he pledged to introduce 'a fundamental shift in the balance of power between the citizen and the state' including reaffirming his Party's commitment to devolution.[48]

In April 1993, Smith went a stage further when he outlined a vision of devolution in the booklet 'Making Britain's Future', which called for new attitudes towards commerce in government, boardrooms, the City and education, as well as proposing 'a sweeping change in Britain's industrial and financial structures'.[49] 'Making Britain's Future' outlined elements of an industrial strategy for Britain, which advocated a reform of company structures including having employees on the board and an overhaul of takeover legislation, bankruptcy laws and accountancy procedures. It also called for 'a full transfer of industrial, financial and political power to the regions with a network of development agencies to support local firms and coordinate investment'.[50] This document offered a taste of what Smith was looking to propose in terms of possible future policy.

Smith's strategy, however, did have its critics. Peter Shore, Labour's former Secretary of State for the Environment during Callaghan's government and author of the 'organic change' policy, created in response to some of the failings of the 1972 Local Government Act, was openly sceptical.[51] Shore cited Smith's Scottishness as a weakness, arguing that a Scottish MP representing a constituency in Scotland – as well as being part of a large cohort of Scottish MPs at the very top of the Labour Party – created a danger of a disconnect 'with the problems which face a large part of England, including London and the South'.[52] Shore acknowledged that Smith shared 'a special sense of Scottish discontent' with Westminster and Whitehall but argued that 'a Scot may ask the question if Scotland can exist within the union of the UK, why can't the UK too live within a European Union?'[53] Shore saw this as being a risk in Smith's overall strategy.

Another common criticism of Smith's devolution policy was the fact that throughout his leadership there was very little detail provided about how a future Labour government would deliver on that pledge. This perpetuated the view that Smith was either being complacent or lazy by some backbench Labour MPs when it came to formulating new and big ideas. This was challenged by Gerald Kaufman in an article titled 'He defied pressure to come up with a big idea. His big idea was to win'. Smith's overriding goal was to win power in order to achieve redistributive socialism.[54]

Jack Straw once argued that the main purpose of the opposition was to not provide detail but hard thought. In this way, he believed that Labour under Smith offered 'a better quality of government'. Straw was also of the belief that, had Smith survived, a Bill of Rights, a Freedom of Information Act, devolution to Scotland, Wales and the English regions, and a referendum on the voting system would have been introduced – all of which would have added up to a huge shift of power to local people and communities at the end of the twentieth century.[55]

At the October 1993 Labour Party conference, there was a perception that despite much optimism and strong poll ratings, which pointed to a future general election victory under Smith's leadership, the party had not only become too inward looking but also stale on policy creation.[56] During his 55-minute leader's speech in Brighton, much of it was devoted towards attacking Major and the Conservative Party's record in government. On the topic of constitutional reform, which was designed to woo voters in the south and within Labour heartlands, Smith argued:

> This is a government that cares less about democracy than about power; that cares less about people than about political dogma; that

cares less about fairness and justice than about defending its own interests and the interests of its own rich benefactors. No wonder people feel disillusioned with politics; no wonder they feel dismayed and disappointed and no wonder they feel disgusted with a government that has proved itself time and time again unfit to run this country.[57]

When commenting on the speech, the journalist Hugo Young argued that towards the end of his tenure as Labour leader, Smith had taken 'a near-Stalinist attitude' towards dissent and created 'an iron curtain' when it came to discussions about a possible centre-left coalition to defeat the Conservatives at a future general election. Unlike Blair and Brown, Smith was totally hostile to the idea of creating a centre-left partnership with Paddy Ashdown's Liberal Democrats and believed that Labour would gain a working majority around 1996 following the early collapse of Major's government.[58]

Alderman and Carter in 1994 asserted that as leader of the Labour Party, Smith had remained aloof from internal party differences between 'modernisers' and 'traditionalists', which presented a danger that divisions would eventually emerge in a struggle for succession.[59] However, there were factions within Labour who felt that by playing a cautious long game based on maintaining party unity at any cost, Smith was not moving quickly enough on policy issues, which seemed evident in relation to devolution and especially Scottish home rule. Former parliamentary under-secretary in the Blair government Peter Kilfoyle has stated that Smith could be 'extremely acerbic' when dealing with modernisers and especially Peter Mandelson, who, having previously served under Kinnock, was deliberately sidelined by Smith and kept at arm's-length from the Labour leadership.[60]

Smith had rejected the notion of New Labour and seemed averse to ideological developments and new campaigning techniques that emerged in the US during the run-up to the election of Bill Clinton as President. Underneath the seams, there was a cross-over of ideas between the modernisers within Labour and Clinton's Democratic Party team.[61] Similar questions about Smith's leadership being reactive rather than proactive were raised in relation to the rapidly changing situation in Northern Ireland.

One of the issues regarding Smith's drive for settling the will of the Scottish people was that the desire for devolution was present, but very little detail about his intentions was displayed. This stance bears parallels with Keir Starmer's Labour during this day and age – both Smith and Starmer share the drive to govern and do things in office, but at the same time, and unlike the Kinnock leadership, do not reveal their hands too publicly.

NORTHERN IRELAND

The journalist Adam Boulton has doubted whether Smith would have given the same priority as Blair to the search for peace in Northern Ireland because 'sectarianism was rife around his constituency in Scotland'.[62] However, Mark Stuart has argued that Smith generally supported Major's attempts to secure a lasting peace and solution to the Troubles. For instance, Smith was regularly briefed by the Prime Minister over negotiations regarding the Downing Street Declaration and supportive of the Conservative government's cross-party collaboration.[63]

Under Smith's leadership, the dynamics of the party's stance towards Northern Ireland's constitutional matters changed significantly from his predecessor. Kinnock's appointment of Kevin McNamara as shadow Secretary of State for Northern Ireland in 1987 meant that both leader and spokesperson were pro-Nationalist in outlook. Smith being from a Protestant background gave the Unionists reassurance, and this was reflected during a visit to Belfast in December that year. However, despite this, Smith believed in a united Ireland by consent and tried to achieve consensus between Republicans and Unionists within the Labour Party itself, particularly amongst backbenchers.[64]

Stuart argues that Smith respected the secrecy involved with Northern Ireland security matters but was always wary about general issues and fearful that the Conservatives would unnecessarily 'tie him in' to a bi-partisan policy.[65] In December 1993, both Major and his Irish counterpart, Albert Reynolds, urged the Irish Republican Army to put down their weapons and negotiate a permanent peace in Northern Ireland in the Downing Street Declaration. At the time, the violence of the Troubles had claimed more than 3,000 lives over a twenty-five year period. The declaration gained widespread support, except from hard-line Unionists, who felt isolated and claimed that the move amounted to treachery.[66]

Smith was highly supportive of the declaration: 'We fervently hope that it will be an important first step in a peace process which will lead to a new political settlement.'[67] He also endorsed Major's appeal for an end to the violence in Northern Ireland and said 'that must be the overwhelming desire of all the people of the British Isles, not least those in Northern Ireland who have suffered the appalling violence of the last 25 years'.[68]

At one stage, just a couple of months before Smith's passing, tensions erupted between both Labour and the Conservative government over Northern Ireland policy when details of a private meeting between Major and Smith to discuss anti-terrorist laws were leaked. Labour demanded an investigation, and the Tories were accused of trying to make political capital out of behind-the-scenes discussions over the Prevention of Terrorism Act.[69] Smith and Blair, as shadow Home Secretary, had reviewed Labour's policy towards the Act and agreed a way forward.[70] From this, it can be inferred that there was more that united Smith and Blair on this issue than divided the two, despite the latter wanting to frantically quicken the pace of reform when modernising the Labour Party. However, differences did emerge between both politicians, which later became magnified once Blair became Labour leader and eventually Prime Minister. Under New Labour, policy became more joined up, with the greater inclusion of the Republic of Ireland in the quest for peace and a solution to the longstanding conflict.[71] In the main, if Smith had remained leader of the Labour Party, there is a suspicion that such dynamism would not have occurred as it did under Blair, as Smith was always more cautious in his approach to politics than Blair.

CONCLUSION

In summary, Smith's greatest legacy was to set in motion the eventual creation of the Scottish Parliament and Welsh Assembly, which would be delivered by Blair's government and, more prominently, his close friend and colleague Donald Dewar, who became Scotland's first ever First Minister.

A major question posited by political journalists, commentators and pundits is not just whether Smith would have been elected as Prime Minister, but also what devolution may have looked like had he led Labour into power, about which much speculation has abounded. The creation of home rule for Scotland was not the panacea to Scottish nationalist ambitions. John Smith's colleague George Robertson, who served as Labour's shadow Scottish Secretary, once predicted in 1995 that devolution would 'kill the SNP stone dead'.[72] According to Irvine, what both Robertson and Dewar had not foreseen was that the 1998 Scotland Act would cause 'major trouble within the Scottish Labour Party', along with splits within its ranks.[73] Such cracks had already started to appear at the very beginning of Smith's leadership.

Irvine has argued that following the 'annihilation' of the Conservatives at the 1997 general election, there was a complacent belief that they would 'remain a spent force there [in Scotland] unless and until they could bring themselves to embrace devolution and the new Scottish parliament'.[74] Along with the Conservatives being deeply unpopular in Scotland due to their neglect of Scotland and its affairs during the Thatcher and Major years, this naive complacency allowed the SNP to gradually gain a political stranglehold once the Scottish Parliament opened on 1 July 1999, which, during the mid-1970s, Thatcher once prophesised would happen.[75]

The 2014 Scottish independence referendum would certainly not have occurred under Smith's leadership had he been Prime Minister. One of the key speakers involved with the Better Together campaign against Scottish independence was Gordon Brown, who has been a torch bearer for many of the ideas about federalism and the reinvigoration of the British union – all of which stemmed from the ideas of Smith and Dewar during the 1980s and early 1990s.[76]

In recent times, some of Brown's ideas have fed into current Labour leader Sir Keir Starmer's vision for the future of Britain, should the party regain power in a future general election.[77] First, Brown set up a commission which proposed how a future Labour government would shift power away from Whitehall and Westminster towards metro mayors and local authorities, with a view towards tackling deep-rooted regional inequalities and a longstanding problem over skills. Brown's proposals also advocated a new second chamber to protect the constitution; parliament and the public to play a stronger role in enforcing better standards in public life, which John Smith had previously campaigned for vigorously; and greater civil service accountability, as well as additional powers for Wales and Scotland with constitutional protections.[78]

Brown's main criticism of previous devolution initiatives is that for many years there has been a missing element, with the centre remaining untouched. Starmer has also vowed to end what he termed as being 'sticking plaster politics'.[79] This argument is shared by another torch bearer who served under Smith in his shadow Cabinet, David Blunkett, who has recently called for 'less preaching and more practice of devolution' as a clarion call to reinvigorate the northern powerhouse and levelling up agendas for the English regions, which if Smith was still alive today he would have fully supported.[80]

However, in 2023, despite Smith's legacy of devolved administrations for Scotland and Wales, there is still ambivalence within Labour and central government about devolution and Northern Ireland, which in recent years has threatened the stability of the UK – a union which Smith sought to protect at any cost. Smith had the foresight and collegiality to seek an end to the Troubles, which his successor as leader and eventual Prime Minister Tony Blair, along with Secretary of State for Northern Ireland Mo Mowlam, would eventually oversee through the 1998 Good Friday Agreement once Labour were finally elected in to government in 1997.[81]

10

JOHN SMITH: LABOUR'S MOST PRO-EUROPEAN LEADER

Richard Johnson

O<small>N THE EVENING OF</small> 11 May 1994, a sea of crisp, white tablecloths and red roses glistened in candlelight at the Park Lane Hotel in London.[1] Five hundred bankers, financiers, industrialists and actors had paid £500 each for the privilege of hearing the man they expected to be the next Prime Minister.* John Smith, star of the evening, boasted that there were probably more capitalists in the ballroom 'than we have ever had at a Labour Party dinner in our history'.[2] The novelist Ken Follett thought that Smith that night 'seemed like a man with the smell of victory in his nostrils'.[3]

The cause of the occasion was the forthcoming European Parliament elections, and the Labour Party was riding high in the polls.

---

* Over £1,000 after adjusting for inflation.

The European question had destroyed the Conservatives' reputation in the preceding years. The economic damage caused by Black Wednesday (16 September 1992) was followed by months of bitter parliamentary ructions over the Maastricht Treaty's ratification, nearly collapsing the government altogether. In contrast, the Labour Party was led by an ardent pro-European, and its Eurosceptic faction, once dominant, had shrivelled to impotence. Bryan Gould, a Eurosceptic and Smith's erstwhile opponent for the Labour leadership, was so disheartened by the party's direction that he announced that he would be resigning as an MP the following week and moving to New Zealand.[4]

At the top table that night, Smith was joined by Pauline Green, leader of the Labour Members of the European Parliament (MEPs). In an interview with the author on the twenty-eighth anniversary of that dinner, Green remembered, 'He was late arriving, and I was a little cross with him.' City slickers streamed into the grand hotel, but the Labour leader had failed to materialise. 'Ah John, for God's sake. All these people are coming in,' she fumed to herself. Then, after nearly all the pre-dinner drinks had been quaffed, 'he came sort of bouncing through the door with Michel Rocard', the leader of the French Socialist Party. Smith gave Green a wink and a thumbs up. He had been delayed because he was plotting, as it turned out, on her behalf. When Smith eventually made his way through the crowd of well-wishers, he gave Green a kiss and whispered in her ear 'you got the French'.[5] Thanks to Smith's machinations, Green became the first – and only – UK Labour leader of the Socialist MEPs in the European Parliament.

Smith's ability to manoeuvre one of his own MEPs into this

powerful position demonstrated a remarkable shift in Labour's attitudes towards European Union membership and the party's reputation within EU institutions.* During the previous decade, the Labour
group of MEPs had been led by Eurosceptics Barbara Castle, Alf
Lomas and Barry Seal, who desperately wanted to press the 'eject'
button on Britain's membership.[6] In 1983, Labour's manifesto advocated withdrawal (or 'Brexit', as it would be later rechristened). Even
in 1987, the party still held out the possibility of leaving the European
Economic Community (EEC) if it intervened unduly in Labour's
programme for economic renewal.[7]

Yet, that night, these transgressions were forgotten. Smith confidently declared to the glittering assembly, 'The Labour Party is now
the European Party in British politics. We are totally committed to
it ... We have a single market. Let's make a success of it.'[8] He received a standing ovation. The Labour Party had, in the words of
one commentator, 'Europeanised'.[9] Smith, a lifelong pro-European,
could look out at a party that was now at the heart of the project of
European integration, leading in Europe rather than contemplating
leaving it.

At 11.35 p.m., John and Elizabeth Smith departed the hotel for
their 35th-floor flat in the Barbican.[10] Just over eight hours later, the
Labour leader rose to prepare for a visit to Basildon to campaign for
Labour MEP candidate Richard Howitt. After showering at 8 a.m.,
Smith suffered a heart attack and collapsed to the bathroom floor.
Efforts were made to resuscitate him but to no avail. Paramedics

---

* The organisation was called the European Economic Community (EEC) from 1957 to 1992. It has been known as
the European Union (EU) since 1993. It will be known as either the EEC or EU in this chapter, depending on the
relevant context.

discovered a weak and inconsistent heartbeat. Minutes later, on the way to St Bartholomew's Hospital, he suffered a second heart attack. He was declared dead soon after arrival.[11]

It is both tragic and fitting that Smith's final speech was made at one of the most enthusiastically pro-European gatherings in the party's history. The following month, Labour won 73 per cent of British seats in the EU Parliament.[*] The Socialists were the largest group, led by a Labour MEP, and Labour, by some considerable distance, was the single largest party in the entire EU Parliament.[†] Gerald Kaufman, a fellow right-wing Labour MP and pro-European, eulogised that if Smith were fated to die prematurely, 'I do not think he would have wanted to die in any other way'.[12]

Although Smith's leadership was short, his role in cementing Labour's pro-European credentials should not be overlooked. Every one of his predecessors, from Clement Attlee to Neil Kinnock, had taken stands against British membership of the EEC. Attlee, Hugh Gaitskell, Harold Wilson, Jim Callaghan and Michael Foot all opposed the Treaty of Rome in 1957 and Britain's application to join the EEC in 1963. Wilson, Callaghan, Foot and Kinnock voted against the European Communities Act in 1972. Three years later, Foot and Kinnock campaigned to leave the EEC. The Labour Party officially remained open to leaving the EEC, unless certain reform criteria were met, until 1988, five years into Kinnock's leadership.

Throughout this time, Smith was an unwavering pro-European. He defied his party whip to vote for the European Communities Act.

---

[*] Sixty-two out of eighty-five in Great Britain. In addition, one of the three Northern Irish seats, elected under a different electoral system, was won by John Hume of Labour's sister party, the SDLP.

[†] The next largest party was the German SPD on forty seats.

He campaigned to remain in the EEC during the 1975 referendum. He was one of the few advocates of joining the European Monetary System as early as 1978. Although he never contemplated joining the pro-EEC Social Democratic Party (SDP), Smith remained proudly identified with the Labour right's pro-European wing, led informally in the 1980s by deputy leader Roy Hattersley. From his position as a shadow Cabinet member in the late 1980s, Smith was one of the foremost advocates of Labour's embrace of European Commission president Jacques Delors's proposals for further integration. More than any other frontbencher, Smith can be credited (or blamed) with Labour's embrace of European economic and monetary union in the early 1990s. During his leadership, Labour officially supported joining the single European currency. Even if he would not use the word himself, Smith was as close to being a European 'federalist' as any Labour leader. He was Labour's most pro-European leader in its history.

SHADOW CHANCELLOR: DEFEATING THE EUROSCEPTICS (1987-9)

A fateful crossroads both for Labour and John Smith followed the party's defeat in the 1987 general election. Leader Neil Kinnock re-shuffled the shadow Cabinet, determined to bring in new blood and elevate talent. The shadow Chief Secretary to the Treasury, Bryan Gould, had been tasked with running Labour's election campaign. Although Labour lost, it was widely agreed that the campaign itself had been run efficiently.[13] Gould was seen as a rising star with leadership potential. In the June 1987 shadow Cabinet elections he topped the poll, receiving 163 votes – substantially higher than the second-place finisher John Prescott on 130. With deputy leader Roy Hattersley set to be moved from shadow Chancellor to shadow Home Secretary, it seemed likely that Kinnock would appoint Gould to replace him.

Gould, however, had two demerits against him. The first was that he was from the (soft) left-wing of the party, a committed Keynesian and a principled believer in active economic planning by government. The second, and not unrelated, disadvantage was that Gould was a committed Eurosceptic, at the time when the party was moving full steam ahead to a pro-European position.

Hattersley intervened. He refused to move from being shadow Chancellor if Kinnock was going to replace him with Gould.[14] If Kinnock insisted on appointing Gould, then Kinnock would have to sack Hattersley from the shadow Cabinet entirely.[15] Having just lost an election four years into the job, Kinnock was at his weakest point as leader. He could not risk enflaming tensions on the party's right, who would have quite happily replaced him with one of their own.

In an interview with the author, Gould reflected:

The opposition he [Kinnock] encountered within his own shadow Cabinet came from the pro-Europeans – Roy Hattersley, John Smith – they were the people who were his most bitter critics, both openly and behind the scenes ... They would not be pacified and stay on side as long as he was seen as anti-Europe.[16]

Hattersley, in effect, forced Kinnock to appoint his Labour right, pro-European ally Smith as shadow Chancellor instead.[17] This was despite Kinnock's apparent political inclinations. Gould attests that in private meetings, Kinnock 'assured me that on issues like the economy and Europe he was very much of my view'.[18] Kinnock confirmed in an interview with historian Colm Murphy that he was personally sympathetic to Gould's arguments in favour of devaluation to boost manufacturing and exports.[19]

In contrast, Kinnock had a 'chilly' relationship with Smith.[20] The new shadow Chancellor had a low opinion of his leader. While publicly loyal, Smith would complain about Kinnock amongst right-wing Labour friends. At one late-night gathering at Smith's home in Edinburgh, the shadow Chancellor told Peter Mandelson, Donald Dewar and Hattersley that Kinnock's leadership was 'froth, pure froth'.[21]

Kinnock's concession to Gould was to appoint him shadow Secretary of State for Trade and Industry (the post Smith had held in government 1978–9) and to award him a major part of the economic brief in Labour's Policy Review in 1988. 'I was bought off in a sense, and it was a reasonable deal,' Gould later assessed.[22] This latter decision was a snub to Smith. The first report of the Policy Review, entitled *Social Justice and Economic Efficiency*, showed Gould's mark. It insisted, 'The Community cannot be allowed to deter Britain from doing what is required to regenerate our economy.'[23] Nonetheless, there was no question of leaving the EEC, with the Labour Party conference finally voting to scrap Labour's threat of withdrawal that same year.

The most important document of the Policy Review was the second-stage report in 1989 known as *Meet the Challenge, Make the Change*. Although it accepted that 'Britain's future is in the European Community as it develops', the document ruled out taking Britain into a European currency union. It also warned against taking sterling into the Exchange Rate Mechanism (ERM) unless and until substantial changes were made to remove its deflationary bias. This sceptical position over fixed exchange rates was largely thanks to Gould's influence.

Soon after the document was endorsed by the Labour Party conference, however, Smith exacted his revenge. In November 1989, Gould was demoted from the trade and industry portfolio to the Department for the Environment. Smith had been behind these manoeuvres, ensuring that Gould would be replaced by Smith's loyal protégé, Gordon Brown.[24] The *Financial Times* reported that Gould's demotion paved the way for Labour to embrace European monetary union.[25]

The final stage of the Policy Review, which produced the 1990 document *Looking to the Future*, demonstrated the shifting sands. This document embraced economic convergence and monetary union, claiming that the ERM would 'provide a stable framework for long-term investment and steady growth'.[26] The last gasp of the Eurosceptic cause materialised in the 1992 leadership election to replace Kinnock, following Labour's fourth consecutive election defeat. Gould stood on a bold economic programme, which resisted further moves to European integration. Smith offered a more cautious programme, but he was an enthusiast of moves towards economic and monetary union. By this point, the party had been chastened by defeat. Many Labour members now regarded the EEC as the more reliable deliverer of social democracy than the British electorate. Smith trounced Gould. Colm Murphy writes that 'a major reason for Smith's victory was his longstanding advocacy of European integration in contrast to Gould's more sceptical positioning'.[27]

ERM: A LUCKY ESCAPE (1989-92)

In the 1960s and 1970s, three economic policy dilemmas bedevilled British governments: maintaining foreign confidence in sterling, preventing excessively inflationary wage settlements, and maintaining prudence in government spending. The ERM of the European Monetary System offered a way of escaping these political problems. It promised high international confidence in sterling in exchange for downward pressure on wage claims and tight fiscal spending rules. Governments would be required to implement austerity, their hand forced by international commitments, but inflation would be held at bay.

Labour had historically been sceptical of efforts to take monetary policy out of politics. This was perhaps most dramatically exemplified by the Attlee government's landmark Bank of England Act of 1946, which nationalised the bank and placed power over monetary policy in the government's hands. From the 1940s until the mid-1980s, few in the Labour Party were willing to stomach the idea of surrendering this democratic control over monetary policy in exchange for greater stability.

However, after the 1987 defeat, the mood shifted. Smith, a lawyer who had no economic training, sought counsel from a group of pro-EEC economists who were enthusiasts of ERM. This was a change from even the earlier years of the Kinnock leadership. Kinnock had previously been advised on economic policy by the Labour peer and economist Nicholas Kaldor, who vociferously warned against ERM. Kaldor, however, died in 1986, and Smith was advised instead by LSE economist Meghnad Desai, who was given a peerage in 1991. Desai viewed the ERM as a way of confronting inflation. He later explained, 'It became essential to have this straitjacket to keep inflation under control, but we had so much hassle from gung-ho Keynesians like Bryan Gould.'[28]

On 27 June 1989, the shadow Cabinet voted to support joining the ERM but on the condition that entry was at a competitive rate. This qualification came at Gould's insistence. He believed that there would never be a competitive rate and so he could stave off joining ERM without having to resign from the shadow Cabinet. This proved to be a tactical miscalculation, as by voting for the principle of joining the ERM, he had dipped his hands in the proverbial blood. Collective shadow Cabinet responsibility made criticism of the fundamentals difficult.

At the Labour Party conference that October, Smith declared that ERM membership would be 'an early objective of [Labour] Government policy'.[29] Two weeks later, he travelled to Brussels to tell MEPs that he was 'eager to negotiate early entry into the Exchange Rate Mechanism of the EMS' and was 'keen to plan a full and constructive part in the debate on progress towards Economic and Monetary Union'.[30] Michael Jones in the *Sunday Times* reflected that Smith's advocacy not just of the ERM but also of currency union put Labour 'down the federalist road. It represents a huge transformation in British politics'.[31]

Some Labour MPs, including Smith, recalled unfavourably how the Wilson and Callaghan governments had been derailed by spiralling wage claims, currency speculation and inflation. The ERM would discipline the unions, leaving them with few options but to accept moderate wage claims or risk unemployment altogether.[32] Being in the ERM meant deficits needed to be brought down, inflation contained by whacking up interest rates and productivity increased. This would mean sacking 'unproductive' workers for those willing to work more hours for less pay.

The most obvious and direct groups to suffer would be those who were in debt, because high interest rates would be one way of propping up sterling's value, and workers seeking higher wages. The Governor of the Bank of England argued that ERM would be a way of helping to ensure that wage inflation did not outstrip general inflation: 'Only an exchange rate policy ... can constitute a sufficiently obvious discipline, even for the dullest of wage negotiators, to break the trend that has bedevilled us for more than a generation.'[33] This was the mindset Labour was now championing – an astonishing about-turn. Eric Shaw wrote that Labour's acceptance of ERM 'completed its conversion to financial orthodoxy'. It entailed 'the discarding of full employment as the overriding economic priority'.[34]

Smith acknowledged that one of the consequences of ERM was 'a certain counter-inflationary discipline' on wages. In a staggering interview with the *Independent on Sunday* in May 1990, Smith was asked what would happen if employers didn't hold down workers' wages. 'Well, there would be unemployment, wouldn't there?' Smith retorted. He added that 'if companies make mistakes', such as paying their workers too much, they will be 'beaten in the competition of the single market, [and] I can't do very much about it'.[35] It was a remarkable statement from a Labour shadow Chancellor and an echo of Margaret Thatcher's assertion in a 1981 *Sunday Times* interview: 'People price themselves out of the market by saying, "come what may, I must have more money." There are times when they have created their own unemployment.'[36]

The logic of this position ruled out a Keynesian strategy. Smith accepted this point openly. He told *Tribune* in September 1990, 'In a sense, we have moved on from the Keynesian concept.'[37] Other staunch pro-Europeans echoed Smith's words. Stuart Holland, who had become an enthusiast of Euro-federalism, wrote in the *New Statesman*, 'Keynes is dead, Beveridge is dead, and the national economy of which they wrote has been transformed by a multinational trade and payments system.'[38]

The new priority was economic stability first. Economic planning had to operate within formalised constraints. If certain tools of national economic planning were surrendered for the sake of stability, this was seen as acceptable.[39] In effect, Smith had shifted Labour from seeing the end of unemployment as its number one economic objective to regarding inflation as enemy number one.[40] Later, Gould and other Keynesians like Labour MP Austin Mitchell would set up the Full Employment Forum to challenge this kind of thinking, but it failed to make a significant impact within the party. The liberal newspaper *The Economist* in April 1990 breathed a sigh of relief that Keynesians like Gould and Michael Meacher had been displaced by the rising prominence of Smith, Brown and Tony Blair in Kinnock's top team.[41]

On 8 October 1990, the final day of the Labour Party conference, Thatcher took Britain into the ERM. Hattersley and Smith (notably not Kinnock) issued a joint statement approving the move.[42] Mark

Stuart writes that, at this point, Labour and the Conservatives 'had virtually the same anti-inflationary strategy'.[43]

On 29 November 1990, the day after Thatcher resigned as Prime Minister, the Labour National Executive Committee voted to support joining the single currency as Labour policy.[44] This was an astonishing decision because convergence to what would become the euro meant the wholesale surrender of control not just over monetary policy but also economic policy, due to the convergence criteria rules. Joining the euro would impose strict limits on budget deficits and demand a low debt-to-GDP ratio. Nonetheless, Smith was a champion of the single currency. He told the House of Commons in November 1991 that a single currency would induce a low rate of inflation, low interest rates and currency stability.[45]

For three years (1989–92), a minority of Labour MPs pleaded with the party leadership to think again on these policies. Gould warned that if Labour committed to ERM and eventual monetary union, 'we would not be waiting for the City to shackle us. We would in effect be offering up our own wrists in advance for the application of the handcuffs'.[46] Austin Mitchell wrote to Kinnock pleading with him to ignore his shadow Chancellor. He warned, 'Abandoning the weapons of national management will not only undermine Labour's ability to fulfil its mission but place the whole burden of sacrifice and suffering on the unions and those we represent for the benefit of a financial sector which will screw us.'[47] Some Labour MPs couldn't believe what the party was signing up for. An April 1992 briefing document on currency union prepared for the Labour MP Peter Shore contains the marginal comment, 'One has to ask: Are we mad?'[48]

These objections were to no avail. In September 1992, the Treasury increased interest rates to such an astonishingly high level to maintain Britain in the ERM that the Major government was eventually forced by political pressure to exit the EMS altogether. The government's economic credibility never recovered from this humiliation, known as Black Wednesday. While Labour reaped the political benefits of this disaster, the reality is that Smith as shadow Chancellor and Leader of the Opposition had been an even more ardent enthusiast of ERM than the Thatcher and Major governments.

After Black Wednesday, Smith's sole substantive critique of the government was that the pound should have been devalued before entering the ERM. The 2.95 Deutschmarks to the pound, Smith would later say, was too high. This was a point, however, which he failed to make at the time. Indeed, in November 1991, Smith ruled out devaluing the pound if Labour entered office.[49] There was also nothing in Labour's 1992 manifesto that criticised the overvaluing of the pound relative to the Deutschmark. In fact, the 1992 manifesto said, 'Labour will maintain the value of the pound within the European Exchange Rate Mechanism.' When Brown became shadow Chancellor after the 1992 election defeat, he spent the months before Black Wednesday insisting that Britain must not devalue.[50] In contrast, Gould warned before Black Wednesday that 'the system is crashing around our ears' and described the whole situation as 'insane'.[51]

The discussion about the pegging at 2.95 Deutschmarks, often cited by Smith's defenders, is a red herring. Whether it was pegged at this level or a lower one, the fundamental fact remained that the ERM was imposing a limit on government economic policy. Whether the pound was valued at 2.95 or 2.50 (with a 6 per cent variance), British economic policy was to be geared around maintaining this valuation at all costs.

By the 1990s, Britain's main economic problem was not the lack of monetary stability anyway. The country's economic woes were due to the depletion of Britain's manufacturing capacity and gross under-investment thanks to the Thatcher and Major governments. Egregiously, North Sea oil was not used to buy productive assets. The 1980s were a decade of credit-based consumption of imported goods, failing even to boost domestic production. What the country needed was a proper industrial policy. Gould chastised the mistaken 'belief that monetary measures matter more than the real economy in which ordinary people live and work'. He criticised the idea 'that one can take a shortcut through fiscal policy and that the mere assertion that we have a strong currency will lead to the economic success we see others enjoy'.[52]

When Black Wednesday occurred, Smith delivered one of his most famous lines, calling Major 'the devalued Prime Minister of a devalued Government'.[53] It was an effective line, but as Major later wrote in his memoirs, it was 'a riot of freewheeling hypocrisy' and showed 'brass neck' from a Labour leader who had supported ERM membership even more enthusiastically than the government.[54]

Black Wednesday caused no serious rethink in the Labour Party about the dangers of its new conversion to Europe. The party celebrated its luck – and that's all it was – that it had lost the 1992 election and that the Conservatives, not Labour, had received the blame for the inevitable consequences of the very policy that Labour had supported. Two weeks later, Gould resigned from the shadow Cabinet, delivering his resignation speech at the fringe Labour Common

Market Safeguards Committee meeting at party conference. Gould was furious that 'none of the major figures in the drama on the Labour side ever hinted for a moment that they might have been wrong'.[55]

MAASTRICHT (1992-3)

The Treaty on European Union was negotiated in Maastricht, Netherlands, in December 1991.[56] The document rechristened the European Economic Community as the European Union, removed some of the ability of governments to veto EU policy and paved the way for a single European currency. It was a thoroughly pro-integrationist document, the kind that Labour would have opposed just a decade earlier. Debate began in the House of Commons in May 1992, following the general election held the previous month. Kinnock remained the lame duck leader until July, when Smith assumed the leadership.

Both parties were split, but the arithmetic worked to Labour's strategic advantage. There was a clear majority of pro-Maastricht MPs in the House of Commons, but the pro-Maastricht majority could not be found on the Conservative benches alone. In order to pass the treaty, Major needed Labour to co-operate, either by voting in favour or abstaining. However, this meant that Labour could conspire with anti-Maastricht Tories to inflict defeats on the government along the way. Smith's handling of Maastricht was a masterclass in political tactics. He was a 'House of Commons man' and it showed. Smith was aided by extremely effective Labour whips. Their goal, as Labour frontbencher George Robertson put it, was 'to harry the Government but not to lose the Treaty'.[57]

Labour whips would, therefore, co-ordinate behind the scenes with the anti-Maastricht Tories in order to inflict bruises against the government but never running things so close that the treaty itself would be endangered. Smith was able to play this game in part because his pro-European credentials were not in doubt. Pro-EU Labour MPs felt safe following the Smith line, trusting him not to sabotage the treaty entirely.

The Parliamentary Labour Party (PLP) was strongly divided over the treaty, even more so than the Conservatives. Nearly half of Labour MPs (138) defied the whips at some point during the Maastricht debates, compared to just forty-nine Conservatives.[58] Tony Benn told the September 1992 Labour Party conference that Maastricht was 'the biggest constitutional change of this century. It transfers powers, won very painfully by the Chartists and the suffragettes, from the electors to the commissioners and bankers'.[59] Gould wrote in the *New Statesman* that same month that Maastricht 'represents a breathtakingly audacious attempt to enshrine forever in treaty law a permanent victory by bankers over democrats'.[60] Mitchell called Maastricht 'The Final Victory of the Right'.[61]

At a March 1993 PLP meeting, viewpoints ranged from Giles Radice arguing in favour of a single currency to Mitchell describing the Maastricht Treaty as a 'charter for Central Bank rule on a monetarist basis'. 'How much more will we swallow?' he asked exasperatedly. David Winnick worried that the fiscal rules required to be in the monetary union, such as limits on deficit spending, were unacceptable and would 'imprison' any future Labour government.[62]

At the May 1993 PLP meeting, on the eve of the third reading of the Maastricht legislation, Shore attacked George Robertson's support for a Treaty that 'handed great chunks of British power to decision-making in the European institutions ... If my honourable friend cannot understand that, he is not fit to speak for my Party'.[63] Shore was supported by Nigel Spearing, who declared that Maastricht was 'against what the Party was founded to do – to battle against bankers' forces'.[64]

As the treaty approached its final hurdle in the House of Commons, Smith wanted to ensure that it would pass, but he wisely understood that whipping Labour MPs to vote in favour would be divisive. He therefore instructed Labour MPs to abstain on the third reading of Maastricht in May 1993.[65] However, seventy-one Labour MPs felt so strongly that they broke the whip. Overwhelmingly, these were Eurosceptics, with sixty-six Labour MPs voting against the treaty and just five in favour. A greater number of Labour MPs voted against Maastricht than Conservatives, who numbered forty-one.[66] One of the Labour rebels was Kate Hoey, a shadow minister in the team led by Mo Mowlam. In an interview with the author, Hoey recalls her frustration: 'It was ridiculous. We had spent weeks debating this, and then being told to abstain was just stupid.' She informed Mowlam of her plans to defy the whip. 'She was very understanding. I got on quite well with her because she was a rebel as well in many ways,' Hoey warmly recounts.

After casting her vote, Hoey returned to her flat to watch the football highlights. 'I got a phone call. And it was John Smith.' He asked his shadow minister to confirm that she had broken the whip that night. 'He got very angry at people who voted against Maastricht,' she remembers. After Hoey confirmed that she was one of the rebels, Smith began to speak. 'Well—'. But at that moment, Hoey let out a cry, momentarily baffling the Labour Leader: 'Oh! Arsenal has just scored!'

'I know this sounds ridiculous,' she candidly reflects years later – but emphasises that she is a great Arsenal fan. Gathering his composure, Smith asked Hoey if she would resign. She retorted, 'Well if you want me to resign, you should sack me.' Smith replied, 'Right. You're sacked.' 'There was only a tiny bit about it in the paper. I mean, I wasn't that important,' reminisces Hoey.[67]

The embrace of Maastricht represented 'a seismic change of attitudes' within the Labour Party.[68] The Labour rebellions demonstrated that there was still a non-trivial minority of Labour MPs who had not signed up fully to the EU integrationist agenda. However, perhaps what is more notable is that, as he had in the early 1970s, Smith was prepared to prop up a Conservative government in order to facilitate passage of a European treaty. If Smith had ordered Labour MPs to vote against Maastricht, it is possible that they could have brought down the government. Labour would likely have won the ensuing general election, making Smith Prime Minister in 1993. To do so, however, would have required Smith abandoning his pro-European principles and may have derailed the creation of the EU.

A SOCIAL AND DEMOCRATIC EUROPE (1993-4)

The repeated electoral defeats during the Thatcher and Major era contributed to a crisis of faith on the part of the Labour Party. Some Labour MPs came to question the willingness of the British public to vote for a socialist government. The traumas of Thatcher's attack on organised labour caused many in the labour movement to look to the EEC as a life raft. They were encouraged to do so by European Commission president Jacques Delors, who promised a Social Chapter, a set of social rights to accompany the integration of the European Single Market. It would be capitalism with a conscience.

While EEC membership entailed the surrendering of a variety of national democratic economic powers, constraints were placed on both left- and right-wing governments. The EEC may have imposed a ceiling on socialist ambitions, but it also created a common floor below which the degradations of capitalism could not sink. Even better, from this pessimistic perspective, the social rights of the Social Chapter would be entrenched by international treaty and could not be undone by elected governments.

Smith was a passionate believer in 'social Europe'. As shadow Chancellor, he admitted, 'There can be no lasting economic convergence and monetary cooperation without a strong commitment to a social Europe.'[69] Major had negotiated an opt out of the Social Chapter, which he regarded as essential to ensure Conservative support for the treaty. Smith, on the other hand, argued that the absence of the Social Chapter was a serious problem. He vowed to sign up to it as soon as Labour entered government.

The promise of Delors's 'social Europe' was, as the Fabian researcher Stephen Tindale surmised, a move from 'Croslandism in one continent' to 'Croslandism in one country' – a reference to the revisionist Labour thinker, and hero of Smith's, Tony Crosland.[70] The offer was, in actual fact, pretty thin gruel. Nearly everything in the Social Chapter was already protected by British law, having been implemented by the Attlee, Wilson and Callaghan governments. It was also not clear what objectives the chapter protected that a Labour government would not legislate for anyway. Tindale writes, 'A genuinely socialist party would have rejected the Delors initiatives and the Social Chapter as a fig leaf.'[71] But, its key strength was that its provisions were protected from the consequences of elections. When Thatcher complained that 'we have not successfully rolled back the frontiers of the state in Britain, only to see them re-imposed at a European level', many on the left wanted desperately to believe her concerns were the truth rather than hyperbole.[72]

By the early 1990s, the Labour Party had become 'significantly more European than public opinion'. Smith showed some self-awareness on this front.[73] He realised that the British public's support of the European project was contingent, not dogmatic. In 1992, he acknowledged that in the previous decades, European integration had been built 'upon shared prosperity'. He warned, 'If the public begin to believe that interdependence is a source of economic weakness and not strength – that it will diminish the opportunities for employment and prosperity – then the clamour for purely national solutions, however misguided, will grow.'[74]

Although Smith was supportive of monetary union, he wanted a politically accountable central bank. This applied both at the national and European level. As shadow Chancellor, Smith argued in 1989:

The constitutional position of the Bank of England in relation to the Government is satisfactory at the moment. I see no reason why that should be changed. A wide range of powers is available to the Chancellor of the Exchequer and no Chancellor should willingly give them up. He should certainly not contemplate handing over power over key economic [and] monetary issues to bankers who are not accountable to the British people.[75]

Smith said he was 'shocked' to hear that the Conservative government was contemplating granting procedural independence to the Bank of England.[76]

The normally enthusiastically pro-European Smith raised concerns over Delors's proposals for institutional reform, which included an independent European Central Bank in charge of Europe-wide monetary policy. He told the House of Commons, in the same debate, the proposals were:

> On the whole dangerously insensitive to the political dimension of economic decision taking and the need for democratic accountability … The Delors report may be a useful starting point for debate and discussion, but it could never be regarded as a blueprint for the future of Europe … Let me make it clear that we would not be willing to accept any system of central banks which would be independent of political control, just as we strongly oppose an independent status for the Bank of England.[77]

In Smith's ideal scenario, the Council of Economic and Finance Ministers (ECOFIN) would set the political direction of monetary policy, including the ability to set interest rates. In a 29 January 1991 speech at Chatham House, Smith argued that ECOFIN 'should become the political supervisory body … capable of adding an effective political dimension to the conduct of monetary policy of the Community'.[78]

Smith repeated that democratic control over monetary policy would be a necessary precondition for Labour's support of a single European currency. He told a Deutsche Bank seminar in Berlin in September 1991, 'It should be recognised that monetary union influences all aspects of economic life and therefore cannot (and in my opinion should not) be detached from democratic decision-making.'[79]

In November 1991, Smith told the House of Commons that the European Central Bank needed to operate in a 'framework of accountability': 'We believe that it is important, for example, that the setting of the external exchange rate for a single currency should be a matter for ECOFIN.'[80] Control over monetary policy had been a key article of faith for the Labour Party since the Attlee government. Roger Berry, a Labour MP who had previously been an economics lecturer at Bristol University, argued at a February 1993 PLP meeting that 'the Maastricht proposals are clearly undemocratic and are deliberately deflationary. Labour should oppose, and oppose vigorously, an independent central bank'.[81]

By this time, however, events had made such a model a fait accompli. Smith was in a bind. He needed Labour to accept Maastricht, but he realised how many Labour MPs regarded central bank independence as a step too far, a view with which he sympathised personally. At the same PLP meeting, Smith promised that he would seek to modify EU institutions once in government to enhance their democratic accountability. In response to this, the veteran Labour MP Peter Shore erupted that Smith's assurances weren't 'worth a damn'. He averred, 'The frontbench hasn't got the guts to stand up for Britain, and if [Smith's motion to accept the central bank] is carried today, it will go down as a day of infamy in the history of the Labour Party.' In spite of this oratory, the PLP voted 112 to forty-six to accept Maastricht, even with its independent central bank provisions.[82]

CONCLUSION

Smith's untimely death, after just twenty-two months as Labour leader, inevitably provokes many questions of 'What if?' On the matter of Europe, the subsequent direction of travel was broadly consistent with the path that he had forged. However, it is fair to say that neither Blair nor Brown were the instinctive Europeans that Smith had been. Famously, on the eve of St George's Day during the 1997 election, Blair vowed, 'I will have no truck with a European superstate. If there are moves to create that dragon, I will slay it.'[83] Blair's Chancellor, Brown, killed off any notions of Britain joining the euro. Although Blair himself was personally supportive, he was not willing to risk his premiership on the question. Jonathan Tonge writes that Blair thought he might lose a referendum on the euro and then be compelled to resign early as Prime Minister.[84] Ian Bache and Andrew Jordan concur, writing that Brown's five tests on the euro were 'a camouflage to disguise the real test: whether the government could win a referendum on entry'.[85]

In the final speech of his life, Smith declared, 'We in the Labour Party believe that our future is truly European.'[86] Under Smith, Labour was self-confidently and, for the first time in its history, unequivocally a pro-European party. There is a good case to be made that Smith was Labour's most passionately pro-EU leader ever. He was certainly the most consistent. While Kinnock's shift was 'tactical and opportunistic' and 'seemed to lack genuine commitment', Smith was a true believer from the start.[87] As his internal opponent Gould later charged, Smith held 'almost religious convictions on the European issue' and showed 'resistance to anyone who did not share the True Faith'.[88]

PART III
PERSPECTIVES

11

A VIEW FROM THE
SHADOW CABINET

Ann Taylor, Baroness Taylor of Bolton

JOHN SMITH WAS A formidable politician who would undoubtedly have won the general election and been a successful
Prime Minister. My abiding memory of John is that he was always
good company. He enjoyed a drink, was very easy to talk to and had
a great sense of humour. He had friends across the spectrum of the
Labour Party. He didn't suffer fools gladly but would often defuse
difficult situations with a well-timed joke.

John became leader after the 1992 election defeat. Prior to that,
Neil Kinnock had led us back from the brink and deserves a good
deal of credit for that. Two things in particular stand out from that
period – Kinnock's bravery in taking on the Militant Tendency and
his modernisation of campaign techniques. But it wasn't enough, as

it turned out, and the defeat was painful – especially as the opinion polls predicted we would win. The defeat gave us a clear sense of purpose, and this was reinforced by the events of Black Wednesday later in the year.

John was always going to win the leadership contest. I recall Bryan Gould ringing me to ask for my support and I urged him to run for deputy leader instead, which he probably would have got – but he didn't take my advice!

I got to know John many years before this, having first been elected in 1974, and had observed him in the House of Commons and later the shadow Cabinet. In both settings, he performed extremely well.

In those days the shadow Cabinet was elected annually by the Parliamentary Labour Party (PLP). Nobody liked going through those elections, but they were a good constraint and kept us in touch with the views of the back benches. It meant that there was diversity of opinion. There were serious discussions but no rows. He allowed individual members to work out their own positions and gave them autonomy to do so, while focusing on the bigger political issues of the day. John was a team player and kept the Cabinet united around its central purpose of winning the next election. He would also allow debate to take place in meetings of the PLP until decisions had been made.

Without doubt, he had command of the House at all times. Whether it was Prime Minister's Questions or set-piece debates, we always had confidence that John would perform well. For whatever reason, he was more confident in the House than Neil had been. He had a command of detail as well as a sense of the bigger picture. I never went into the House of Commons worried about how he would perform – he was on top of things.

John inherited the issue of electoral reform, which some in the party had become interested in, and Neil had set up a committee to examine it. I never got the feeling he did want to move towards proportional representation (PR). In this he was right. I always felt that the constituency link and direct sense of accountability under the existing system was crucial. There was a clear sense of a mandate being given to the winning party. Under PR the tail wags the dog, as smaller parties have considerably more influence than their parliamentary position warrants. I never shared the enthusiasm of some who believed in changing the system, either because they wanted a more pluralistic form of politics or something more similar to the Continent.

He was right to push through the changes modernising the relationship between the party and the trades unions. He also established the Social Justice Commission, which I think was an important step forward, as it would provide a more comprehensive approach to policymaking.

John didn't need to spin as much as Tony Blair felt he had to do because he had known many of the political journalists a long time and they knew him. He felt he could be straight with them.

He was on the right of the party but it was the inside right – recognising that there were different opinions within the party and that it was necessary to try to keep it united. This frustrated some who wanted to go further and faster.

He would have won the 1997 general election, with a smaller

majority than Tony, and he would have gone on to win the 2001 election in all likelihood. We would still have had increased public spending on hospitals and schools, probably a higher rate of income tax on top earners and a focus on reducing inequalities, as John was guided above all by a strong sense of social justice. He would have been a very able Prime Minister.

12

BEING JOHN SMITH

Bryan Gould

ALTHOUGH JOHN SMITH AND I ended up as rivals and opponents, our relationship in the early days of our acquaintance was cordial, even fraternal. Indeed, my first meeting with him was when, after I had returned to the House as MP for Dagenham in 1983, he approached me and asked if I would, after his appointment as shadow Secretary of State for Trade and Industry, act as parliamentary private secretary with special responsibilities for City affairs – that is, financial services. Accordingly, we worked together on the standing committee stage of a bill on some aspect of financial regulation. John was the senior partner and I worked with him as a sort of deputy – and I recall that we congratulated each other at the end of the committee process on forming a pretty good team.

The next stage in our relationship, however, was less convivial. I found myself, as a new member of the shadow Cabinet in 1987, providing regular support to party leader Neil Kinnock, who, as I have observed elsewhere, had to contend with a shadow Cabinet in which virtually none of the members had voted for him in the leadership election, following Michael Foot's resignation.

Principal amongst this group of Kinnock doubters was John Smith. It was not that he was more outspoken and antagonistic than others; rather, he was the focal point around whom the doubters coalesced and who provided them with some kind of common identity. He seemed, in other words, to be their natural leader, sharing with them, as he did, their pro-European sentiments and their innate suspicion of anything too radical and risk taking. These factors inevitably meant that, when any question about the Kinnock leadership arose, John's name entered the conversation as the most likely successor.

Our own personal relationship remained amicable, to the extent that John felt able sometimes to reveal to me, as we sat side by side on the front bench, his concerns about what he saw as Neil's errors and weaknesses. I grew accustomed to seeing him as belonging to a different wing of the party from mine. I had not, at that point, seen him in leadership terms, but I formed an opinion of him and of his politics that I saw no reason to change over the later stages of our relationship.

I observed that his approach to politics was very much an expression of his personality. I was tempted at the time to see him as what I described as a 'machine politician', by which I mean that he saw the business of politics as being conducted through the relationships developed in the context of political organisation.

In his case, the relevant organisation was the Scottish Labour Party. He was quintessentially a product of the Scottish Labour Party; most of his political friends (and allies) came from that source. It was that bond, it seemed to me, that was the most important political fact in his life – more important than policies or political deals or principles or any of the other considerations that might weigh with others.

He chose his political colleagues not according to whether their political views matched his own but on the basis that they came from the same political organisation. This approach was very much borne out when it came to seeking support from his colleagues, such as when he was campaigning for the leadership of the party. John directed most of his efforts not to propounding policy or to explaining where he stood on particular issues but to reinforcing his links with those he could count on as allies because they came from the same and familiar political origins.

This meant that his most effective campaigning was done while sharing a whisky with trusted colleagues on the House of Commons terrace. On such occasions, he was, in the words of one observer, 'the life and soul of the party'.

In a wider sense, it also meant that winning support was not about – and did not require – the establishment of common political ground. It was enough to 'be John Smith' – to be the recognisably four-square and reliable figure suggested by the very plainness of his name – the figure who everyone knew where they were with.

I had some evidence of this perception and its political significance during the 1992 election campaign. The Labour Party was faced with the problem familiar to all left-wing parties – how to overcome the constant efforts of the right-wing tabloid press to persuade the voters that managing the economy could not be entrusted to a party whose sole economic policy would be to increase taxation.

Some effort had been made in advance of the election campaign to resolve this by appointing John to the post of shadow Chancellor. As it turned out, John proved to have little interest in or ability to address the economic problems that the British economy suffered as a consequence of more than a decade of Thatcherite neglect. As far as I could see, he had no ability to analyse the broader macroeconomic picture or to recommend changes for the better. He therefore had little ability to make an effective critique of Tory economic management or to offer a convincing alternative on behalf of a newly elected Labour government.

Where he came into his own, however, was in rebutting the constant efforts of the Tories and their allies in the popular press to frighten the voters with stories about the tax increases that a Labour government would introduce. It was thought that the best way to rebut these tactics would be to 'come clean' about any changes that Labour planned to make to the tax system.

John had recognised that National Insurance contributions, while not strictly part of the income tax structure, were nevertheless indistinguishable in the popular mind from any other tax. He recognised that some reform of the National Insurance scheme was required, which would be a palatable form of change, and that to reveal the detail of what was proposed would show that nothing more sinister was intended. John was put up to do precisely this, in the confident belief that his 'honest John' image would satisfy the electorate that there was nothing more frightening being hidden from them.

It is hard to know whether and to what extent this belief was justified, but what became clear was that, whenever the campaign appeared to be flagging, John was again put up to focus attention on the proposed changes to National Insurance contributions. I could only shake my head in disbelief when we repeatedly used our few opportunities to campaign on issues of our own choosing to return to the ground that favoured our opponents.

The episode illustrates very well the strengths, real or perceived, that John was thought to embody. The decision was, however, very 'Smithian', in that personality was counted on as more significant than policy.

The election defeat in 1992 produced, of course, the immediate prospect of a new leadership election, following Neil's post-election resignation. I have recounted elsewhere what went through my mind about how that process might unfold. There was no doubt, of course, that given his prominence and the role he had played in the campaign, John was virtually certain to inherit the leadership. He had for so long been touted in the press as the next leader that there was a virtually unstoppable belief that his accession was a done deal.

I was concerned that, after the fourth election defeat in a row, the Labour Party would, without a moment's reflection about what had or had not worked, saddle itself with a long-heralded new leader with no opportunity to reflect and debate on whether a change of direction of some sort was needed.

As I have recounted elsewhere, Neil advised me not to throw my hat in the ring. 'Smithy,' he said, 'has got it all sewn up.' And he went further: 'He won't last the course. You should stick around to pick up the pieces.' I do not know whether this last remark was occasioned by some inside knowledge about John's health, but it proved to be remarkably prescient.

The campaign for the leadership was pretty much a non-event.

John, in effect, claimed his inheritance. He had been surprised, puzzled and disappointed when he learned that I had thrown my hat in the ring, but he set about doing what he knew best – calling in old debts and strengthening old links. The big trade unions fell into line; even those to whom I had been helpful in policy terms and with whom I had had a productive working relationship did not bother to talk to me. My candidature was seen as a challenge to the natural order of things.

There was little opportunity for the candidates to test each other. We had, if I remember correctly, just two chances to cross swords: one when we both addressed a meeting of the parliamentary party and a second organised by the Fabian Society. I felt both had gone quite well for me.

The campaign, such as it was, nevertheless provided me with an opportunity to observe John at close quarters and from a different vantage point. I discovered nothing that I did not already know. If stability, solidity, taking no risks, not frightening the horses was what you wanted, then John was your man. If innovation, inspiration, bringing about change and reform, shaking things up was your bag, then look elsewhere.

But John, of course, knew himself better than anyone else did. He knew that he could be confident that just 'being John Smith' was enough to produce victory, that he did not need to break sweat or pretend to be something he wasn't. His public image as Mr Reliable and calling in old debts arising from long-standing relationships would do the trick.

When the result was declared, John's reaction and his treatment of me were impeccable. He was neither unduly triumphant or unconvincingly solicitous. In the conversations we had once the dust had settled, in which we tried to sort out what job I might do under his leadership, he unsurprisingly made it clear that he would not offer me the task of shadowing any of the great offices of state. We eventually agreed that I would take on the heritage portfolio.

It took me only a short time, however, to become alarmed at the direction – on issues like Europe and the economy, which I saw as closely intertwined – in which John was taking party policy. At the same time, I was approached about a job that would require me to return to my native New Zealand. I decided that I should make a new start. John did not pretend that he was sorry.

With his untimely death, we never got the chance to see what sort of fist he would make of running the country. It would certainly have been in safe hands. Whether that would have been enough, we shall never know. One thing I know – his death meant that we lost a good and decent man.

13

THE MYTH OF
'ONE MORE HEAVE'

David Ward

SINCE HIS EARLY DEATH on 12 May 1994, the voice most missed about John Smith's leadership has been his own. Like Hugh Gaitskell, the other Labour leader who had the misfortune to die in office, Smith was denied the opportunity of autobiography. His story has been told by others with a strong bias of self-justification. The architects of New Labour especially – even as they sincerely mourned his death – have caricatured Smith's leadership as cautious and complacent.

Tony Blair, the late Philip Gould and, recently, David Miliband have portrayed Smith as an exponent of 'one more heave', unable to embrace the change they believed necessary for Labour's return to power.[1] Blair's closest advisor, Anji Hunter, a few years ago dismissed Smith as 'a perfectly nice guy, but not a massive reformer, not a massive progressive, a bit of a statist'.[2] I worked for John Smith from 1988 to 1994 when he was shadow Chancellor of the Exchequer and Leader of the Opposition. I hope I can give a more nuanced and authentic account of his leadership.

The passage of time inevitably distances us from Smith's period in office, but the legacy of his leadership still has a large impact on public life. In less than two years as Leader of the Opposition, he revived Labour's electoral prospects, reformed the party's relationship with trades unions and established legislative priorities – particularly on constitutional reform – that remain amongst the lasting achievements of the Blair government elected in 1997.[3]

Smith was a man of supreme self-confidence, sure in his beliefs, informed by a Presbyterian faith instilled during his upbringing in the West Highlands and supported by a loving family. His good friend the late Donald Dewar described Smith's character as 'formidable'.[4] His training as a lawyer combined with his great natural wit and debating prowess made him a master of the House of Commons Chamber. Smith's ambition was to lead a country that would 'harness the extraordinary potential of ordinary people'.[5] He was inspired by a vision of social justice and democratic citizenship and opposed to a society dominated by entitled elites or opaque market forces.

When Smith was elected as Labour leader by a landslide over Bryan Gould in July 1992, he did not dispute that the party needed further reform. The issue was the pace, style and content of change. The 'modernisers', led by Blair, believed that Labour's defeat in the 1992 general election was proof that Neil Kinnock's reform of the party had been too timid and slow. They wanted to make a binary differentiation between 'Old' and 'New' Labour. In contrast, Smith had no interest in rebranding Labour in a way that implicitly repudiated its past. He was proud to have joined the party at sixteen, become a Labour MP in 1970 and served as a Cabinet minister in the government of Jim Callaghan.

Rooted in Labour's social democratic tradition, Smith felt that the tide of political ideas was moving his way. He did not have a political past he wanted to resile from. Rather than run against 'Old' Labour, he wanted to concentrate his fire on a Conservative Party that, after more than twelve years in office, was very vulnerable to attack. Smith knew that further modernisation was necessary for Labour to win, but he preferred to use the arts of persuasion, rather than confrontation, especially for a party still licking its wounds after the 1992 defeat. Alastair Campbell described the tension between the 'modernisers' and Smith as a struggle between 'frantics' and 'long gamers'.[6] In managing the party for another period in opposition, strategic patience was the key to Smith's approach. His style of leadership was cat-like: capable of bold jumps but wanting to be sure of his footing.

Smith was determined to avoid the difficulties that faced his predecessor, Kinnock. After the 1987 election, Kinnock initiated a much-needed policy review. However, its work was completed as early as 1989. This locked in policy pledges that left the party vulnerable to exaggerated Tory costings and the Tories' 'Labour's going for broke' campaign launched in June 1991 and then relaunched as the 'tax bombshell' poster in early 1992. This, rather than Smith's shadow Budget in March 1992, was the strategic mistake that limited Labour's policy options ahead of the 1992 election.[7]

Smith's plan was to divide the parliament into two distinct phases. The first phase, up to the 1994 European elections, had three main priorities: firstly, to complete the one member, one vote (OMOV) reforms to reduce trade union influence in the elections for the party leader and parliamentary candidates; secondly, to maximise Tory divisions over the Maastricht Treaty, securing ratification while minimising Labour rebellions; and thirdly, to launch a policy review that would begin with constitutional reform, which had minimal implications for government expenditure. The second phase, from mid-1994, would enable Smith to set out Labour's vision and new agenda for Britain, while leading a relentless attack on a Tory government that was increasingly mired in sleaze and scandal.

In following this plan, Smith was determined to avoid internal rows over 'Clintonisation' of the Labour party or revisit the debate over Clause IV, believing that both would distract from achieving his objectives. Of course, Smith was encouraged by Bill Clinton's victory in the US presidential election in November 1992.* However, he was bemused and frustrated that the Democrat's success quickly shifted from a cause of Labour celebration to a source of internal argument.† Nor did he welcome proposals by Jack Straw that Clause IV of the party's constitution – calling for 'common ownership of the means of production' – should be rewritten. Smith warned Straw that to do so would stir up a hornet's nest and that it should be left to wither on the vine.[8]

Far more important for Smith was to win the battle for OMOV. This was the *sine qua non* of Labour's modernisation agenda that he

---

* Smith asked Labour's National Executive Committee to prepare a briefing on the US election, which was carried out by the party's senior organisational officer John Braggins, and I also prepared a review of the Democrats' election platform.

† Shadow Cabinet members Clare Short and John Prescott warned against importing what they saw as Clinton's centrist agenda, while Blair and Gordon Brown saw his success as a blueprint for Labour.

had inherited unfinished from Kinnock. It was a reform strongly opposed by some major trade unions including Smith's own, the GMB, who fiercely resented any reduction in their influence over candidate selection and leadership elections. Smith was convinced that trying to win OMOV and simultaneously take on Clause IV would commit the fatal error of fighting battles on two fronts at once. Meanwhile, Smith faced competing pressure from 'modernisers' like Blair, who was impatient to adopt the 'purest' form of OMOV, and his deputy Margaret Beckett, who would have preferred to drop further reform entirely.[9]

After the 1992 election, Kinnock's team were convinced that an OMOV deal was achievable at the party conference that October. Smith disagreed. He had been given warnings from friendly trade union leaders, such as the late Rodney Bickerstaffe, that promises of support made previously to Kinnock could not be relied upon. Smith would have to win his own deal, and delaying the decision by a year would give him more time to do so. Another key factor was that the size of the union block vote at the party conference was going to be reduced in 1993 from 90 per cent to 70 per cent, making it easier to secure these vital reforms. Smith's subsequent win on OMOV – assisted by a powerful supportive speech from John Prescott – by a very narrow margin showed that the decision to delay had been astute. Had he gone for OMOV in October 1992 and lost, the defeat would have been disastrous, both for Smith and the party.

Instead, that autumn, Smith was free to concentrate his energy on attacking the Tories, and no better opportunity came than after Black Wednesday in September 1992. The pound's humiliating exit from the Exchange Rate Mechanism (ERM) destroyed the credibility of

Conservative economic policy. Smith's parliamentary performances at this time were magisterial, combing wit with a devastating demolition of Major as the 'devalued Prime Minister of a devalued government'.

Smith was able to exploit this decisive political moment because he had moved quickly to shift Labour's ERM policy immediately after the 1992 election.[10] During the leadership election, Smith had proposed a managed realignment of the ERM, which was already advocated by the German Bundesbank and could have avoided the chaos of Black Wednesday.[11] Smith's swift recalibration of Labour's ERM policy reaped immediate political rewards. Labour took over the lead in the polls as the party best able to handle the economy and quickly established a huge 22-point poll advantage over the Conservatives.

If Black Wednesday decisively wrecked the Tory's reputation for economic competence, it was the Maastricht Treaty ratification crisis that destroyed their ability to govern. Labour's strategy, crafted by Smith with Labour's then European spokesperson George Robertson, was to drag out the legislative process as long as possible and table a 'ticking time bomb' amendment on the Social Chapter opt out, which led to a defeat for the government.[12]

Smith, a committed supporter of Britain's membership of the European Community, was determined to support the treaty's provision for a framework of social and employment rights, which was strongly opposed by the Tories.* But he was also willing to exploit deep Conservative divisions over Europe and encourage Tory rebels to destabilise John Major's government. Calling some of his

---

* On 28 October 1971, Smith was one of sixty-nine Labour MPs to defy a three-line whip and vote in favour of Britian's entry into the European Common Market.

colleagues 'bastards', the embattled Prime Minister was forced to resort to a motion of confidence to get the treaty through the Commons. Threatened with annihilation, the rebellion ended, but the damage to Major's authority was severe. In marked contrast, Smith had kept Labour's own Maastricht divisions under control. This was achieved by taking the highly unusual step of allowing a series of debates in the Parliamentary Labour Party before the shadow Cabinet agreed the whip. All the PLP votes went Smith's way, but his inclusive style earned respect from Labour's Maastricht rebels, including a then largely unknown backbencher, Jeremy Corbyn.

This consensual approach was also used to introduce significant reforms to Labour's policymaking process. Smith pressed ahead with the creation of a National Policy Forum (NPF) that had been originally proposed by Kinnock in 1990.[13] The NPF was launched in May 1993 as a more inclusive and deliberative process than conference resolutions, which were often determined by union block votes. Another significant step was to outsource new thinking on key policy areas. Smith was fully aware that Labour's tax and welfare policies needed review but also had to be insulated from future Tory 'tax bombshell' attacks. To allow fresh thinking, while avoiding this trap, Smith established the independent Commission for Social Justice, hosted by the Institute for Public Policy Research and chaired by Gordon Borrie. The NPF and the commission were important innovations that avoided the pitfalls of Labour's 1987–9 policy review.

Meanwhile, Smith pushed forwards with a bold agenda of constitutional reform. He strongly felt this was his unfinished business, dating back to his ministerial role promoting Scottish devolution in Callaghan's government. Smith wanted Labour to adopt an ambitious reform agenda but felt that an early draft prepared by Blair, then shadow Home Secretary, lacked energy and vision. So, in March 1993, Smith took the initiative himself by giving a major speech to the constitutional and electoral reform campaign, Charter 88.

In his speech, titled 'A Citizen's Democracy', Smith set out the most comprehensive agenda on constitutional and democratic reform made by any Labour leader.[14] Warning that Britain had become an overcentralised elective dictatorship, he called for a new 'dynamic framework of government' empowered by 'municipal, regional, national and European decision-making'.[15] Smith supported devolution in Scotland and Wales and incorporation of the European Convention on Human Rights into British law. He was scathing about Whitehall's obsession with secrecy and pledged to introduce a Freedom of Information Act. Not exactly the typical policy agenda of 'a bit of a statist', as alleged by Anji Hunter. Ironically, the modernisation of the UK's democratic governance that Blair's government subsequently implemented was largely based on the commitments made by Smith in his speech to Charter 88.

By May 1994, Smith had successfully completed the main objectives of the first phase of his leadership. All that remained was the campaign for the 1994 elections to the European Parliament. At a gala dinner held in London with leader of the French Socialist Party Michel Rocard, Smith was confident that Labour would do well. He concluded his speech with words that are now a poignant testament to Smith's commitment to public service: 'The opportunity to serve our country – that is all we ask.' Tragically, he died the following morning. Less than a month later, Labour won 42.6 per cent of the vote and sixty-two out of eighty-seven seats in the European elections.

Presided over by the party's acting leader, Margaret Beckett, the European election result almost matched Blair's landslide in 1997 and showed that Labour was fully capable of converting its strong lead in opinion polls into votes in the ballot box.*

Had Smith lived, Labour's European election landslide would have provided a superb platform to launch the second phase of his leadership. It would have served as a strong endorsement of Smith's commitment to Europe, his agenda of social justice, economic opportunity and democratic reform. However, it was not to be. Smith's absence has allowed a continuation of the 'one more heave' mythology to suggest that Smith would have rested on his laurels rather than take the fight to Major's divided and decaying government. In fact, with the battles over OMOV and the Maastricht Treaty behind him, Smith was looking forward to presenting his own vision of Labour in government, preparing for the twenty-first century. He was planning to reinvigorate Labour's core aims and values in a document to be launched at the 1994 party conference. It would have been his alternative to rewriting Clause IV and intended to move the party beyond arcane constitutional debates. Work on Smith's statement was to have begun immediately after the European elections and to be based on principles and policies that he had set out in a series of speeches given in 1993.[16]

In his R. H. Tawney Memorial Lecture, Smith used the often-overlooked progressive writings of the classical economist Adam Smith to undermine the Conservative's laissez-faire ideology.† Smith argued

---

* Labour's vote share in the 1994 European elections was 42.6 per cent compared with 43.2 per cent in the 1997 general election.

† The altruistic themes of Adam Smith's *Theory of Moral Sentiments* (1759) are less well known than his work of classical economics *An Inquiry into the Nature and Causes of the Wealth of Nations* (1776).

in favour of 'a richer conception of freedom of the individual', which was 'only meaningful and achievable in society', and 'our ultimate moral goal'.[17] He strongly believed that social justice and economic prosperity were intertwined. Speaking to the Trades Union Congress, Smith made a clear commitment to full employment, a national minimum wage and the introduction of a new charter to put part-time and full-time workers on the same footing. At the time his speech caused disquiet amongst Labour's modernisers, but today, with the emergence of the 'gig' economy and zero-hour contracts, Smith's concern for workplace rights looks far-sighted.

Addressing the substance of the Clause IV issue at Labour's local government conference, Smith dismissed the 'largely sterile debate about the ownership of industry and services as if privatisation and nationalisation are the only conceivable choices in economic policy'.[18] For Smith, the modern alternative to old-style nationalisation was a more dynamic and smart approach to corporate regulation and a willingness to be robust in tackling monopolies or market failures that were detrimental to the public interest. Smith's pragmatism and confidence was informed by his time as Minister of State for Energy in the mid-1970s, where he proved to be a tough negotiator and secured North Sea licensing agreements with multinational oil companies.[19]

After Black Wednesday, Smith had also become increasingly concerned about excessive liberalisation of financial markets. He raised concerns about the risks of financial deregulation and the growth of derivatives with sister European Socialist and Social Democratic parties. At his request, these concerns were included in a 'Declaration of Party Leaders', adopted in April 1994.[20] Smith's warnings about derivative trading now seems powerfully prescient, but, unfortunately, they were not followed up by Blair or Brown. Rather than strengthen regulation, the opposite was encouraged both in the US and the UK. The Glass-Steagall Act, which maintained a wall between commercial and investment banking, was abolished by Clinton, while New Labour also supported a 'light touch' regulatory regime for the City of London. Their indulgence of the banking sector was exposed by the onset of the financial crisis in 2008 and severely damaged Labour's reputation for economic competence, just as the ERM crisis did to the Tories in 1992.

There is a sad redundancy to the 'what if' speculation about what would have happened had John Smith lived. For what they are worth, here are my own reflections. Smith's victory – certain I think, though probably with a smaller majority than Blair – would have denied New Labour its self-serving mythology that only their rebranded version of Labour could have won in 1997.

Smith's social justice agenda would have been explicitly redistributive and included a top-rate tax band of 50 per cent. His strong European commitment would not have extended to adopting a single currency, about which he was extremely cautious, but he would have been a strong supporter of the single market and its growing role as a regulatory superpower. He would reluctantly have accepted Brown's proposal to make the Bank of England independent but as quid pro quo would have wanted to push back against financial deregulation. On constitutional reform, he would not have seen the necessity for referenda ahead of Scottish and Welsh devolution but would have carried through with the pledge to hold a referendum on proportional representation.[21] Finally, I believe Smith would have opposed the invasion of Iraq and emulated Harold Wilson's resistance to requests from Lyndon B. Johnson for the UK to send troops to Vietnam in the 1960s.

Thirty years on, rather than debate what might have been, I think the most appropriate act of reflection is to acknowledge Smith's substantial achievements as Labour leader. After the pain of defeat in April 1992, in less than two years Smith's Labour Party was comfortably outpolling the Tories, united and committed to policies that would create a lasting legacy in government. I believe Smith was a great Labour leader, whose bequest to Blair in May 1994 was to leave the party resurgent and ready for office, in as good a shape as any other leader before or since. Rather than recycle the tired mythology of 'one more heave', it would be refreshing if New Labour's advocates could show the good grace to admit how lucky they were to have inherited the party's leadership from the formidable John Smith.

14

BUILT TO LAST?

John Rentoul

TONY BLAIR SEEMS TO have been in two minds about whether John Smith, had he lived, could have won the 1997 election. At one point in his memoir, *A Journey*, Blair wrote, 'I assessed that there were three types of Labour: old-fashioned Labour, which could never win; modernised Labour, which could win and keep winning, which was my ambition from the outset; and plain Labour, which could win once, but essentially as a reaction to an unpopular Conservative government.'[1]

In this taxonomy, Smith was 'plain Labour', possibly with a touch of 'old-fashioned' about him. Blair was pleased that Smith recognised the desirability of reducing the power of trade union block votes in the party but otherwise thought that Smith was complacent about the need for thoroughgoing modernisation.

Elsewhere in his memoir, however, Blair hinted that he thought Smith would lose. He criticised Smith for proposing, as shadow Chancellor, higher taxes for those earning more than £30,000 a year in the 1992 election and accused him of doing so 'partly' to curry favour with party members and trade unionists, who would choose the next leader if Labour lost. 'John knew that afterwards he might be contesting the leadership,' Blair wrote, stating that his proposed tax rises 'were great for the party faithful but plainly problematic for the public'. He further commented, cryptically, 'Once we were beaten, somehow I felt that the next election would not be John's.'[2] This may have referred to Smith's health, although that was not the subject of this section; the implication is that Smith's selfishness disqualified him from being Prime Minister.

This ambiguous assessment lies at the core of the modernisers' view of Smith. They liked him personally; they admired his parliamentary skills, but they were disparaging in private about what they regarded as the strategic failings of his leadership. 'He didn't believe you had to go out to win,' one of the leading Blairite ministers said. 'If you just happened to occupy the post of leader of the Labour Party, your turn would come.'[3] In fact, if that had been Smith's view, it had some justification. As David Ward, Smith's head of policy, has pointed out, the crisis of the European Exchange Rate Mechanism in late 1992 'is almost entirely overlooked' by the modernisers. The humiliation of John Major's government, brilliantly exploited by Smith, had a big and lasting effect on its popularity.[4]

There are two other important points to be made about Blair's view of Smith as recorded in *A Journey*. One is that even in 1992, when the term 'modernisers' gained currency in analysis of the Labour Party, its leading members did not hold a single view. Blair was already beginning to separate himself from Gordon Brown. Brown was closer to Smith and Peter Mandelson further away – indeed, Mandelson, elected as MP for Hartlepool in 1992, was regarded with suspicion by Smith and was kept at arm's length. Blair's criticism of Smith is closely linked to his view that Brown should have challenged Smith for the leadership after the 1992 election, which in turn is linked to Blair's view of himself as the bolder of the two. Part of Blair's justification for seizing the leadership – when Brown, his friend and ally, thought he was entitled to it – was that Brown had had his chance and passed it up.

This leads on to the second point, which is that Blair wrote his memoirs after leaving office and many years after the events of 1992–4, so there is likely to be an element of self-justification and self-mythologisation in his account. Even so, my conversations at the time and since confirm that Blair's account of the view of 'the modernisers', however defined, is broadly accurate. They blamed Smith's shadow Budget for losing the 1992 election, and they thought that his passive approach to preparing for the following election risked losing it. After the election, of course, this was a harder position to maintain because it was won by such a large margin; hence the claim that Smith could have won once, with a much smaller majority, but he would have encountered problems in government and might have lost a subsequent election.

The extent to which this is true is an issue at the heart of the debate in the Labour Party about Blair's legacy. Neal Lawson, a former advisor to Brown and chair of Compass, a Labour pressure group, wrote an open letter to Blair in *The Guardian* on 1 January 2015:

If he had lived, John Smith would have won in 1997 – not by as much as you, granted – but then your majority was too big, wasn't it? ... In hindsight the wrong people were voting Labour. The tent was too big and you spent the next 10 years trying to keep the wrong people in it: the very rich, for example. What meaningful project includes everyone?[5]

Lawson's argument is that it would have been better for Labour to have won with a smaller majority on a more 'left-wing' manifesto. The same debate takes place in the Labour Party before every election: that the leader should make 'bolder' promises, even at the cost of putting off a few potential voters, in order to win a mandate for 'radical' change. Otherwise, it is said, Labour risks being just a continuation of the Conservative government with different faces. However, those who look back wistfully on Smith as representing a politics that was both 'more Labour' than New Labour and capable of winning an election can do so only in hindsight. They overlook the fact that, despite the ERM debacle and despite the opinion polls, Blair could not be sure that he would win. The opinion polls had got it wrong in 1992 and so few Labourites took victory for granted. It was only afterwards that the 'if only' school of thought took hold – mostly some time afterwards, when disappointment with Blair's foreign policy grew.

'If only' Smith had lived, it was said, Blair would not have 'overdone' the reassurance of Tory Middle England. 'If only' Smith had lived, we would never have joined the US in invading Iraq. Well, who can say? But there is ample evidence that things would have been different. Look, for example, at the changes Blair made in his three years as Leader of the Opposition to the Labour policies he inherited from

Smith. One of the most significant was on tax. Despite the view that Smith had helped lose Labour the 1992 election by proposing to raise taxes on higher incomes, as leader he still intended to impose higher taxes on the better-off. The lesson he took from his 1992 shadow Budget was that he had planned to hit people at too low a level, at £30,000 a year; for the next election he and his shadow Chancellor Brown 'shared the assumption' that a higher tax rate would apply to incomes over 'something like' £70,000 to £100,000.[6] Brown dissuaded Smith in the autumn of 1993 from confirming that there would be a 50p top rate of income tax above what was then the highest rate of 40p, on the grounds that there was no need to be specific at that stage, but they both assumed that there would be a higher rate.

Blair, however, took a sharply different view and insisted that Labour should promise not to raise any rates of income tax at all. When Ed Balls, Brown's advisor, suggested in a pre-election meeting that they could responsibly propose a 50p rate on incomes over £100,000 a year, Blair told him to 'wash your mouth out'.[7] Blair thought that a significant part of the electorate would regard such a tax as confiscatory, even if it fell on a tiny minority of taxpayers, and would fear that it would be extended lower down the income scale. This difference between Smith and Blair on tax would not have altered the finances of a Labour government much: as it was, Brown's change to pensions taxation raised a much larger sum. But it would have reduced Labour's electoral appeal, given that those enthused by taxing the rich would already be voting Labour.

There were three other important changes that Blair made, which Smith would not have. Blair shifted to a more sceptical policy on the European single currency, he insisted on referendums before legislating for Scottish and Welsh devolution and he in effect changed the name of the party to New Labour.

Under Smith, Labour had been in favour of joining the single currency in principle – indeed Smith opposed the opt-out secured by Major in the Maastricht Treaty that allowed the UK to choose whether or not to take part. Smith thought that Britain should join the currency when it was launched. By the time he died, the launch date had not been decided but was likely to be 1999 (as indeed it turned out to be). Soon after Blair became leader, he said that the case for joining depended on whether the British and continental economies had converged sufficiently, and Robin Cook, his shadow Foreign Secretary, said 'the probability is' that a government would be 'looking towards the subsequent parliament' to join.[8] Smith might have resisted this adjustment – although he, like Blair, would probably have followed Major in promising a referendum if the government ever decided in favour of joining. According to Ward, Smith intended to hold a referendum in government anyway.[9] He recognised, as Blair did, that it would be disastrous for any Prime Minister to try to join without a referendum.

We cannot know if Smith would actually have tried to join the euro when it was launched in January 1999 if he had been Prime Minister. He was a longstanding pro-European, who had voted with Roy Jenkins against the Labour whip in 1971 to join the European Economic Community. But he was also a politician and would not have wanted to put the euro question to a referendum if he was likely to lose it. Blair never thought a referendum was winnable, and Smith would probably have come to the same conclusion.

On devolution, though, we can be surer that Smith would have taken a different course. Blair, advised by Derry Irvine, decided that referenda would help get the legislation through the House of Lords, where Labour did not have a majority. Smith was a friend of Irvine's but as a fellow Scot – indeed as the minister who had taken the legislation for devolution through Parliament in the Callaghan government – might have thought he knew better. Despite the failure of that attempt, scuppered by a post-legislative referendum, Smith regarded a Scottish Parliament as the settled will of the Scottish people. Ward said, 'I don't think John would have been persuaded and his instinct would have been to make a clear manifesto commitment that would give a Labour government all the mandate it required to act on both Scottish and Welsh devolution.'[10]

Nor would Smith have entertained the idea of rebranding the party as 'New Labour'. He was suspicious of marketing, and his sharpest difference with Blair, and to a lesser extent Brown, was his pride in Labour history and Labour values.

Blair made a number of other changes, some of which Smith might have made but probably not all. Blair retained the policy of a minimum wage but abandoned the formula for setting it at half of median male earnings (it was brought in, in 1999, at below this rate). He scrapped Smith's promise of full rights for employees from day one in a job. He ditched the promise of an elected second chamber, committing only to removing hereditary peers from the House of Lords as 'a minimum first step'.[11] He ended Labour's opposition to school league tables based on exam results. And he shifted to a neutral position between Unionism and Nationalism in Northern Ireland. 'In each case,' I comment in my biography of him, 'policy change moved Labour closer to the Conservatives.'[12]

If Smith had kept any of those policies, they might have cost Labour votes – in addition to the votes lost by a tax rise on higher earners, a more enthusiastic approach to the euro and a more old-fashioned presentation of the party as 'plain' Labour. Or they might have caused Labour difficulty in government – in addition to the potential for delay and the eating up of parliamentary time of devolution legislation. It is easy to imagine Smith gleefully doing a deal with Tory peers behind the back of their leader in the Commons, in the way Blair did, to avoid Lords reform snarling up the rest of the Labour government's legislative programme – but equally, he was more likely to be tripped up by something else, such as his promise of a referendum on the voting system. Blair simply reneged on that promise in government.

So, when it is said that Smith would have kept Britain out of the Iraq War in 2003, the question is not so much whether he would have joined the US invasion – and Ward said, 'I am confident he would not have' – but whether Smith would have won the second election in 2001 or 2002.[13] Certainly, Smith would have won a smaller majority than Blair in 1997. On the balance of probabilities, he would have lost support during his government, and it is likely that the Conservative opposition would have been in better shape, probably led by a 'moderniser' in the form of Michael Portillo, who would have held his seat.

However, we are now deep into the realms of hypothetical history, buttressed by the benefit of hindsight. In many ways, the dispute between John Smith and the modernisers is a false one, in that Smith and Blair pursued different strategies suited to their characters. Smith was unconvincing as 'a modern man ... part of the rock 'n' roll generation', as Blair once described himself, and so Smith sought to reassure swing voters with a show of party unity and the solidity of traditional Labour values.[14] Blair, on the other hand, could take liberties with Labour history and lay claim to the future by leading 'almost literally a new party'.[15] The difference is also a false one: Neal Lawson's complaint that Blair won 'too big' a majority implies that it was possible before the 1997 election to calibrate exactly how many vote-losing policies to ditch in order to maximise the 'radical' mandate and still win. That is the sort of thing that can be said only after the votes have been counted. It must be doubted that John Smith would have had anything to do with such a speculative and theoretical analysis.

15

RETROSPECT

Andy Burnham

T WICE IN THE HISTORY of the Labour Party has the leader died on the verge of ending long periods of Conservative dominance. In 1963, Hugh Gaitskell died after leading the party since 1955. The death of John Smith on 12 May 1994 was a moment that stays firmly in the memory. In his tragically short period of time as leader, John had secured public trust and the confidence of his party. He would have won the next general election and served as Prime Minister. He was a very able politician and a man of personal integrity.

John always recognised that the Labour Party is a broad church, containing people with diverse views, and maintained good relations with members from different wings of the party. He had served as a minister in the 1970s under Tony Benn and Michael Foot, working well with both. At no point did he contemplate leaving the Labour Party in the long period of opposition after the 1979 general election defeat. With John as leader, everyone in the parliamentary party felt that they had a fair hearing. The Labour Party is at its strongest when it is united around its core principles of equality and social justice with a set of credible policies to make these beliefs a reality. John provided this sense of unity.

John's second legacy is devolution. In the 1970s, he attempted to introduce legislative devolution for Scotland and Wales. During the Thatcher governments power was centralised, and support for devolution grew. Devolving power was a key objective of his leadership, and the final establishment of the Scottish Parliament and Welsh Assembly after Tony Blair was elected in 1997 was seen, rightly, as a continuation of John's unfinished agenda. Despite the granting of further powers to the devolved bodies in Scotland and Wales and the introduction of elected mayors in major English cities, Britain remains very centralised. The result is that policies are implemented which benefit London and the south-east. The fate of HS2 and Northern Powerhouse Rail shows what happens when decisions are not taken closer to the people. That is why I, and other elected mayors, have campaigned for further powers so that decisions can be taken in the interests of the areas we represent. If levelling up is ever to be a reality, then this has to happen. So, John was right to believe in devolution, and it is an issue that remains very relevant today.

Therefore, although thirty years have passed since his death, his twin concerns of party unity and devolution of power remain as relevant as ever.

NOTES

INTRODUCTION

1 A. McSmith, *John Smith: A Life, 1938–94* (London: Mandarin, 1994) and M. Stuart, *John Smith: A Life* (London: Politico's, 2005).

2 A. Crines and K. Hickson (eds.) *Harold Wilson: The Unprincipled Prime Minister?* (London: Biteback, 2016); K. Hickson and J. Miles (eds.) *James Callaghan: An Underrated Prime Minister?* (London: Biteback, 2020); K. Hickson and B. Williams (eds.) *John Major: An Unsuccessful Prime Minister?* (London: Biteback, 2017) and K. Hickson (ed.) *Neil Kinnock: Saving the Labour Party?* (London: Routledge, 2022).

1. TRIBUNE OF THE PEOPLE: THE POPULARITY, APPEAL AND LEGACY OF JOHN SMITH

1 Voting intentions (Westminster) – all companies' polls 1992-1997; https://www.ipsos.com/en-uk/voting-intentions-westminster-all-companies-polls-1992-1997. This provides the list of all opinion polls between 1992 and 1997, the date of the sampling, the size of the sample, and the political support for the major political parties. They are constantly shifting sands. In mid-July 1993, the Harris/*Observer* poll had the Conservatives at 44 points, 6 points ahead of Labour, although the ICM/*Guardian* poll had this at 41 for the Conservatives in 7–8 August 1992 to 40 for Labour. There were many similar polls in October 1993, all with a substantial lead for Labour. The 27 October–1 November Gallup/*Daily Telegraph* poll gave 24 points to the Conservatives and 46.5 per cent to Labour. On the 4–9 May 1994 survey by Gallup/*Daily Telegraph*, the last before Smith's death, the figures were 24.5 to the Conservatives, 45.5 to Labour, 25 to the Liberal Democrats and 5 between the rest.

2 *Open Democracy*, 'John Smith and the path Britain did not take', 12 May 2019, https://www.opendemocracy.net/en/opendemocracyuk/john-smith-and-path-britain-did-not-take/

3 Ibid.

4 B. Brivati (ed.) *Guiding Light: The Collected Speeches of John Smith* (London: Politico's, 2000), pp. xiii–xxvii

5 Ibid., p.162, and most newspapers, including *Halifax Evening Courier*, *The Guardian* and *The Times*, 20 July and 21 July 1992. The fine details of the vote can be found in the survey of the 1992 Labour Leadership Election located in the Labour Leadership Special Conference 18 July 1992 file at the Labour History Archive and Study Centre, People's History Museum, Manchester.

6 D. Butler and G. Butler, *British Political Facts, 1900–1994* (London: Macmillan, 1994) p.137. This indicates that the trade unions held 40 per cent of the vote, the Constituency Labour Parties 30 per cent and the MPs 30 per cent. Of these, the proportion of the vote for trade unions was 38.518 to 1.482; for the Constituency Labour Parties 29.311 to 0.689; and for the MPs 23.187 to 6.813, giving an overall total of 91.016 of the vote for Smith and 8.984 for Gould.

7 *Halifax Evening Courier*, 20 July 1992 and 21 July 1993

8 Figures from D. Butler and G. Butler, *Twentieth-Century British Political Facts, 1900–2000* (London: Macmillan, 2000), pp.277–8

9 See note 1.

10 C. Bryant (ed.) *Reclaiming the Ground: Christianity and Socialism* (London: Spire, 1993). John Smith's article 'Reclaiming the Ground' appears pp.127–42.

11 Ibid. p.127

12   J. Smith, 'Reclaiming the Ground: Freedom and the Value of Society', in C. Bryant, *Reclaiming the Ground*, pp. 127–42

13   P. Snowden, *The Individual Under Socialism* (London: Independent Labour Party, 1903)

14   T. H. Marshall, *Citizenship and Social Class: And Other Essays* (Cambridge: Cambridge University Press, 1950). It was also republished by Pluto Press as a Pluto Classic in 1992.

15   Smith, 'Reclaiming the Ground', p.135

16   The R. H. Tawney Lecture by John Smith 'Reclaiming the Ground', delivered on 20 March 1993, is reproduced in Brivati, *Guiding Light*, pp.212–25, p.216, p.217

17   Ibid. p.216

18   Ibid. p.220

19   'The Eighth John Mackintosh Lecture', republished in Brivati, *Guiding Light*, pp. 53–77, p.65. The Tory view of protecting the rich was reiterated by Liz Truss in Prime Minister's Questions, during her brief and disastrous period of office at the end of 2022.

20   John Smith, speech to the Nottingham Rally, 28 May 1987. MSS 389/6/13/343 in the Modern Records Centre, University of Warwick.

21   Ibid.

22   John Smith, 'A Commitment to Change', delivered at the Royal Horticultural Hall, London, 18 July 1992 and republished in Brivati, *Guiding Light*, pp. 167–76, p.175

23   HC Debs, 28 October 1971, col. 2213. Also *The Independent*, 13 May 1994, referred to in a tribute by Tam Dalyell MP.

24   HC Debs, 21 November 1991, col. 505–12

25   'Editorial', *The Independent*, 17 September 1992

26   The ICM/*Guardian* poll conducted 4–5 September 1992 and published 10 September gave the Conservatives 38 points, Labour 38 points, the Liberal Democrats 19 and others 5. The Harris/*Observer* poll of 16–17 September 1991, published 20 September, had the figures as 36, 44, 16 and 4 respectively. The Gallup/*Daily Telegraph* poll conducted 16–17 September 1992 had it as 37, 42, 14 and 4. Thereafter, Labour ran a substantial lead.

27   Quoted in Stuart, p.259

28   'The ball is in Labour's court'; *The Independent*, 17 September 1992

29   John Smith, 'The Standards of and Practice of Government', delivered to the Labour, Finance and Industry Group, 28 January 1993 and republished in Brivati, *Guiding Light,* pp.202–12, p.202.

30   Ibid. p.202

31   Ibid. p.207

32   Parliamentary Labour Party (PLP) Parliamentary Committee, minutes 12 January 1994, in the Labour History Archive and Study Centre, People's History Museum, Manchester. The PLP minutes are also in this archive.

33   Ibid.

34   *Report of the Inquiry into the Export of Defence Equipment and Dual-Use Goods to Iraq and Related Prosecutions* (London: HMSO, 1996) and the Records of the Inquiry, National Archives, KF1.

35   PLP Parliamentary Committee, minutes 26 January 1994

36   Ibid.

37   Ibid., minutes 29 July 1992

38   *Halifax Evening Courier*, 20 July 1992 and PLP Parliamentary Committee minutes, 29 July 1992

39   Quoted in M. Stuart, 'John Smith 1992–4', in T. Heppell (ed.) *Leaders of the Opposition from Churchill to Cameron* (London: Palgrave, 2012), p.166

40   M. Stuart, 'Managing the Bloody Infantry: The Parliamentary Labour Party under John Smith 1992–4', *Parliamentary Affairs* (2006), vol. 59 no. 3, pp.401–19. The PLP Minutes, which I have also consulted, are in the Labour Study and Archive Centre, People's History Museum, Manchester.

41   PLP Parliamentary Committee, minutes 17 February 1993

42   *The Sunday Times*, 28 February 1993; *The Times*, 2 March 1993

43   Stuart, 'Managing the Bloody Infantry', p.410

44   Brivati, *Guiding Light*, p.160; *The Guardian*, 15 April 1992

45   Brivati, *Guiding Light*, p.166

46   M. Prescott, *The Sunday Times*, 6 June 1993

47   John Smith, speech to the TUC 456 conference, delivered 7 September 1993. Available at the Bickerstaffe Collection, MSS 389/6/13/343, pp.2–3

48   Ibid. p.11

49   A. Grice, 'Smith Faces Defeat on Block Vote', *Sunday Times*, 5 September 1993

50   Ibid.

51   'Brighton Labour Party Conference', *The Independent*, 27 September 1993

52 A. Grice and M. Prescott, 'The Invisible Man', *Sunday Times*, 26 September 1993; 'Go Further Mr. Smith', *The Independent*, 29 September 1993

53 P. Murphy, 'Rank and file could see Smith scrape in', *Yorkshire Post*, 29 September 1993

54 *Labour Party Annual Conference Report* 1993, John Prescott speech pp.161–4, p.162

55 Ibid. p.164

56 'Big Ripple in Brighton', *The Independent*, 30 September 1993

57 Rodney Bickerstaffe papers. Available at Modern Records Centre, Warwick, Gov/TRA/1

58 Recording of BBC Radio Four *The World at One*, 12 May 1994. An interview by Nick Clarke of Rodney Bickerstaffe, conducted little more than an hour after the announcement of the death of John Smith, a copy of which is in the Bickerstaffe Papers at the Modern Records Centre, University of Warwick.

59 *Labour Party Annual Conference Report* 1993, pp.152–4

60 R. Hattersley, *50 Years On: A Prejudiced History of Britain since the War* (London: Little, Brown and Company, 1997), p.374

61 C. J. Wilkinson, *John Smith: A Reappraisal: A Critical Analysis of the Labour Party's Lost Leader* (Lichfield: Blacklist Press Ltd, 2022), Kindle edition.

62 A. Howard, 'John Smith obituary', *The Times*, 13 May 1994. Also appears in an edition of A. Howard, *Lives Remembered: Times Obituaries* (Berkshire: Blewberry Books, 1996).

63 '1993 United Kingdom local elections', https://en.wikipedia.org/wiki/1993_United_Kingdom_local_elections; '1994 United Kingdom local elections', https://en.wikipedia.org/wiki/1994_United_Kingdom_local_elections

64 Open Council Data UK, cited in P. Walker and J. Elgot, 'Expectation management: Labour wary of Tories' claim they could lose 1,000 seats', *The Guardian*, 22 April 2023. The graph suggests that in 1994 and 1995, the peak period for Labour, Labour held about 47 per cent of council seats in Great Britain, compared to the Tories' 19 per cent.

65 C. Haddon, 'Making Policy in Opposition: The Commission on Social Justice, 1992–1994', *Institute for Government*, https://www.instituteforgovernment.org.uk/sites/default/files/publications/CSJ%20final_0.pdf

66 N. Timmins, 'Labour's think tank', *The Independent*, 9 July 1990

67 Commission on Social Justice, *Social Justice* (London: Random House, 1994), p.ix

68 Ibid. p.8. Pages 1–13 offer the executive summary of the report.

69 Ibid. p.10

70 Ibid. p.11

71 Quoted in C Haddon, 'Making Policy in Opposition', p.9

72 R. Hattersley, 'New Labour's Poverty Gap', *The Guardian*, 16 July 2001; Laybourn, *A Century of Labour: A History of the Labour Party, 1900–2000* (Stroud: Sutton, 2001), p.145

73 J. Rentoul, *Tony Blair* (London: Little, Brown and Company, 1995), pp.342, 346–7

74 Laybourn, *A Century of Labour*, p.134

75 BBC Radio Four, *The World at One*, 12 May 1994

2. JOHN SMITH AND IDEOLOGY

1 J. Smith, 'Reclaiming the Ground' in B. Brivati (ed.) *Guiding Light: The Collected Speeches of John Smith* (London: Politico's, 2000), p.214

2 M. Stuart, *John Smith: A Life* (London: Politico's, 2005), p.65

3 Ibid. pp.115–17

4 C. A. R. Crosland, *The Future of Socialism* (London: Jonathan Cape, 1956)

5 C. A. R. Crosland, 'Socialism Now' in D. Leonard (ed.) *Socialism Now and Other Essays* (London: Jonathan Cape, 1974)

6 J. Smith, 'A Commitment to Change', in Brivati, *Guiding Light*, p.170

7 For a discussion of Plant's ideas see M. Beech and K. Hickson (eds.) *The Idea of the Good Society: Essays in Honour of Raymond Plant* (Oxford: Oxford University Press, forthcoming)

8 R. Hattersley, *Choose Freedom: The Future for Democratic Socialism* (London: Michael Joseph, 1987)

9 Smith, 'A Commitment to Change', p.170

10 J. Smith, 'Reclaiming the Ground', in Brivati, *Guiding Light*, pp.212–25. See also C. Bryant (ed.) *Reclaiming the Ground: Christianity and Politics* (London: Hodder and Stoughton, 1993)

11 Stuart, *John Smith*, p.305

12 Smith, 'Reclaiming the Ground', p.218

13 Ibid. p.225

14 M. Beech and K. Hickson, *Labour's Thinkers* (London: I. B. Tauris, 2007), pp.235–6

15 Ibid. p.236

16 Smith, 'Reclaiming the Ground', p.215

17 A. Giddens, *Beyond Left and Right: The Future of Radical Politics* (Cambridge: Polity Press, 1994); A. Giddens, *The Third Way: The Renewal of Social Democracy* (Cambridge: Polity Press, 1998)
18 J. Smith, 'The Eighth John Mackintosh Memorial Lecture', in Brivati (ed.) *Guiding Light*, pp.53–77, p.60
19 Stuart, *John Smith*, p.302
20 J. Smith, 'European Community', in Brivati (ed.) *Guiding Light*, p.147
21 Ibid. p.161
22 Brivati notes that this was, in part, 'simply a conversion born of regular defeat'. Ibid. p.154
23 Smith, 'Reclaiming the Ground', p.221, where he highlights the changing position of John Gray.
24 Ibid. p.214
25 Ibid. p.221

3. OCCUPYING THE PALACE: JOHN SMITH AND PARLIAMENT

1   P. Norton, *The 1922 Committee: Power Behind the Scenes* (Manchester: Manchester University Press, 2023), pp.1–13
2   P. Norton, 'Power Behind the Scenes: The Importance of Informal Space in Legislatures', *Parliamentary Affairs* (2019), vol. 72, no.2, pp.245–66
3   E. Smith, 'Introduction', in G. Brown and J. Naughtie (eds.) *John Smith: Life and Soul of the Party* (Edinburgh: Mainstream, 1994), p.12
4   Ibid. p.12
5   HC Debs, 28 October 1971, cols. 2211–18. See also U. Kitzinger, *Diplomacy and Persuasion* (London: Thames and Hudson, 1973), chapter 13 and appendix 1
6   T. Jones, *Remaking the Labour Party* (London: Routledge, 1996), p.131
7   J. Naughtie, 'A Political Life Observed', in Brown and Naughtie (eds.) *John Smith: Life and Soul of the Party*, p.33
8   Ibid. p.35
9   N. Lawson, *Memoirs of a Tory Radical* (London: Biteback, 2010), p.584
10 A. McSmith, *John Smith: A Life 1938–1994* (London: Mandarin, 1994), p.149
11 K. O. Morgan, *Michael Foot: A Life* (London: Harper Press, 2007), p.334
12 M. Stuart, *John Smith: A Life* (London: Politico's, 2005), p.136
13 Lawson, *Memoirs of a Tory Radical*, p.584
14 HC Debs, 7 June 1989, col. 249
15 HC Debs, 24 October 1989, col. 688
16 Ibid.
17 G. Brown, 'John Smith's Socialism: His Writings and Speeches', in Brown and Naughtie (eds) *John Smith: Life and Soul of the Party*, p.81
18 G. Brandreth, *Breaking the Code* (London: Phoenix, 1999), p.119
19 Lord Irvine of Lairg, 'Tribute', in Brown and Naughtie (eds.) *John Smith: Life and Soul of the Party*, p.106
20 A. Seldon, *Major: A Political Life* (London: Weidenfeld & Nicolson, 1997), p.322
21 J. Major, *John Major: The Autobiography* (London: HarperCollins, 1999), p.339
22 Brandreth, *Breaking the Code*, pp.187–8
23 C. Clarke, 'The View from the Left', in K. Hickson and B. Williams (eds.) *John Major: An Unsuccessful Prime Minister?* (London: Biteback, 2017), p.315
24 Brandreth, *Breaking the Code*, p.201
25 Lord Blunkett to author, August 2023
26 Stuart, *John Smith: A Life*, p.261
27 M. Stuart, 'Managing the Poor Bloody Infantry: The Parliamentary Labour Party under John Smith, 1992–94', *Parliamentary Affairs* (2006), vol. 59, no. 3, pp.401–19
28 Ibid. p.407
29 P. Cowley and P. Norton with M. Stuart and M. Bailey, 'Blair's Bastards: Discontent within the Parliamentary Labour Party', *Legislative Studies* (1996) vol. 1, no. 96, University of Hull: Centre for Legislative Studies, pp.20–21
30 P. Seyd, 'Tony Blair and New Labour', in A. King (ed.) *New Labour Triumphs: Britain at the Polls* (Chatham, NJ: Chatham House Publishers, 1998), pp.66–7
31 Baroness Taylor of Bolton to author, September 2023
32 Norton, 'Power Behind the Scenes', pp.245–66
33 Ibid. pp.258–9
34 P. Norton, 'Staying in the Saddle: James Callaghan and Parliament', in K. Hickson and J. Miles (eds.) *James Callaghan: An Underrated Prime Minister* (London: Biteback, 2020), pp.55–70
35 McSmith, *John Smith: A Life*, p.66
36 Morgan, *Michael Foot: A Life*, p.335

37 *The Observer*, 15 May 1994. Cited in Jones, *Remaking the Labour Party*, p.131n2

38 Stuart, *John Smith: A Life*, p.347

39 Naughtie, 'A Political Life Observed', p.23

40 Lord Blunkett to author, August 2023

41 Lord Grocott to author, September 2023

42 Baroness Taylor of Bolton to author, September 2023

43 Lord Grocott to author, September 2023

44 Brandreth, *Breaking the Code*, p.251

45 Brandreth, *Breaking the Code*, pp.251–2

46 HC Debs, 12 May 1994, col. 429

4. ONE MORE HEAVE? OPINION POLLS AND ELECTIONS DURING JOHN SMITH'S LEADERSHIP

1 A. McSmith, *John Smith: A Life, 1938–1994* (London: Mandarin, 1994), p.299

2 P. Gould, *The Unfinished Revolution: How the Modernisers saved the Labour Party* (London: Little, Brown and Company, 1998), p.177

3 Ibid. p.178

4 Ibid. p.182

5 Ibid. p.179

6 H. Young, *The Hugo Young Papers: Thirty Years of British Politics – Off the Record* (London: Allen Lane, 2008), p.379

7 M. Stuart, *John Smith: A Life* (London: Politico's, 2005), p.294

5. ECONOMIC POLICY

1 D. Ward, 'John Smith and the mythology of "One More Heave"', *Mile End Institute Blog*, https://www.qmul.ac.uk/mei/news-and-opinion/items/john-smith-and-the-mythology-of-one-more-heave.html

2 D. Ward, 'John Smith Remembered', *John Smith Centre*, https://www.johnsmithcentre.com/research-blog/john-smith-remembered-david-ward/

3 D. Ward, 'John Smith's Shadow Budget 1992 – Myths and Lessons for Labour', *Mile End Institute*, https://www.qmul.ac.uk/mei/media/mei/tgc-media/filesx2fpublications/140_22-MILEEND_REPORT_Budget-1992_v3_web.pdf

4 N. Lamont, *In Office* (London: Little, Brown and Company, 1999), p.179

5 J. Naughtie, 'A Political Life Observed', in G. Brown and J. Naughtie (eds.) *John Smith: Life and Soul of the Party* (Edinburgh: Mainstream, 1994), pp.21–55, p.29

6 Ibid. p.28

7 G. Carey, 'Memorial Service for the Rt Hon John Smith QC, MP: Address by the Archbishop of Canterbury', in Brown and Naughtie (eds.) *John Smith*, pp.107–10, p.109

8 M. Stuart, *John Smith: A Life* (London: Politico's, 2005), p.305

9 Ibid. p.305

10 Ibid. p.409

11 Ibid. p.50

12 Ibid. p.73

13 Ibid. p.125

14 Anonymous, personal communication, 10 August 2023

15 Quoted in Ward, 'John Smith Remembered'

16 D. Butler and D. Kavanagh, *The British General Election of 1992* (Basingstoke: Macmillan, 1992), p.49

17 Ibid. p.50

18 Quoted in Stuart, *John Smith*, p.189

19 Ibid. p.190

20 Butler and Kavanagh, *The British General Election of 1992*, p.90

21 Stuart, *John Smith*, p.204

22 Naughtie, 'A Political Life Observed', p.46

23 Stuart, *John Smith*, p.206

24 Butler and Kavanagh, *The British General Election of 1992*, p. 90

25 Lamont, *In Office*, p.180

26 Ibid. p.174

27 Stuart, *John Smith*, p.232

28 Lamont, *In Office*, p.180

29 Stuart, *John Smith*, p.212
30 J. Major, *John Major: The Autobiography* (London: HarperCollins, 1999), p.295
31 Ward, 'John Smith's Shadow Budget'
32 Butler and Kavanagh, *The British General Election of 1992*, p.252
33 Stuart, *John Smith*, p.207
34 Ibid. p.218
35 A. Heath, R. Jowell and J. Curtice, 'Can Labour Win?', in A. Heath, R. Jowell and J. Curtice (eds.) *Labour's Last Chance: The 1992 Election and Beyond* (Aldershot: Dartmouth, 1994), pp.275–99, p.290
36 Ibid. p. 292
37 Ward, 'John Smith's Shadow Budget'
38 Ibid.
39 Ibid.
40 G. Brown, 'John Smith's Socialism: His Writing and Speeches', in Brown and Naughtie (eds) *John Smith*, pp.61–103, p.83
41 Naughtie, 'A Political Life Observed', p.50
42 G. Brown, *My Life, Our Times* (London: Bodley Head, 2017), p.91
43 Lamont, *In Office*, p.268
44 Major, *The Autobiography*, p.324
45 Stuart, *John Smith*, p.297
46 B. Brivati (ed.) 'John Smith's Final Speech', *Guiding Light: The Collected Speeches of John Smith* (London: Politico's, 2000), pp.143–9
47 Ibid. p.145
48 Ward, 'One More Heave'
49 Naughtie, 'A Political Life', p.50
50 Stuart, *John Smith*, p.194

6. SOCIAL POLICY

1   See B. Williams, *The Evolution of Conservative Party Social Policy* (Basingstoke: Palgrave, 2015), chapter 2. See also C. Moore, *Margaret Thatcher: The Authorised Biography*, volume 2 (Penguin: London, 2016), pp.94–5, where the Thatcher social policy approach is referred to as being secondary to its economic agenda: 'Social policy was not on the back burner, (but) on a neighbouring work surface.'
2   B. Williams, 'Social Policy', in K. Hickson and B. Williams (eds.) *John Major: An Unsuccessful Prime Minister?* (London: Biteback, 2017)
3   B. Williams, 'Social Policy', in K. Hickson (ed.) *Neil Kinnock: Saving the Labour Party?* (London: Routledge, 2022), p.135
4   M. Stuart, *John Smith: A Life* (London: Politico's, 2005), chapter 21
5   Ibid. chapter 16
6   P. Sloman, 'Better off with Labour? Fiscal policy, electoral strategy and the road to John Smith's shadow budget, 1979–92', *Historical Research* (2022), vol. 95 no. 267, pp.132–50, p.138
7   B. Williams, 'Social Policy', in K. Hickson and J. Miles (eds.) *James Callaghan: An Underrated Prime Minister?* (London: Biteback, 2020)
8   P. Gould, *The Unfinished Revolution: How the Modernisers Saved the Labour Party* (London: Little, Brown and Company, 1998), pp.189–90
9   J. Straw, *Last Man Standing: Memoirs of a Political Survivor* (Basingstoke: Macmillan, 2012), p.189
10 P. Gould, *The Unfinished Revolution*, p.161
11 P. Mandelson, *The Third Man: Life at the Heart of New Labour* (London: Harper Press, 2010), p.134
12 Stuart, *John Smith*, pp.289–90
13 Mandelson, *The Third Man*, p.130
14 C. Haddon, 'Making Policy in Opposition: the Commission on Social Justice, 1992–1994', *Institute for Government*, p.5, https://www.instituteforgovernment.org.uk/sites/default/files/publications/CSJ%20final_0.pdf
15 D. Butler and D. Kavanagh, *The British General Election of 1992* (Basingstoke: Macmillan, 1992), p.256
16 Haddon, 'Making Policy in Opposition', p.7
17 The Report of the Commission on Social Justice, *Social Justice: Strategies for National Renewal* (London: Vintage, 1994), https://www.ippr.org/files/publications/pdf/commission-on-social-justice_final_2014.pdf, p.1
18 J. Smith, Leader's speech to the Labour Party conference, Brighton, 29 September 1992, http://britishpoliticalspeech.org/speech-archive.htm?speech=198
19 John Smith, Leader's speech to the Labour Party conference, Brighton, 28 September 1993, http://www.britishpoliticalspeech.org/speech-archive.htm?speech=199

20   Haddon, 'Making Policy in Opposition', p.6
21   Williams, 'Social Policy' (2022), p.136
22   K. Hickson and B. Williams, 'The Beveridge Report at 80', *Political Insight Journal* (2022), vol. 13, no. 1, https://journals.sagepub.com/doi/10.1177/20419058221091635
23   Haddon, 'Making Policy in Opposition', p.5
24   N. Timmins, 'Smith Launches "Big Idea" for Welfare State', *The Independent*, 18 December 1992, https://www.independent.co.uk/news/uk/politics/smith-launches-big-idea-for-welfare-state-1564161.html
25   Haddon, 'Making Policy in Opposition', p.6
26   Ibid. p.6. See also Stuart, *John Smith*, p.296
27   Haddon, 'Making Policy in Opposition', p.6
28   Stuart, *John Smith*, p.297. See also R. Cowe, 'Lord Borrie obituary', *The Guardian*, 23 October 2016, https://web.archive.org/web/20161220171120/https://www.theguardian.com/business/2016/oct/23/lord-borrie-obituary
29   Cited in Stuart, *John Smith*, p.297
30   'Commission on Social Justice: Labour's election defeat fuelled inquiry', *The Independent*, 25 October 1994, https://www.independent.co.uk/news/uk/commission-on-social-justice-labour-s-election-defeat-fuelled-inquiry-1444838.html
31   Haddon, 'Making Policy in Opposition', p.8
32   Stuart, *John Smith*, p.297
33   'Commission on Social Justice: Labour's election defeat fuelled inquiry'
34   Stuart, *John Smith*, p.297
35   Ibid. p.297
36   W. Keegan, *The Prudence of Mr. Gordon Brown* (Oxford: John Wiley, 2004)
37   Cited in Stuart, *John Smith*, p.297
38   Haddon, 'Making Policy in Opposition', p.7
39   Williams, 'Social Policy' (2022), pp.133–5
40   Stuart, *John Smith*, p.298
41   Haddon, 'Making Policy in Opposition', p.8
42   Timmins, 'Smith Launches "Big Idea" for Welfare State'
43   Stuart, *John Smith*, p.292
44   Ibid. p.298
45   Haddon, 'Making Policy in Opposition', p.10
46   Ibid. p.11
47   Ibid. p.10
48   The Report of the Commission on Social Justice, *Social Justice*
49   M. White and L. Elliott, 'Brown Buries the Tax and Spend Image', *The Guardian*, 21 January 1997, https://www.theguardian.com/politics/1997/jan/21/economy.uk
50   Haddon, 'Making Policy in Opposition', p.10
51   F. Field, *Making Welfare Work: Reconstructing Welfare for the Millennium* (London: Institute of Community Studies, 1995)
52   Stuart, *John Smith*, p.299
53   Haddon, 'Making Policy in Opposition', p.8
54   Stuart, *John Smith*, p.298
55   R. Hattersley, *Fifty Years On: A Prejudiced History of Britain Since the War* (London: Little, Brown and Company, 1997), p.374

7. SCOTTISH HEART, ENGLISH HEAD: LABOUR'S EDUCATION POLICY, 1992-4

1   'Interview with Anthony Howard and Andrew Neil', *On the Record*, BBC One, 7 February 1993, https://www.bbc.co.uk/otr/intext92-93/Howard-Neil7.2.93.html
2   P. Webster, 'Citizen Smith ends Labour backing for state control', *The Times*, 8 February 1993, p.1
3   Labour Party, *Opening Doors to a Learning Society* (London: Labour Party, 1994)
4   S. Tomlinson, *The Politics of Race, Class and Special Education: The selected works of Sally Tomlinson* (Abingdon: Routledge, 2014), p.7
5   A. McSmith, *John Smith: A Life 1938–1994* (London: Mandarin, 1994), p.16
6   M. Stuart, *John Smith: A Life* (London: Politico's, 2005), p.10
7   Ibid. pp.63–4
8   A. McSmith, *John Smith*, pp.56–7; Stuart, *John Smith*, p.65
9   D. Barker, 'Wily woman wins team place at last', *The Guardian*, 25 October 1990, p.7; 'Age 25 and 26', *The Guardian*, 11 October 1974, p.1

10 'Spokesmen who will put case for the Opposition', *The Guardian*, 27 June 1979, p.2

11 I. Aitken, 'Foot to tempt Rodgers with a senior post', *The Guardian*, 16 December 1980, p.22

12 J. Carvel, '"Retread" MPs join Labour frontbenchers', *The Guardian*, 20 July 1987, p.2; P. Wintour, 'Blunkett and green trio in Labour team', *The Guardian*, 11 November 1988, p.8

13 T. Alan and P. Wintour, 'Brown moves up in Kinnock reshuffle', *The Guardian*, 2 November 1989, p.1

14 M. White, 'Labour give Taylor high profile job', *The Guardian*, 26 October 1990, p.27

15 A. Travis, 'Smith goes for team with modern appeal', *The Guardian*, 25 July 1992, p.4

16 E. Ledgerwood, 'Interview with Baroness Taylor of Bolton', *The History of Parliament oral history project*, House of Lords, 7 November 2013 [audio at 2:01:00], https://sounds.bl.uk/sounds/baroness-taylor-of-bolton-interviewed-by-emmeline-ledgerwood-1001107741240x000002

17 A. Travis, 'Short back on Labour front bench', *The Guardian*, 31 July 1992, p.2

18 S. Tomlinson, *The Politics of Race, Class and Special Education: The selected works of Sally Tomlinson* (Abingdon: Routledge, 2014), p.7

19 S. Bates, 'Labour now prepared to reverse opt-outs', *The Guardian*, 26 September 1992, p.9

20 C. Chitty, *New Labour and Secondary Education, 1994–2010* (New York: Palgrave, 2013), p.69

21 M. Beech, K. Hickson and R. Plant (eds.) *The Struggle for Labour's Soul: Understanding Labour's Political Thought since 1945*, 2nd edition (Abingdon: Routledge, 2018)

22 J. Smith, 'Message from Rt Hon John Smith QC MP, Leader of Her Majesty's Opposition', in *Opening Doors to a Learning Society* (London: Labour Party, 1994)

23 J. Tiplady, 'Education Policy', in K. Hickson (ed.) *Neil Kinnock: Saving the Labour Party?* (London: Routledge, 2022), p.144

24 Ibid. p.5 and p.33

25 J. Meikle, 'Labour may back charging students tuition fees', *The Guardian*, 28 November 1992, p.3

26 J. Meikle, 'Labour shies from tuition costs debate', *The Guardian*, 22 September 1993, p.5

27 J. Meikle, 'Universities place on a lower priority', *The Guardian*, 24 September 1993, p.5

28 D. Rubenstein, *The Labour Party and British Society: 1880–2005* (Brighton: Sussex Academic Press, 2006) p. 171

29 P. Wintour, 'Sacked Labour education spokesman to disseminate proposals for tuition fees', *The Guardian*, 20 December 1993, p.4

30 D. Finegold et al., *A British 'Baccalaureat': Ending the Division between Education & Training (Education & Training Paper 1)* (London: IPPR, 1990); D. Miliband, *Learning by Right: An Entitlement to Paid Education and Training (Education & Training Paper 2)* (London: IPPR, 1990); D. Miliband, *Markets, Politics and Education: Beyond the Education Reform Act (Education & Training Paper 3)* (London: IPPR, 1991)

31 S. Tomlinson, *Educational Reform and its Consequences* (London: IPPR, 1994); T. Wragg and F. Jarvis, (eds.) *Education: A Different Vision* (London: IPPR, 1993)

32 M. Barber and T. Brighouse, *Partners in Change: Enhancing the Teaching Profession* (London: IPPR, 1992)

33 M. Barber, 'The Dark Side of the Moon: Imagining an End to Failure in Urban Education', in L. Stoll and K. Myers (eds.) *No Quick Fixes: Perspectives on Schools in Difficulty* (London: Falmer Press, 1998); M. Barber, *How to Do the Impossible: A Guide for Politicians with a Passion for Education* (London: Institute of Education, 1997); M. Barber, *The Learning Game: Arguments for an Education Revolution* (London: Victor Gollancz, 1996)

34 M. Barber, *Instruction to Deliver: Tony Blair, Public Services and the Challenge of Achieving Targets* (London: Politico's, 2007), p.22

35 C. Haddon, 'Making Policy in Opposition: The Commission on Social Justice, 1992–1994', *Institute for Government*, https://www.instituteforgovernment.org.uk/sites/default/files/publications/CSJ%20final_0.pdf

8. JOHN SMITH AND THE BRITISH CONSTITUTION: A COMMITTED REFORMER?

1 J. Smith, 'Reforming our Democracy', speech at Strathclyde University, 23 October 1992, in B. Brivati, (ed.) *Guiding Light: The Collected Speeches of John Smith* (London: Politico's, 2000), p.178

2 J. Morrison, *Reforming Britain: New Labour, New Constitution?* (London: Reuters, 2001), p.38

3 A. Barnett, 'John Smith and the path Britain did not take', *Open Democracy*, https://www.opendemocracy.net/en/opendemocracyuk/john-smith-and-path-britain-did-not-take/

4 A. McSmith, *John Smith: A Life 1938–1994* (London: Mandarin, 1994), p.326

5 G. Brown, 'John Smith's Socialism: His Writings and Speeches' in G. Brown and J. Naughtie, *John Smith: Life and Soul of the Party* (Edinburgh: Mainstream, 1994), p.98

6 A. Crosland, *The Future of Socialism* (London: Constable, 2006), p.52

7 N. Randall, 'Understanding Labour's Ideological Trajectory', in J. Callaghan, S. Fielding and S. Ludlam (eds.) *Interpreting the Labour Party: Approaches to Labour Politics and History* (Manchester: Manchester University Press, 2003), pp.8–22

8 J. Miles, 'The Labour Party and Electoral Reform' (London: Bloomsbury, 2023)

9   T. Benn and A. Hood, *Commons Sense: A New Constitution for Britain* (London: Hutchinson, 1993); T. Benn, *Arguments for Democracy* (London: Cape, 1981) quoted in A. Gamble, *Between Europe and America: The Future of British Politics* (Hampshire: Palgrave, 2003), p.23

10 R. Johnson and Y. Y. Zhu, 'Introduction: The Case for the Political Constitution', in R. Johnson and Y. Y. Zhu (eds.) *Sceptical Perspectives on the Changing Constitution of the United Kingdom* (Oxford: Hart, 2023) pp.1–18

11 R. Cook, 'No PR, no future', *New Statesman & Society*, 8 January 1993, pp.22–3

12 W. Hutton, 'Why Labour's constitutional battle is so vital. The end fame of modernising the party – its 'big idea' – is to adopt democracy as a battering ram to change state and society', *The Guardian*, 19 July 1993

13 R. Miliband, *Parliamentary Socialism: A Study in the Politics of Labour* (London: Allen & Unwin, 1961)

14 Quoted in G. Hassan and E. Shaw, *The People's Flag and the Union Jack: An Alternative History of Britain and the Labour Party* (London: Biteback, 2019), p.15

15 M. Stuart, *John Smith: A Life* (London: Methuen, 2005), p.292

16 'Smith pledges new paths for "listening leadership": The front-runner in the Labour contest sets out his personal manifesto', *The Guardian*, 1 May 1992

17 J. Smith, Leader's speech to the Labour Party conference, Brighton, 29 September 1992, http:// britishpoliticalspeech.org/speech-archive.htm?speech=198

18 J. Smith 'Reforming our Democracy', in Brivati, *Guiding Light*, p.180

19 J. Smith, speech titled 'The Standards and Practice of Government', London, 28 January 1993, cited in Brown, 'John Smith's Socialism' in Brown and Naughtie, *John Smith*, p.97

20 Barnett, 'John Smith and the path Britain did not take'

21 J. Smith, speech titled 'A Citizens' Democracy', London, 1 March 1993, cited in Brown, 'John Smith's Socialism', p.98

22 Ibid. p.98

23 Quoted in Barnett, 'John Smith and the path Britain did not take'

24 'A New Agenda for Democracy: Labour's Proposals for Constitutional Reform (1993)', in R. Blackburn and R. Plant (eds.) *Constitutional Reform: The Labour Government's Constitutional Reform Agenda* (London: Longman, 1999), p.446

25 Ibid., pp.461–2

26 Ibid., pp. 462–7

27 Quoted in Miles, *The Labour Party and Electoral Reform*, p.82

28 Quoted in 'Kinnock's heirs divided over electoral change', *The Times*, Tuesday 23 June 1992

29 McSmith, *John Smith*, pp.326–7

30 Stuart, *John Smith*, p.293

31 Barnett, 'John Smith and the path Britain did not take'

32 Quoted in Morrison, *Reforming Britain*, p.33

33 'Mr Smith plays the deadest of bats', *The Guardian*, 20 May 1993

34 M. Evans, *Charter 88: A Successful Challenge to the British Political Tradition?* (Aldershot: Dartmouth, 1995), p.181

35 Cited in 'The Labour Party's long-standing lethargy over House of Lords reform', The Constitution Unit Blog (constitution-unit.com)

36 Morrison, *Reforming Britain*, p.33

37 Cited in Morrison, *Reforming Britain*, pp.38–9; Barnett, 'John Smith and the path Britain did not take'

38 'A New Agenda for Democracy', *Constitutional Reform*, p. 467

9. JOHN SMITH: DEVOLUTION AND NORTHERN IRELAND

1   J. Smith, 'Reforming our Democracy', Strathclyde University, 23 October 1992, in B. Brivati (ed.)*Guiding Light: The collected speeches of John Smith* (London: Politico's, 2000), p.181

2   HC Debs, 10 May 1976, cols.24–7

3   M. Stuart, *John Smith: A Life* (London: Politico's, 2005), pp.88–90

4   J. Shepherd, *Crisis? What Crisis? The Callaghan Government and the British Winter of Discontent* (Manchester: Manchester University Press, 2015)

5   R. McNeil, 'Honest John Smith may have stopped basketcase Britain going doolally', *The Herald*, 9 April 2023, https://www.heraldscotland.com/politics/23445004.honest-john-smith-may-stopped-basketcase-britain-going-doolally/

6   The National Archives, PREM 16/126, *HOME AFFAIRS. Devolution in UK: Report of Kilbrandon Commission on the Constitution; part 2*, 3 June 1974 to 22 July 1974, Bernard Donoughue to Harold Wilson, 'Scotland and Devolution', 19 July 1974; W. Alexander (ed.) *Donald Dewar: Scotland's First First Minister* (Edinburgh: Mainstream, 2005), pp.59–60, 87–9; A. McSmith, *John Smith: A Life, 1938–1994* (London: Mandarin, 1994), p.79

7   The National Archives, PREM 16/126, *HOME AFFAIRS. Devolution in UK: Report of Kilbrandon Commission on the Constitution; part 2*, 3 June 1974 to 22 July 1974, 'Attitudes of the Scottish group of Labour Members of Parliament' in 'Devolution' enclosures from Sir John Hunt to Prime Minister Harold Wilson, 18 July 1974

8   D. Ward, 'Long Read: John Smith and the mythology of "One More Heave"', *Mile End Institute (MEI) Blog*, 17 July 2022, https://www.qmul.ac.uk/mei/news-and-opinion/items/long-read-john-smith-and-the-mythology-of-one-more-heave.html

9   McSmith, *John Smith*, p.326

10 J. Smith, 'Reforming our Democracy', p.186

11 The National Archives, PREM 19/3789, *HOME AFFAIRS. Devolution: the question of the government of Scotland, part 1*, H (79) 62, Cabinet Home and Social Affairs Committee, 'Government of Scotland – Memorandum by the Secretary of State for Scotland and the Chancellor of the Duchy of Lancaster, 10 October 1979.

12 The National Archives, PREM 19/3789, *HOME AFFAIRS. Devolution: the question of the government of Scotland; part 1*. This file contains numerous archival documents relating to Scottish devolution debates during the Margaret Thatcher and John Major years of Conservative governments.

13 P. Wintour, 'Scotland referendum: David Cameron throws down the gauntlet to Salmond', *The Guardian*, 9 January 2012, https://www.theguardian.com/uk/2012/jan/09/scotland-referendum-david-cameron-salmond

14 'Over-unionised', *The Times*, 20 January 1992

15 T. Travers, 'Local Government: Margaret Thatcher's 11-year war', *The Guardian*, 9 April 2013, https://www.theguardian.com/local-government-network/2013/apr/09/local-government-margaret-thatcher-war-politics

16 R. Martin, 'The Political Economy of Britain's North-South Divide', *Transactions of the Institute of British Geographers* (1988), vol. 13, no. 4, pp.389–418, https://doi.org/10.2307/622738; E. Fieldhouse, 'Thatcher's Legacy Still Looms Large: The North-South divide in Britain's electoral support', *British Election Study*, 7 May 2014, https://www.britishelectionstudy.com/bes-findings/thatchers-legacy-still-looms-large-the-north-south-divide-in-britains-electoral-support/

17 The National Archives, PREM 19/3789, *HOME AFFAIRS. Devolution: the question of the government of Scotland; part 1*, Michael Ancram, 'Devolution – Why Not?' enclosure within letter sent from David Crawley, Private Secretary to Secretary of State for Scotland to Nigel Wicks, Principal Private Secretary at 10 Downing Street, 22 April 1988

18 A. Barnett, 'John Smith and the path Britain did not take', *Open Democracy*, https://www.opendemocracy.net/en/opendemocracyuk/john-smith-and-path-britain-did-not-take/; W. Alexander, 'Foundations, Frustrations and Hopes', in W. Alexander (ed.) Donald Dewar, *Scotland's First First Minister* (London: Mainstream Publishing, 2005), pp.208–13

19 M. Elder, *Donald Dewar 1937–2000: A Book of Tribute* (Norwich: Stationery Office, 2000), p.110

20 The National Archives, PREM 16/126, *HOME AFFAIRS. Devolution in UK: Report of Kilbrandon Commission on the Constitution, part 2*, 3 June 1974 to 22 July 1974, Bernard Donoughue to Harold Wilson, 'Scotland and Devolution', 19 July 1974

21 D. Irvine, 'A Skilful Advocate', in Alexander, *Donald Dewar*, p.127

22 Ibid.

23 The National Archives, PREM 19/3789, *HOME AFFAIRS. Devolution: the question of the government of Scotland, part 1*, Prime Minister John Major to Lord Armstrong of Ilminster, GCB and CVO, 21 April 1992

24 P. Hetherington, 'Scottish rebels to defy Smith on home rule', *The Guardian*, 21 July 1992

25 A. Travis, 'Smith goes for team with modern appeal', *The Guardian*, 25 July 1992, p.4

26 E. MacAskill, 'Donald Dewar', *The Guardian*, 12 October 2000, p.22

27 Stuart, *John Smith*, p.242

28 The National Archives, PREM 19/3789, *HOME AFFAIRS. Devolution: the question of the government of Scotland, part 1*, Andrew Turnbull, 'Note for the Record: Scotland and the Constitution', 29 April 1992

29 Ibid.

30 S. Tudor, 'The Barnett formula: How it operates and proposals for change', *House of Lords Library*, 6 March 2023, https://lordslibrary.parliament.uk/the-barnett-formula-how-it-operates-and-proposals-for-change/

31 The National Archives, PREM 19/3789, *HOME AFFAIRS. Devolution: the question of the government of Scotland, part 1*, Sir M. Quinlan GCB, Permanent Under-Secretary of State, Ministry of Defence to Sir Robin Butler KCB CVO Cabinet Office, 'Devolution and enclosure Spring Sunningdale – Regional Government', 30 March 1992

32 J. Smith, 'Reforming our Democracy', in Brivati, *Guiding Light*, p.180

33 D. Healey, *The Time of My Life* (London: Michael Joseph, 1989), p.461

34 P. Riddell, 'Call them unaccountable', *The Times*, 18 January 1993, p.14

35 J. Smith, 'A Commitment to Change', Royal Horticultural Hall, London, 18 July 1992, in B. Brivati (ed.) *Guiding Light: The collected speeches of John Smith* (London: Politico's, 2000), p.172

36 F. Mount, *The British Constitution Now: Recovery or Decline?* (London: Mandarin, 1993)

37 P. Riddell, 'Call them unaccountable', p.14

38 P. Webster, R. Morgan, 'Labour leader vows to end "spiral of decline" in Britain', *The Times*, 30 September 1992.

39 'The Rise of the SNP', *BBC News*, BBC One, 17 May 2015; 'Radical devolution can mend the broken fabric of Britain's communities, says Lord Heseltine', *Mile End Institute*, 20 October 2016, https://www.qmul.ac.uk/media/news/2016/hss/radical-devolution-can-mend-the-broken-fabric-of-britains-communities-says-lord-heseltine.html; G. Blakeley and B. Evans, *Devolution in Greater Manchester and Liverpool City Region: The First Mayoral Term* (Manchester: Manchester University Press, 2023)

40 'Power to the Regions', *Labour Weekly*, 24 September 1982, p.15

41 H. Mulholland, 'North-east voters reject regional assembly', *The Guardian*, 5 November 2004, https://www.theguardian.com/society/2004/nov/05/regionalgovernment.politics

42 J. Ball, 'John Prescott: the Northern Powerhouse is "not devolution, really"', *New Statesman*, 25 February 2019, https://www.newstatesman.com/spotlight/2019/02/john-prescott-northern-powerhouse-not-devolution-really

43 J. McDevitt, 'Dominic Cummings honed strategy in 2004 vote, video reveals', *The Guardian*, 12 November 2019, https://www.theguardian.com/politics/2019/nov/12/dominic-cummings-honed-strategy-2004-vote-north-east

44 J. Smith, 'The Standards and Practice of Government' in Brivati, *Guiding Light*, p.211

45 A. Campbell, 'Time for Smith to make much of Major's misery', *Sunday Telegraph*, 7 February 1993, p.22

46 Ibid.

47 S. Hoggart, 'Smith spells out sweeping constitutional reforms', *The Observer*, 28 February 1993, p.2

48 J. Smith, 'A Citizen's Democracy', Charter 88, Westminster, 1 March 1993; https://www.daviddjward.com/wp-content/uploads/2019/05/Citizens-Democracy-large.pdf; A. Barnett, 'John Smith and the path Britain did not take', *Open Democracy*, 12 May 2019, https://www.opendemocracy.net/en/opendemocracyuk/john-smith-and-path-britain-did-not-take/

49 S. Bates, 'Labour goes for industry rethink', *The Guardian*, 7 April 1993, p.2

50 Ibid.

51 The National Archives, PREM 16/1359, LOCAL GOVERNMENT. Organic change in local government in England: devolution and the English dimension, 13 October 1976 to 4 August 1977; PREM 16/2157, LOCAL GOVERNMENT. Devolution in England; organic change in local government; draft White Paper; part 3, 18 January 1978 to 16 January 1979; PREM 16/2158, LOCAL GOVERNMENT. Devolution in England; organic change in local government; draft White Paper; part 4, 19 January 1979 to 12 February 1979

52 P. Shore, 'Shore on Smith', *The Guardian*, 24 September 1993, pp.28–9.

53 Ibid.

54 G. Kaufman, 'He defied pressure to come up with a big idea. His big idea was to win', *Daily Telegraph*, 13 May 1994, p.2; A. Massie, 'The decent democrat', *Daily Telegraph*, 13 May 1994, p.13

55 J. Straw, 'Better off with no policies', *The Independent on Sunday*, 10 April 1994, p.19

56 'Labour and the Party we need', *The Guardian*, 27 September 1993

57 M. White, 'Smith claims the high ground: Tories put power before democracy', *The Guardian*, 29 September 1993

58 H. Young, 'Labour gambles with southern discomfort', *The Guardian*, 15 February 1994

59 K. Alderman and N. Carter, 'The Labour Party Leadership and Deputy Leadership Elections of 1994', *Parliamentary Affairs* (1995), vol. 48, no. 3, pp.438–55, https://doi-org.liverpool.idm.oclc.org/10.1093/oxfordjournals.pa.a052544

60 P. Kilfoyle, *Left Behind: Lessons from Labour's Heartland* (London: Politico's, 2000), p.304

61 R. Carr, *March of the Moderates: Bill Clinton, Tony Blair and the Rebirth of Progressive Politics* (London: I. B. Tauris, 2019), pp.134–5; p.137; pp.180–4

62 A. Boulton, 'Sky Views: How John Smith's death changed the course of British history', *Sky News*, 4 May 2019, https://news.sky.com/story/sky-views-how-john-smiths-death-changed-the-course-of-british-history-11710748

63 Stuart, *John Smith*, pp.264–5

64 Ibid. p.265

65 Ibid.

66 P. Webster, 'Ulster holds its breath on peace accord', *The Times*, 16 December 1993, pp.1, 3

67 Ibid.

68 J. Sherman, R. Morgan, A. Thomson, 'Platform for peace "not a sell-out"', *The Times*, 16 December 1993, p.3

69 Stuart, *John Smith*, pp.264–7

70 Ibid.

71 M. Sutton, 'Anglo-Irish diplomatic relations and the British Labour Party, 1981–94', in L. Marley (ed.) *The British Labour Party and Twentieth-Century Ireland: The cause of Ireland, the cause of Labour* (Manchester: Manchester University Press, 2016), p.227–8.

72 B. Taylor, 'How is the "killing the SNP stone dead" project going?', *BBC News*, 4 February 2015, https://www.bbc.co.uk/news/uk-scotland-31129382

73 D. Irvine, 'A Skilful Advocate' in Alexander, *Donald Dewar*, p.126

74 Ibid. p.128

75 The National Archives, PREM 16/926, *HOME AFFAIRS. Devolution: planning for legislation; Scots Private Law; possible consensus with Conservative Party in Parliament*; part 13, 7 June 1976 to 27 July 1976, 'Extract from a meeting between PM and Mrs Thatcher', PM's Meeting Room, House of Commons, 21 July 1976; Kenneth Stowe to James Callaghan, 'Devolution', 23 July 1976

76 N. Watt, 'Gordon Brown makes passionate appeal to Labour voters in final no rally', *The Guardian*, 17 September 2014, https://www.theguardian.com/politics/2014/sep/17/gordon-brown-appeals-to-labour-voters-vote-no

77 'Report of the Commission on the UK's Future: A New Britain – Renewing our Democracy and Rebuilding our Economy', *Labour Party*, December 2022, https://labour.org.uk/wp-content/uploads/2022/12/Commission-on-the-UKs-Future.pdf; F. Brown, 'Gordon Brown forms group with Labour politicians calling for UK democracy reform', *Sky News*, 1 June 2023, https://news.sky.com/story/gordon-brown-forms-group-with-labour-politicians-calling-for-uk-democracy-reform-12894543

78 H. White, T. Pope, A. Paun, A. Thomas, T. Durrant, J. Sargeant, 'Comment: Five things we've learned about the Brown Commission on the UK's future', *Institute for Government*, 5 December 2022.

79 Reuters, 'Keir Starmer: constitutional reform report a "turning point" for UK economy – video', *The Guardian*, 5 December 2022, https://www.theguardian.com/politics/video/2022/dec/05/keir-starmer-constitutional-reform-report-a-turning-point-for-uk-economy-video; P. Walker, J. Elgot, S. Carrell, 'Labour plan to reform constitution will end "sticking plaster politics" says Starmer', *The Guardian*, 5 December 2022, https://www.theguardian.com/politics/2022/dec/05/labour-plan-reform-constitution-keir-starmer

80 D. Blunkett, 'Collaborate or get left behind, says Blunkett', *Sheffield Star*, 29 June 2023, https://www.thestar.co.uk/news/opinion/columnists/collaborate-or-get-left-behind-says-blunkett-4201843; 'Council of Skills Advisors' Report: Learning and skills for economic recovery, social cohesion and a more equal Britain', *Labour Party*, 19 October 2022, https://labour.org.uk/wp-content/uploads/2022/10/WR-16813_22-Labour-Skills-Council-report-Edit-19-10-22.pdf

81 L. O'Carroll, 'How did the Good Friday agreement come about and why is it so significant?', *The Guardian*, 7 April 2023, https://www.theguardian.com/world/2023/apr/07/how-did-the-good-friday-agreement-come-about-and-why-is-it-so-significant

10. JOHN SMITH: LABOUR'S MOST PRO-EUROPEAN LEADER

1   M. Bragg, 'The last hours with my good friend John', *Daily Express*, 13 May 1994

2   Quoted in B. Brivati (ed.) *Guiding Light: The Collected Speeches of John Smith* (London: Politico's, 2000), p.276

3   'Smith in Good Form', *Newcastle Journal*, 13 May 1994

4   'Will Gould now stay?', *Evening Standard*, 12 May 1994

5   Interview with Pauline Green, 11 May 2022

6   R. Johnson, 'The European Parliamentary Labour Party', in D. Hayter and D. Harley (eds.) *The Forgotten Tribe: British MEPs, 1979–2020* (London: John Harper, 2021)

7   R. Johnson, 'Neil Kinnock and Labour's European Policy', in K. Hickson (ed.) *Neil Kinnock: Saving the Labour Party?* (London: Routledge, 2022)

8   J. Smith, 'The Opportunity to Serve', speech to European Gala Dinner, 11 May 1994, in Brivati, *Guiding Light*, p.277

9   A. Geddes, 'Labour and the European Community, 1973–93: Pro-Europeanism, Europeanisation, and their Implications', *Contemporary Record* (1994), vol. 8, no. 2, pp.370–80

10 A. Johnson, 'A man with the smell of victory', *The Guardian*, 13 May 1994

11 '70-min fight to save his life', *Daily Telegraph*, 13 May 1994

12 G. Kaufman, 'He defied pressure to come up with a big idea', *Daily Telegraph*, 13 May 1994

13 M. Garnett, G. Hyman and R. Johnson, *Keeping the Red Flag Flying: Labour in Opposition since 1922* (Cambridge: Polity Press, 2024)

14 Interview with Bryan Gould, 30 June 2023

15 B. Gould, *Goodbye to All That* (London: Macmillan, 1995)

16 Interview with Bryan Gould, 30 June 2023

17 R. Hattersley, *Who Goes Home?* (London: Abacus, 1995)

18 Gould, *Goodbye to All That*, p.154

19 C. Murphy, *Futures of Socialism: Modernisation, the Labour Party, and the British Left, 1973–1997* (Cambridge: Cambridge University Press, 2023)

20 M. Stuart, *John Smith: A Life* (London: Politico's, 2005), p.145

21 Quoted in D. Macintyre, *Mandelson: The Biography* (New York: HarperCollins, 1999), p.157

22 Interview with Bryan Gould, 30 June 2023

23 Labour Party, *Social Justice and Economic Efficiency: First Report of Labour's Policy Review for the 1990s* (London: Labour Party, 1988)

24 Stuart, *John Smith*

25 'UK Labour Party puts EMS entry as early policy objective', *Financial Times*, 2 October 1989

26 Labour Party, *Looking to the Future* (London: Labour Party, 1990)

27 Murphy, *Futures of Socialism*, p.112

28 Quoted in Stuart, *John Smith*, p.170

29 P. Stephens, 'UK Labour Party puts EMS entry as early policy objective', *Financial Times*, 2 October 1989

30 Quoted in Stuart, *John Smith*, p.181

31 'It's all change for the role reversal express', *Sunday Times*, 22 October 1989

32 S. Tindale, 'Learning to Love the Market: Labour and the European Community', *Political Quarterly* (1992), vol. 63, no. 3, pp.276–300, p.280

33 Quoted in W. Bonefeld, 'Politics of European Monetary Union: Class, Identity, and Critique', *Economic & Political Weekly* (1998), vol. 33, no. 35, pp.55–69, p.66

34 E. Shaw, *The Labour Party since 1979* (London: Routledge, 1994), p.114

35 C. Huhne and R. Lander, 'Labour's Luncheon Offensive', *Independent on Sunday*, 6 May 1990

36 R. Butt, 'Mrs Thatcher: The First Two Years', *Sunday Times*, 3 May 1981

37 *Tribune*, September 1990

38 S. Holland, 'Towards a People's Europe', *New Statesman*, 2 October 1992

39 *Tribune*, September 1990

40 Interview with Bryan Gould, 30 June 2023

41 *The Economist*, 14 April 1990

42 R. Broad, *Labour's European Dilemmas: From Bevin to Blair* (London: Palgrave, 2001)

43 Stuart, *John Smith*, p.162

44 Broad, *Labour's European Dilemmas*

45 HC Debs, 21 November 1991, col. 507

46 Gould, *Goodbye to All That*, pp.216–17

47 Letter from Austin Mitchell MP to Neil Kinnock (21 December 1990), KNNK/1/3/52 (Kinnock Papers, Churchill College Archives, Cambridge)

48 Quoted in Murphy, *Futures of Socialism*, p.41

49 I. Aitken, 'There's no such thing as a free vote', *The Guardian*, 25 November 1991

50 'Devalue the £ now', *Nottingham Evening Post*, 10 September 1992

51 Ibid.

52 Quoted in A. Turner, *A Classless Society: Britain in the 1990s* (London: Aurum, 2013), pp.42–3

53 HC Debs, 24 September 1992, col. 22

54 J. Major, *John Major: The Autobiography* (New York: HarperCollins, 1999), p.339

55 Gould, *Goodbye to All That*, p.266

56 D. Gow, P. Webster, J. Palmer, 'Maastricht Treaty hailed as great leap forward despite Major concessions', *The Guardian*, 12 December 1991

57 Quoted in Stuart, *John Smith*, p.276

58 Stuart, *John Smith*, p.271

59 S. Goodwin and A. Bevins, 'Maastricht referendum call is rejected', *The Independent*, 28 September 1992

60 Bryan Gould, 'After the Tea Party', *New Statesman*, 25 September 1992

61 KNNK/8/87, Neil Kinnock Papers (Churchill College Archives, Cambridge)

62 Quoted in Stuart, *John Smith*, p.284

63 Quoted in Stuart, *John Smith*, p.282

64 Quoted in Stuart, *John Smith*, p.284

65 'Shadow Cabinet decides to abstain on Maastricht Third Reading', *The Independent*, 12 May 1993

66 M. White, 'Tory Revolt Fails to Halt Treaty Bill', *The Guardian*, 21 May 1993

67 Interview with Kate Hoey, 2 February 2022

68 M. Bainbridge, P. Whyman and A. Mullen, 'The 1975 Referendum on Europe', *The European Legacy* (2006), vol. 17, no. 4, p.71

69 HC Debs, 2 November 1989, col. 502

70 Tindale, 'Learning to Love the Market', p.276

71 Ibid. p.282

72 M. Thatcher, speech to the College of Europe, Bruges, 20 September 1988

73 Tindale, 'Learning to Love the Market', p.278

74 J. Smith, speech entitled 'Europe and the World', Lothian Lecture, University of Edinburgh, 20 November 1992, quoted in Brivati, *Guiding Light*, pp.191–2
75 HC Debs, 2 November 1989, col. 502
76 Ibid.
77 Ibid.
78 Quoted in Stuart, *John Smith*
79 Ibid.
80 HC Debs, 21 November 1991, col. 507
81 Quoted in Stuart, *John Smith*, p.282
82 Stuart, *John Smith*, p.283
83 T. Blair, 'We'll See Off the Euro Dragons', *The Sun*, 22 April 1997
84 J. Tonge, 'Conclusion', in T Casey (ed.) *The Blair Legacy* (Basingstoke: Palgrave Macmillan, 2009). See also O. Daddow, *New Labour and the European Union: Blair and Brown's Logic of History* (Manchester: Manchester University Press, 2011)
85 I. Bache and A. Jordan, 'Britain in Europe and Europe in Britain', in I. Bache and A. Jordan (eds.) *The Europeanisation of British Politics* (Basingstoke: Palgrave Macmillan, 2006), p.9
86 J. Smith, speech entitled 'The Opportunity to Serve', European Gala Dinner, 11 May 1994, quoted in Brivati, *Guiding Light*, p.277
87 K. Featherstone, 'The British Labour Party from Kinnock to Blair: Europeanism and Europeanization', paper presented to the Biennial Conference of the European Community Studies Association, 2–5 June 1999, Pittsburgh, Pennsylvania, p.9
88 Gould, *Goodbye to All That*, p.215

13. THE MYTH OF 'ONE MORE HEAVE'

1   D. Miliband, 'Between the Obsolete and the Utopian: How to Understand the 1997 "Project"', speech to the Mile End Institute, 6 May 2022, https://www.qmul.ac.uk/mei/media/mei/tgc-media/filesx2fpublications/Between-the-Obsolete-and-the-Utopian,-6-May-2022.pdf
2   J. Rentoul, 'Anji Hunter, Tony Blair's longest-serving adviser, on his rise to power', *The Independent*, 17 January 2020, https://www.independent.co.uk/voices/blair-anji-hunter-kings-college-course-rentoul-davis-a9288846.html
3   Gallup monthly polls from September 1992 to May 1994 show a comfortable Labour lead over the Conservatives and by John Smith over John Major. See: D. Butler, *British Political Facts 1900–2000* (London: Macmillan, 2000), pp.277–8
4   D. Dewar, 'Foreword', in B. Brivati (ed.) *Guiding Light: The Collected Speeches of John Smith* (London: Politico's, 2000), p.vii
5   This quote, a favourite of John Smith's, was by R. H. Tawney. Included in Smith's 'R. H. Tawney Memorial Lecture', 20 March 1993, in Brivati, *Guiding Light*
6   M. Stuart, *John Smith: A Life* (London: Politico's, 2005) p.138
7   For a full account of the origins of the shadow Budget see D. Ward, 'John Smith's Shadow Budget 1992 – Myths and Lessons for Labour', *Mile End Institute*, https://www.qmul.ac.uk/mei/media/mei/tgc-media/filesx2fpublications/140_22-MILEEND_REPORT_Budget-1992_v3_web.pdf
8   Stuart, *John Smith*, p.343
9   L. Minkin, *The Blair Supremacy: A Study in the Politics of Labour's Party Management* (Manchester: Manchester University Press, 2014), pp.91–2
10 The evolution of Labour's policy is described in D. Ward, 'Black Wednesday 30 years on', *Mile End Institute*, https://www.qmul.ac.uk/mei/media/mei/tgc-media/filesx2fpublications/Black-Wednesday-30-Years-On.pdf
11 J. Smith, speech to the European Parliamentary Labour Party, Strasbourg, 9 June 1992; HC Debs, 2 July 1992, col. 1050
12 D. Ward, 'Major Clean Bowled: The Maastricht Confidence Motion 30 Years On', *Mile End Institute*, https://www.qmul.ac.uk/mei/news-and-opinion/items/major-clean-bowled-the-maastricht-confidence-motion-30-years-on.html
13 C. Massey, *The Modernisation of the Labour Party, 1979–97* (Manchester: Manchester University Press, 2021)
14 A. Barnett, 'John Smith and the path Britain did not take', *Open Democracy*, https://www.opendemocracy.net/en/opendemocracyuk/john-smith-and-path-britain-did-not-take/
15 'A Citizen's Democracy', 1 March 1993
16 Speech to Labour local government conference, 7 February 1993; 'A Citizen's Democracy', 1 March 1993; 'Reclaiming the Ground', R. H. Tawney Memorial Lecture, 20 March 1993; speech to the Trades Union Congress, 8 September 1993.
17 'Reclaiming the Ground', 20 March 1993

18 J. Smith, speech to the Labour Local Government Conference, Bournemouth, 7 February 1993

19 Stuart, *John Smith*, p.70

20 Declaration of Party Leaders, 'The European Employment Initiative' adopted by the PES on 6 April 1994, section 5.4, page 11. This document was prepared by a working group under the chairmanship of Allan Larsson, the Swedish Finance Minister, in which I served as John Smith's representative.

21 The author hopes that in a referendum, Smith would have decided to remain publicly neutral. For a perspective on Smith's attitude to electoral reform see D. Ward, 'Labour must learn from its old mistakes and commit to fairer elections', *Open Democracy*, https://www.opendemocracy.net/en/proportional-representation-electoral-reform-labour-tony-blair-john-smith-charter-88/

14. BUILT TO LAST?

1   T. Blair, *A Journey* (London: Hutchinson, 2010), p.83

2   Ibid. p.50

3   Confidential interview

4   D. Ward, 'John Smith and the Mythology of "One More Heave"', https://www.daviddjward.com/john-smith-and-the-mythology-of-one-more-heave/

5   N. Lawson, 'Dear Tony Blair, maybe it's your fault if the electorate hasn't shifted to the left', *The Guardian*, 1 January 2015, https://www.theguardian.com/commentisfree/2015/jan/01/dear-tony-blair-electorate-shifted-left-ed-miliband

6   D. Ward, cited in J. Rentoul, *Tony Blair: Prime Minister* (London: Faber and Faber, 2013), p.298

7   J. Rentoul, *Tony Blair: Prime Minister*, p.642

8   Ibid. p.311

9   Ibid. p.472

10 David Ward, personal communication, 25 August 2023

11 J. Rentoul, *Tony Blair: Prime Minister*, p.287

12 Ibid. p.264

13 Ward, 'John Smith and the Mythology of "One More Heave"'

14 J. Rentoul, *Tony Blair: Prime Minister*, p.667

15 Ibid. p.565

CONTRIBUTORS

Dame Margaret Beckett MP was deputy leader of the Labour Party under John Smith and acting leader after his death. She was first elected to Parliament in 1974 and has held numerous Cabinet posts, including as Foreign Secretary 2006–7.

Andy Burnham has been Mayor of Greater Manchester since 2017. He was previously the MP for Leigh from 2001 to 2017, a member of Gordon Brown's Cabinet and a member of Labour's shadow Cabinets from 2010.

David Denver is Emeritus Professor of Politics at Lancaster University. He is widely recognised as a leading expert on electoral politics in the UK. His books include (with Mark Garnett) *British General Elections since 1964* (Oxford University Press, 2021).

Mark Garnett is Senior Lecturer in Politics at Lancaster University, where he teaches and researches on British politics and contemporary political history, especially in relation to the Conservative Party and think tanks.

Bryan Gould was Labour MP for Southampton Test (1974–9) and Dagenham (1983–94). He served in Neil Kinnock's shadow Cabinet and was campaign co-ordinator for the 1987 general election. In 1992, he stood for leadership of the Labour Party. He subsequently served as Vice Chancellor of the University of Waikato.

Wyn Grant is Emeritus Professor of Politics at the University of Warwick and has written extensively on economic policy, pressure groups and the politics of agriculture. He is a past chair of the Political Studies Association.

Kevin Hickson is Senior Lecturer in British Politics at the University of Liverpool, where he has taught for twenty years. He has published seventeen books and numerous journal articles on aspects of British politics and political history.

Richard Johnson is Senior Lecturer in Politics at Queen Mary University of London. He has published widely on UK and US politics. He is the author (with Mark Garnett and Gavin Hyman) of *Keeping the Red Flag Flying: The Labour Party in Opposition since 1922* (Polity Press, 2024).

Keith Laybourn is Diamond Jubilee Professor Emeritus of the University of Huddersfield and Visiting Professor at York St John University. He has authored and edited fifty-one books. He is president of the Society for the Study of Labour History and associate editor of the journal *Labour History*.

Jasper Miles is a Lecturer in Politics at the University of Lincoln, specialising in British politics. His monograph *The Labour Party and Electoral Reform* was published in 2023 by Bloomsbury. He has also co-authored a biography of Peter Shore and co-edited a volume exploring James Callaghan's premiership.

Philip Norton, Lord Norton of Louth is Professor of Government at the University of Hull. He has published extensively on the constitution and the work of Parliament. He sits in the House of Lords as a Conservative peer. His latest book *The 1922 Committee: Power Behind the Scenes* was published in 2023 by Manchester University Press.

Neil Pye is Lecturer in Politics at the University of Liverpool and a member of the Political Studies Association's Local Politics and Governance specialist group. He specialises in the post-war history of the Labour Party, devolution and metro mayors, British political ideologies and post-war politics in Liverpool.

John Rentoul has been the chief political commentator of *The Independent* since 2016, having worked for the newspaper since 1995. He previously worked at the BBC and the *New Statesman* and is currently Visiting Professor at King's College London. He is a biographer of Tony Blair.

Ann Taylor, Baroness Taylor of Bolton was first elected to Parliament in October 1974. She was an assistant whip in James Callaghan's government. Later she was a shadow Minister under Neil Kinnock and a member of the shadow Cabinets of John Smith and Tony Blair. She served in the Labour Cabinet from 1997 to 2001. Since 2005 she has sat in the House of Lords.

Joseph Tiplady is a political historian who teaches at the University of Hull, where he was awarded the Alan Johnson scholarship and where he completed his PhD on New Labour's education reforms.

David Ward was John Smith's head of policy as Leader of the Opposition and his policy advisor as shadow Chancellor of the Exchequer. He was the campaigns officer of the Parliamentary Labour Party from July 1985 to September 1987. He is currently the secretary of the Weald of Kent Labour Party and the executive president of the Towards Zero Foundation.

Ben Williams lectures in Politics and Social Sciences at Edge Hill and Manchester Metropolitan Universities. He has written extensively on post-war British politics and political ideology and frequently appears on media interviews and political podcasts.

ACKNOWLEDGEMENTS

M<small>Y GRATITUDE TOWARDS THE</small> contributors to this volume should not be underestimated. All are busy with numerous commitments and still gave their time to contribute to what will hopefully be an important volume, reappraising the short, yet important, leadership of John Smith from 1992 until his tragic death two years later. John stood for integrity in public life, something which has sadly been in short supply in recent times.

The book brings together academics, politicians, journalists and advisors with a range of perspectives, allowing the reader to judge for themselves what John Smith's contribution and legacy are. The debates with which he engaged and views he held seem strikingly relevant to British politics now, thirty years on.

My thanks to Biteback for once again publishing a book from me and especially the commissioning editor, Olivia Beattie.

Finally, I would like to put on record my appreciation for the tolerance shown by my mum for all the time I have been shut away in my study when I should have been more attentive.

Kevin Hickson
Weston, Cheshire
May 2024

INDEX